THE STALKING
OF KRISTIN

THE STALKING
OF KRISTIN

A Father Investigates
the Murder of His Daughter

GEORGE LARDNER JR.

THE ATLANTIC MONTHLY PRESS
NEW YORK

Published simultaneously in Canada
Printed in the United States of America

FIRST EDITION

Library of Congress Cataloging-in-Publication Data

Lardner, George, Jr.
The stalking of Kristin: a father investigates the murder of his
daughter / George Lardner Jr.
ISBN 0-87113-613-9
1. Homicide—Massachusetts—Boston.   2. Abused women—Crimes
against—Massachusetts—Boston.   3. Fathers and daughters—
Massachusetts—Boston.   4. Lardner, Kristin, 1970–1992.
5. Cartier, Michael, d. 1992.   I. Title.
HV6534.B6L37   1995   364.1′523′092—dc20
[B] 95-14575

Design by Laura Hammond Hough

The Atlantic Monthly Press
841 Broadway
New York, NY 10003

10 9 8 7 6 5 4 3 2

For Kristin

CONTENTS

INTRODUCTION

As I write this, trying to decide how to begin, I can see my grand-daughter, Casey Kristin Lardner, running onto the beach at Jekyll Island and striding into the ocean for the first time in her life. "Pool!" she decides. "My pool!" She is nineteen months old and she is absolutely fearless. She has curly brown hair and large brown eyes, and the world belongs to her as it did twenty-four years ago to the girl she was named after, my daughter, Kristin.

Kristin should be here, too, watching her niece from her favorite beach chair. Instead, she lies buried in a cemetery just outside Washington, D.C.

What happened to Kristin could, I'm afraid, happen to anyone's child. We can't hold on to them forever. They have to strike out on their own. When they do, we have to rely on their good sense and judgment to keep them safe. We rely on that and the law. Kristin had good judgment, most of the time, but she could be impulsive, as young people are sometimes inclined to be. In Boston, studying to be an artist, she saw a young man she wanted to meet and arranged an introduction. They started dating.

At first he was lavish with attention and affection. He had a criminal record, but he told Kristin only what he wanted her to know about it. He told her more about his tortured childhood. She felt sorry for him. But soon his affection turned to jealousy and violence, and finally to murder. He shot and killed her on a sunlit sidewalk only a few months after they met, a few weeks after she refused to see him again.

A large part of this story first appeared in the *Washington Post* in late November 1992, almost six months after Kristin was killed. At first, I wasn't at all sure I would be able to do it, but I had to try. I knew it would be painful to write about what happened, but it would have been more painful to say nothing. The violence Kristin encountered before the shooting is happening to women all across the country and in some cases to men, too. I'm a newspaper reporter, and so I went up to Boston after the funeral to find out more. Thanks to a Brookline police lieutenant, who challenged me in just the right way at just the right time, I kept at it.

What I wrote for the *Post* won a Pulitzer Prize for feature writing in 1993. I was stunned, elated, and sad all at once. Journalists are always chasing "the big story," the big scandal, the big exposé. And by looking for it, we tend to ignore the bits and pieces. We brush them aside as inconsequential, as not worth writing about, and in doing that, we help make the worst happen. I'd always been chasing the headlines myself. As my wife, Rosemary, sometimes reminded me, I wasn't paying enough attention to our little girl. Then I won a Pulitzer Prize for writing about her murder. Winning a Pulitzer is every journalist's dream, but I never knew that dreams could hurt so much. When I first heard about it, I knew that I could tell Rosemary only by apologizing. And by saying that I think Kristin would have been pleased. Rosemary cried anyway.

In the end, Rosemary approved of what I'd written for the *Post.* She felt it helped wake people up to some of the flaws in the way the legal system handles domestic violence. But she did not want me to write this book. She said she felt it would serve mostly to enhance my reputation. I hope she's wrong. I thought writing the book would be easier than what I'd done for the *Post,* but it wasn't. I'd only scratched the surface. There was much more to be learned and more to be said, about Kristin, about the young man she met, and about the disjointed system of justice that left him free to stalk and kill her. This is Kristin's story. I'd give anything not to have written it.

Jekyll Island, Georgia

THE STALKING
OF KRISTIN

I

The phone was ringing insistently, hurrying me back to my desk. My daughter Helen was on the line, sobbing so hard she could barely catch her breath.

"Dad!" she shouted. "Come home! Right away!"

I was stunned. I had never heard her like this before. "What's wrong?" I asked. "What happened?"

I could hear my wife, Rosemary, crying in the background, making awful, tormented sounds. She wanted the answer to wait until I got home. "Don't tell him, don't tell him," I could hear her saying in the background. Helen hesitated for a few moments. She said something about a shooting and a hospital, but it didn't register. "What's wrong?" I asked her again.

"It's—it's Kristin. She's been shot . . . and killed."

Kristin? My Kristin? Our Kristin? I'd talked to her the afternoon before. Her last words to me were, "I love you, Dad." Suddenly I had trouble breathing myself.

It was 7:30 P.M., Saturday, May 30, 1992, near the end of a glorious spring day. Just ninety minutes before that devastating phone call, Kristin Lardner had been hurrying down Commonwealth Avenue in Boston to meet a roommate on the corner. A twenty-one-year-old art student, she was dressed all in black, her favorite non-color. She was looking forward to a big going-away party that weekend for the friend she was rushing to meet. Then, without warning, she was murdered, shot in the head and face by an ex-boyfriend who was under court orders to stay away from her.

What happened to Kristin was a crime that could and should have been prevented. There are no excuses for what her killer did, but the law made it easy for him. He should have been in jail that awful Saturday. But his case was far from unusual. The system of justice that failed to protect her is failing us all. It is a system that is making our streets, and homes, more dangerous in the name of making them safe. Every day, in every courthouse in the country, we keep recycling the same criminals onto the streets to give them another chance, a chance they then seize to commit more crimes. "To wink at a fault causes trouble," the Book of Proverbs says. Ours is a system that is addicted to winking, especially at the evil done to women.

At the *Washington Post,* where I worked covering "sin and corruption," as I usually told people who asked what I did, Helen's phone call left me fumbling around at my desk, compulsively picking up documents for a bank scandal story I was working on, then dumping them down again. I distractedly announced what I'd just been told and headed for the elevators. Two good friends from the *Post*'s national desk came with me to make sure I didn't drive off the road. I had no idea who had shot Kristin or why. I kept thinking that she must have been killed in a holdup at the liquor store where she was a part-time cashier and scolded myself for not seeing the dangers in such a job. And of course, I kept hoping that it was all some dreadful mistake. Someone had stolen Kristin's wallet about two weeks earlier and charged more than $2,000 to her American Express card. Perhaps it was someone else. It could have been anyone's child, anyone's beautiful daughter.

It was Kristin. Her big sister, Helen, would not have told me it was without making sure. Helen had been visiting with Rosemary when Kristin's roommate, Lauren Mace, called around seven that evening. "There's been a shooting," Lauren said and then broke down. Another roommate, Brian Fazekas, came on the line and said police wouldn't give them any details because they weren't relatives. Helen, a lawyer, quickly called the Boston police number Brian gave her. They patched her through to the emergency room at Brigham & Women's Hospital.

Dr. Alex Souther, the physician on duty, took the call. He didn't want to say anything over the phone, but Helen persisted. Finally, he asked her if Kristin had any distinguishing marks such as a birthmark or tattoo. I would have said no. Helen knew better. She said yes, she has a tattoo around her ankle. "I'm sorry to tell you this on the phone, but that young woman is dead," Souther told her in a flat, professional tone that sounded curt, cold, and final.

Rosemary was red with tears when I came in the door. I hugged her as hard as I could, but it didn't help. She doubled over in pain, clutching her stomach. "Oh no, oh no," she kept saying. The grief hit me, too. It boils up inside you, and it hurts, intensely, physically. I'd never felt it like that before, even when my mother died as I was sitting by her bedside. I knew that was coming. Nothing can prepare you for the death of your child. Helen told me of the phone calls from and to Boston. I remember thinking numbly: "Tattoo? What tattoo? Nobody told me about any tattoo." As it turned out, Kristin had designed it herself. She thought it was quite elegant.

There was a lot more, I'm ashamed to say, that I didn't know. But I was, slowly, painfully, about to find out. Helen gave me the Boston police number to call. The desk officer transferred me to homicide. Detective William Dwyer brought me out of the tiny cloud of ignorance I was still trying to hide behind. He did it as gently as he could.

"Is she gone?" I asked him.

"Yes," he said. "Apparently it was a boyfriend. He found out about a restraining order she had gotten. He waited for her to get out of work."

I was startled. A boyfriend? Kristin had told me just the day before that she wasn't dating anyone. I had been delighted to hear it. The last boyfriend I knew about had accidentally killed a little kitten he gave her. They had been dating for only a few weeks. I suggested she get rid of him, and I thought she had. I didn't know she had gotten a restraining order. I couldn't even remember his name.

"It's Michael Cartier," Dwyer told me. "He's in his early twenties. He shot her three times in the head."

Three times! In the head! This was unbelievable. This was a death sentence. She never had a chance to recover.

Dwyer told me the police had tracked Cartier to a nearby apartment building where he lived. Witnesses spotted him running into it after he killed Kristin. A police operations team was making plans to storm his apartment at the time I spoke with Dwyer. I found myself hoping that Cartier would not come out of it alive. When police burst into his apartment about fifteen minutes later, they found him sprawled on his bed, dead from a final act of self-pity. The .38 he used to kill Kristin was in his right hand. "He's dead," Dwyer told me when I called him back. "He shot himself dead."

Dwyer gave me the address and phone number of the medical examiner's office in Boston and told me to check in with them the next morning. He gave me directions on how to get to the morgue once we got to Boston, but I was beginning to wonder if we would ever get there. I had started calling the airlines, one after another, but they were in the midst of a big fare war that weekend. All I could get from any of them was a recorded message, and it was getting close to 10 P.M., when no more commercial flights would be taking off from Washington's National Airport. Frantic, I began thinking of trying to drive to Boston, but it was too far and I was too numb. Kristin was dead, but we needed to be there, to be with her, to find out what happened. The worst torture would have been an endless night at home.

The phone rang again, luckily this time. A good friend from the *Post,* Walter Pincus, had heard what happened and called to see if there was anything he could do. I told him Thanks, there wasn't, not unless he could commandeer an airline. He came close. He called *Post* publisher Don Graham, who generously arranged for us to use his chartered plane. Another old friend, George Wilson, drove us to the airport, where pilot Mark Lacagnina was filling out the necessary papers. Quiet and understanding, Lacagnina took off for Boston shortly after midnight, taxiing past darkened terminals that were taking no more travelers. It was a smooth and unremittingly dreadful flight. The only sounds were the engines, occasional chatter with control towers, and Rosemary's anguished cries. I hugged her, as much for my benefit as hers, and wept as quietly as I could.

My mind jumped back to the Sunday before, a lustrous morning on the towpath alongside the Chesapeake and Ohio canal. The trail is about the width of a pickup truck, stretching for miles along the banks of the Potomac, and if you get there early enough after sunrise and park above Chain Bridge, you can have it almost all to yourself. We had Helen's Irish wolfhound, Butler, with us. We walked him, or vice versa. A soft breeze ruffled the waters and made the leaves flutter with a lively rhythm. Butler and I ran up and down the towpath for about three miles while Rosemary walked. Everything seemed right with the world. All five children were either doing well in college or had decent jobs. "You know," I told Rosemary, "things have never been better for us."

Was someone listening? Six days later, I felt like Job. "When I looked for good, evil came. And when I waited for light, darkness came. . . . My lyre is turned to mourning, and my pipe to the voice of those who weep."

We crept into a hotel room in Boston around 3 A.M. that Sunday. Rosemary stared at the ceiling until sunrise, then dozed off. I got a few hours of fitful sleep. My education was about to begin. When Kristin went off to college there in 1988, we were delighted. Boston was a mecca for college students. A wonderful place to study art, find new friends, and spread her wings. Our minds were still in the 1950s, when we went to school, when violence on—and off—campus was relatively rare. Given the crime rates in D.C., murder capital of the nation, we thought we were sending her away from danger, not into it.

We didn't know how perilous it was for young women to try to get a college education without being harassed, attacked, molested, or worse. At least, I didn't know. I can't tell you how many fathers are in my boat, but I must confess that Rosemary has always accused me, at least until recently, of being a male chauvinist. I can remember her sputtering indignantly about the first lecture, delivered by an earnest Jesuit named George Bischofberger, in a Christian Marriage course that she took at Marquette University in Milwaukee, where we met years ago. "Now, girls," he told them, "you've got to remember: They're gonna hit ya." I used to think that was funny.

I called the morgue around 8:30 A.M. and talked briefly with the acting medical examiner, Dr. Stanton Kessler. He said Kristin was shot "twice—two shots in the face," but the examination was not yet complete. In fact, I later learned, it had yet to begin. He told me to call back around noon, after the autopsy was completed, and ask for Mr. Taralli, the chief technician. I said I wanted to see her. I'd been in morgues before. I've seen bodies rolled out of what amounts to big filing cabinets, shot up, mutilated, sliced, and crudely stitched back up as though they were burlap bags. I didn't mention any of that, but I was trying to serve notice that I did not want Kristin so defiled. I thought I could steel myself enough for a close-up look at her face, but I wasn't at all sure. Kessler said, rather stiffly I thought, "You may want to wait until after the funeral home gets her."

I tried to get the detective, Billy Dwyer. No luck. He was on the night shift. Call back at six, I was told. What next? We didn't want to go to Kristin's house yet. Her roommates, if they were lucky, would still be asleep. At loose ends, we went to mass at St. Cecilia's, a Back Bay church near our hotel. I knew where it was. I'd gone there for the first time on the first day of spring in 1988, when I took Kristin to Boston for interviews at and tours of the art schools she had in mind. Rosemary and I looked for an empty back row and found we had an ample choice. The priest gave an eloquent sermon on the senselessness of civil strife. He had very few listeners.

We looked for a breakfast spot that was open and bought the Boston papers from a nearby newsstand. Rosemary burst into tears as she read the *Herald*'s five-inch story on Kristin, chiseled into the bottom of an inside page. It was headlined: "Woman Killed in Allston Shootings," and it depicted Kristin as a twenty-five-year-old liquor store worker killed by a thirty-year-old man she had recently broken up with. "It makes it sound like some cheap liaison," Rosemary said. To me, it sounded like a hurry-up job, compiled over the phone and stuffed into the paper at the last minute on a Saturday night when most reporters had gone home. The *Herald*'s coverage would improve greatly in the next few days, but that morning all our news came from the *Globe*.

By coincidence, the *Globe*'s early editions carried the first of a thorough, insightful series on the explosion of family violence in Massachusetts. It was already claiming a life every eight days, most often of women who had obtained restraining orders or taken other legal steps to keep their abusive partners away. The presses were about to start rolling Saturday night when Kristin was killed. Her death was further proof of the problem. The *Globe* assigned three reporters to turn out a detailed article for the late editions under a front-page headline that said: "Brookline Woman Shot to Death by Ex-Boyfriend on Allston Street."

The story quoted Kristin's roommates; an anonymous friend of Cartier's; workers at Marty's, the store where Kristin worked, and at Bunratty's, the nightclub that employed Cartier; police; and others. I wiped away tears as I read how Kristin had been shot three times near a sandwich shop on Commonwealth Avenue as the restaurant's patrons looked on:

> Sonny Souarit, an employee of the sandwich shop, said Cartier shot Lardner once from a distance of 20 feet, then shot her twice more in the head as she lay on the ground.
>
> "It happened so fast," said Souarit. "We heard one pop and then we saw this man walk past the window. He had his gun in the air. He walked up, crouched down, and then we heard 'pop, pop.'"

One of the most maddening things about the article was the suggestion that the killing was somehow an act of love. "He loved her a lot, and it was probably a crime of passion," said a man who identified himself as a friend of Cartier's but wouldn't give his name. "He was in love—he didn't do it because he was nuts." He said they broke off "after Lardner said she wanted to date other people."

Cartier may have said that, but I don't think Kristin ever did. She'd had her fill of boyfriends for a while. She probably told Cartier she didn't want to see him anymore, and he jealously assumed there must have been someone else she wanted to date.

For me, the story was full of surprises. "He abused her once, and she drew the line there," Lauren Mace told the *Globe*. She said Cartier often called Kristin after their breakup, asking her for help. Mace said Kristin told him to seek counseling. "She cared about him, she thought he was a good person," Mace said. "The reason she got a restraining order was because she was afraid of him." Mace said Cartier grew up in foster homes, and Kristin was the only person he felt cared for him.

Cartier, I would later discover, told that to all the girls. It was very effective. It made them feel sorry for him, until it was too late.

I didn't know any of that at the time. I was just trying to make my way through the Sunday paper without making a scene. But I was taken aback at the twenty-second paragraph, anonymously quoting Cartier's "former boss" at Bunratty's about how he had almost called "Cartier's parole officer" because he "beat her quite a lot."

Parole officer? The phrase jumped out at me. So this Cartier had a criminal record? For what? And how often had he beaten her? Once or quite a lot? Once would have been more than enough for Kristin, I thought. The *Globe* said nothing more.

Up in Salem, Massachusetts, a young woman named Rose Ryan read the *Globe* that morning, too. She was dismayed by its superficial treatment of Cartier as a forlorn suitor driven to desperate measures. "They didn't have any information about him," she said. "All they had was some unknown friend who said that he wasn't crazy, that he really loved her, that this was a crime of passion." Rose Ryan knew that was nonsense. She had been Cartier's girlfriend before he started dating Kristin. Rose knew how vicious he could be, and she was exasperated that no one else was talking about it. She was already fuming over a phone call from a friend of Cartier's on Saturday night, right after the late-night TV news broadcasts about Kristin's murder. Rose was at her boyfriend Sean Casey's house when the call came. "Hey, did you guys hear what happened?" the caller asked. "Did you hear what Mike did? Wow, he's got balls!" Rose started yelling at him, and then she and Sean hung up on him.

Back at the hotel, we started making tentative funeral arrangements. At noon, I called the medical examiner's office and, as instructed, asked for Mr. Taralli. "The autopsy's done," he said. "It's going to be necessary for a member of her family to identify her." Kristin's roommate Brian Fazekas had already identified her, but that wasn't sufficient.

I said I'd come by later in the day and asked what the autopsy showed. "Two shots," Taralli recalled. "I did see two in the face. I'm not sure about a third. I wasn't present at the autopsy." I asked for Kessler. "Dr. Kessler left about ten minutes ago," Taralli said. "The assistants who helped him are not available." I was annoyed and upset. Had Kessler told me to call back by noon because he planned to be out the door by then? "Maybe he's on the golf course," I told Rosemary.

It took an interminable cab ride to get to Kristin's flat on Winchester Street in Brookline. Our cab driver couldn't even find Brookline, much less Winchester Street, without stopping twice to ask for directions. When we finally got to the address, we saw why Kristin liked it so much. It is a two-story brick house on a high slope above the road, with a clear view of the tall church steeples and high-rise buildings of downtown Boston. Kristin and her roommates occupied the first floor, a comfortable three-bedroom flat with spacious living and dining rooms and the worn, somewhat battered furniture that college students manage to collect.

Kristin's roommates, Lauren, Brian, and Matt Newton, and some other friends were in the living room, their faces as glum and depressed as ours. A frisky orange tiger kitten jumped across our path. She was Kristin's, bought by a close friend to replace the one Cartier had killed. Kristin named her Stubby, after a slight break in her tail, and had been teaching her to retrieve wadded-up pieces of paper, which is just what she was doing when she skittered past us into the dining room.

Stubby pounced on the paper ball and brought it back to me, pur-
ring as I scratched her ears. I tossed the ball and saw it land near a
striking nude portrait in angry reds, oranges, and yellows with a dark
green bruise on the subject's upper left leg. It was Kristin. Her roommates said she'd painted it after a brutal beating Cartier had given her
on their last date in April. It was a powerful work of art. I was stunned,
and impressed, and angry. I began groping for happier days.

Fathers always exaggerate, I know, but you can take my word for
it: She was quite beautiful, even if she always complained that her nose
was too big. We always told her it was a fine Sicilian nose, a gift from
her grandmother Rosetta, who was born in New York's Little Italy
shortly after the turn of the century. But that was the least of it. What
captivated you was her smile. Her bounce. Her exuberance. She was a
joy to be with. She made life sparkle.

Kristin was, at twenty-one, the youngest of our five children, all
of whom were very close to one another. She was born in D.C. at the
Columbia Hospital for Women on July 28, 1970, and got her first air-
plane ride five days later, jetting down with her mother to join the rest
of us for the traditional summer vacation on Jekyll Island off the coast
of Georgia. Everyone called her "tree frog" for the way she dug in her
legs when you picked her up.

Chevy Chase, D.C., where Kristin grew up, is a comfortable, tree-
lined neighborhood of old homes, heavily populated by teachers, lawyers, journalists, government workers, congressional staffers, and other
professionals. The trolley line made its way up there along Connecticut
Avenue in the 1890s. Many of the houses were turn-of-the-century pre-
fabs from Sears & Roebuck; now they cost hundreds of thousands of
dollars. It was still relatively inexpensive real estate in the mid-1960s,
when we arrived. Now children who grew up there wait for the day
they can make enough money to move back in. It's still in the city but
close to Rock Creek Park and sprinkled with wildlife like the big gray
owl and the portly raccoon Kristin once saw fighting in the back yard
and the ill-tempered possum that snuck into the basement and couldn't

find its way out. With all sorts of stores as well as a library and community center just a few blocks away on Connecticut Avenue, it has, as local architect Reena Racki points out, "all the conveniences of a big city in a small town setting: a place to shop, drop in for a cup of coffee or a bite to eat, to run errands or just meet your neighbors. And best of all you can bike or walk to it, with your stroller or shopping cart." It was a great place to grow up in, and Kristin attacked it with zest, eyes bright, chin forward, even when she was a little unsure of herself. Kindergarten lasted for only half a day when she attended, so she went twice, in the mornings at Blessed Sacrament and in the afternoons at Lafayette Elementary, while both parents worked. But it wasn't always smooth sailing, or spelling.

"For kindergarten [at Lafayette] I was in Ms. Jones class," she wrote a few years later. "About the only thing I rember [*sic*] was the time the class went to the zoo. I didn't bring in my permission slip until the day we went. I wasn't allowed to go."

There were other deprivations. Our Dodge Dart died on Interstate 270 when Rosemary was trying to take the older boys, Edmund and Richard, to Boy Scout camp at Deep Creek Lake, Maryland. We slowly got around to buying another car, a mammoth red Buick station wagon, but that was totaled in 1978 when a pickup truck hauling an air compressor slammed into the backside with Richard at the wheel. Luckily, no one was hurt. Also around that time the TV set expired. We decided to do without another car or TV for as long as possible, a decision that lasted into the early eighties for the TV, the late eighties for the car. Kristin, like the other children, missed the car, but she took the loss of the TV stoically. She plunged into books, which she read for hours on end before going to sleep in what she called her cotton "light-down." Fairy tales. Dr. Seuss. Ghost stories. And every Nancy Drew mystery that her sister Helen collected, which was just about all of them.

Kristin loved Halloween and the Fourth of July, costumes and fireworks. She went trick-or-treating dressed as Greta Garbo and played one of the witches in *Macbeth*. She had a grand time in tap-dancing class, even when she forgetfully showed up in her sneakers, and she produced a colorful collection of pottery in ceramics classes at the Community Center. When I came home from work, the other children usually took the arrival for granted. Kristin would come bounding down the stairs, arms out for a hug, saying "Hi, my dad." She put a rosy finish on the dreariest of days.

Some nights when I got home with time to spare, which wasn't often, I would tell her and Charlie, our youngest son, the adventures of Otto the Otter, a character my father had created for me. I made up the stories on the spot, not being able to recall my father's much better concoctions, but the children had no basis for comparison and were quite content with whatever I managed to dream up.

Her oldest brothers, Edmund, who was ten when she was born, and Richard, who was nine, doted on her despite occasional spats. She was always ready for adventure, never daunted by the odds. Once, when she was about five, they decided to take her over to Connecticut Avenue for a trip to the novelty shop. Ed had a black Huffy bike with a narrow rack on the back. It wasn't meant for sitting, but they were supposed to be babysitting, so they literally strapped Kristin to the rack and took off. They zipped down Northampton Street and were getting ready to cut through an alley when Kristin slipped a bit and cut her foot against the back spokes. She cried a little, but she didn't want to go back home. She impressed her big brothers even more by not saying a word about what happened to Mom or Dad.

I got a sense of what a brave girl Kristin was when she was nine. To Rosemary's longstanding chagrin, the doctor who delivered Kristin left her with a belly button protruding out of her tummy as though it had been tied by a bumbling Cub Scout. Kristin didn't like it, either, and would have liked it less and less as she grew older. So one day I took her over to Children's Hospital for the requisite surgery. She was eager to go at first, but she clasped my hand tightly as she was wheeled toward the doors of the operating room. She asked me if she would be all right. She nodded when I told her yes and furrowed her brow with a determined look. I went back to the waiting room to worry until the doctor came out to announce success. Kristin was delighted with the new look. She could face age in double digits. Two-piece bathing suits were now acceptable.

When she was small, she always got up in time for me to take her to Saturday morning cartoons at the Chevy Chase Library and then over to the neighborhood Drug Fair (now a video store), which still had a cafeteria. We would talk about the best cartoons of the morning or her friends or school, or sometimes we'd just sit in silence, thinking our own thoughts. Keeping silent company is an old family tradition. Then we would hurry back home, where there was always a pet waiting for attention. Like the older children, Kristin loved pets and she took cheerful care of a steady succession of cats, mice, gerbils, hamsters, and guinea pigs. Ed was the most assiduous collector, acquiring rabbits, tropical fish, lizards, and, for a short time, six black snakes that he brought back from summer camp at Deep Creek Lake. He wanted Rosemary to buy him a twenty-gallon tank for the collection, but she balked at the price, whatever it was in those days. Ed began scouting the classified ads for a secondhand purchase, but it was too late for the snakes. All escaped from the box he put them in and slithered into the yard and the world beyond. Our first formal notice of this came when Jocelyn Rotter began screaming in the next-door garage where she kept her bike.

Unfortunately, Mr. Sarni, who lived across the alley, got there first and killed the snake with a hoe. He was just doing his duty as he saw it, but the Lardner children never forgave him. Most of the other snakes made their way into nearby compost heaps or other refuges and were never seen again. Number six turned up the next spring, hanging from still another neighbor's pine tree. Rosemary told Richard to take it over to Rock Creek Park and leave it there. It was not the last of the line. Edmund found a queen snake, barely a foot long, that got loose in the upstairs hallway one Sunday and scared the daylights out of his great aunt Leona on a trip to the bathroom. The longest lasting was a little green snake that Helen brought home from a visit with relatives in Wisconsin and kept in an aquarium in her and Kristin's room.

Kristin eventually outdid them all. She bought a pet ball python her third year in college. It grew to be about four feet long and was quite friendly. Kristin liked to drape it around her neck. She called it Circe, after the sorceress who turned men into swine.

At Lafayette, the public school just a block and a half from our house, Kristin made many good friends and spent busy afternoons with them in classes at the Community Center. With Rosemary and I both working full-time, Kristin went from the Community Center to the adjoining library until Rosemary picked her up. The children's librarian, Barbara Roberts, kept a close watch on her and helped her find the books she wanted. Kristin's memories of those days, reflected in a little diary she composed in sixth grade as a class assignment, were bittersweet.

She remembered a stuffed bunny that I got for her in second grade. She named it Peter Rabbit or "Bunny for short" and brought it to school for show and tell. "Accidentally my friend threw it on the roof," she wrote. "I never saw it again." Third grade spotlighted some persistent spelling problems. "I rember [*sic*] not being able to spell 'gril,' I mean 'girl,' " she said. "It took me two weeks to remember [she got it right this time] it was 'ir,' not 'ri.' " Fourth grade was undistinguished. "I seem to have blocked [it] out of my mind." Fifth grade was exciting. "I had my old friends, Natasha R., Kim T. and Elise G. And I met new ones," she said. "The most memorable experience was when Lisa hung out the window (we were on the second floor) and almost got killed 'cause I wanted to know what it would feel like."

Spelling aside, she liked to write. My favorite is from the fourth grade; she titled it "The Bee That Roared." It reads, in its entirety:

> The first day I went to school I saw a bee. It said, Rrrr. I was very fritened. I thought it was a Loin! I ran under a table. That bee said Rrrrr all day. The next day it was saying Rrrr. I don't know how he held his breath so long.

Kristin's best friend at Lafayette was "Kim T.," Kim Thompson. They spent long hours together, especially at Kim's house, where they had an attic bedroom all to themselves and only those with the secret password could enter. Kristin would organize the fun and games, from making funny faces with Shrinky Dinks to playing elaborate card games that took up an entire bedspread. To Peg Thompson, Kim's mother, Kristin was like a second daughter. "She was so imaginative and always so much fun," Peg Thompson said. "I remember, I would read them stories. Kristin would stop me right in the middle and say, 'Wait, why is this happening?' Or she'd ask questions at the end. 'What does it mean?' You never knew what to expect from her." When Kristin stayed over on Saturday nights, she would get up early and take Kim with her to the folk mass at Blessed Sacrament Church, celebrated with guitar music. "Kim was so antireligious," her mother said. "Kristin would drag her. Kim absolutely loved it."

The most exciting excursions were on Friday night for the *Rocky Horror Picture Show* at Georgetown's Key Theater. Before the movie, the audience would get revved up by dancing in the aisles to punk videos. Participation was the point. When someone in the movie said, "Let's have a toast," the fans in the theater would raise their cups or throw toast. When it rained in the movie, the Key would turn on the sprinkler system, or everyone would squirt one another with water guns. Kim and Kristin went as often as they could. Peg Thompson would drive them down and then retrieve them for the ride back home. "I could not believe I was doing this," she said. "Here I was in Georgetown in the middle of the night, waiting to pick up these two little girls." After a while, Kim said, they went on their own.

Lisa Galaty (Elise G.), another close friend, used to hang out with Kim and Kristin, too. At Lafayette, Lisa and Kristin often traded lunches. Kristin usually had ham and swiss cheese on soft white bread with mustard. "I loved those sandwiches," Lisa remembers. "I always had bologna on whole wheat with mayonnaise. I would give mine to Kristin but I don't know if she ate it. She would just give me half of hers." After school, Kristin would bring Lisa home and they'd make some more. Then they went to a favorite corner of the living room and played rummy, Go Fish, or Kristin's favorite, an ingenious battery-operated game called "Dark Tower." I liked to play it with Kristin on weekends myself.

Sometimes, the action would switch to Lisa's house, two blocks away. One summery day, around the end of fourth grade, she and Kristin got nostalgic for Christmas, so they collected all the gift wrapping paper they could find in both houses and got to work.

"We would wrap a plate, anything," Lisa said. "It was fun. We put Christmas records on and we just wrapped and wrapped. Then we opened everything up."

Hanging out the second-floor window at Lafayette sticks in Lisa's mind, too. Some of the girls in Mrs. Lambros' fifth-grade class—Kristin, Kim, Lisa, and Juliet Eilprin—frequently took over a study carrel in the back of the room. One day, at Kristin's instigation, they persuaded Lisa to drape herself out the window and tell them how it felt.

"Somehow it wasn't scary," Lisa said. "They were looking out the window at me and we were all singing 'Slip Slidin' Away' by Paul Simon. I think there was a ledge beneath me to fall on. Maybe they were laughing at me for being so stupid, but I felt real brave. I don't remember how I got back in. I may have hung out with my elbows. Maybe they helped pull me up."

The girls were halfway through fifth grade when they fell in love with the Beatles. Kristin was at Lisa's house when they heard on the radio that John Lennon had been killed, and the news report prompted them to find out more. Kristin knew there were a good number of Beatles records in the Lardner house, thanks to her brothers and sister, and the ten-year-olds were soon enthralled.

"We always did things as a unit," Elise said. "We were just obsessed. We would sit there at lunch in the cafeteria at Lafayette and talk about them. We made up a fan club. We decided which Beatle we were. Kristin was George Harrison because she had bushy eyebrows. I was Paul McCartney because I had puppy dog eyes, eyes that sagged. Juliet had round glasses so she was John Lennon. Kim was Ringo Starr because of her nose. . . . We all hated our noses. I remember fantasizing about getting a nose job."

The new fan club listened to all the Beatles records they could, rented a Beatles record video called the Magical Mystery Tour that they watched repeatedly, and talked for hours about seeing a Beatles concert with all of them there. They decided they would give their right arms to bring John Lennon back for the show. (Kristin would have been delighted to know that technology has now made that come true.)

Kristin liked to be different. Often she took her cue from books. There was always something new to read since she shared a room with

Helen, who was twelve years older. When she was nine, she was captivated by Pippi Longstocking with her fantastic strength and powers of invention second to none. More than that, Pippi was very irreverent and didn't hearken to authority. And she was only nine years old herself. Like Pippi, Kristin soon took to sleeping with her feet on the pillow and head way down under the quilt. She seemed to enjoy it. As Pippi said, "It's the only real way to sleep." Kristin probably even dreamed of tossing bothersome boys in the air like Pippi did.

When she was in high school, she took up weightlifting, using her brothers' equipment to build up her biceps and triceps. I thought it was good exercise until she showed me a bodybuilding magazine with glistening illustrations of the musclebound female physique she had in mind. Suddenly I began to yearn for the junior high days when she thought of becoming a model and took cosmetics courses at Neiman Marcus, a gift from sister Helen, to help her along. She still wasn't happy with her nose, but she knew how to ham it up for the camera. Kim Thompson, an aspiring photographer, made a portfolio for her. "She was gorgeous, so exotic," said Peg Thompson, an unabashed admirer. "And she played it up. She really had style." Kristin took the portfolio with her to sound out a couple of modeling studios. One turned her down, but the other was impressed. "They told her to come back when she was 5'7"," said Kim, who went with her. "But when she got to be 5'7", she was no longer into it. We were in eighth grade when I made the portfolio for her. We both wanted to be models. Kristin taught me how to put on eyeliner, shave my legs, do all that beauty stuff."

Kristin enjoyed giving presents. On one of Kim's birthdays, Kristin gave her a necklace of a horse that she bought at the National Zoo. It said "genuine pewter" on the back. Kim loved horses. She liked the necklace and put it on, but Kristin was even more pleased with it. "It's genuine pewter," she kept saying. At another party, she gave Kim a pair of sunglasses with a leopard-pattern frame that she bought at a shop in Georgetown called Commander Salamander. Kristin could hardly contain her enthusiasm. "She was so excited about the presents she gave," Lisa said. "They jumped out at you."

The exuberance was contagious, but sometimes it could be exasperating, too. Kristin reached puberty before a lot of her friends. She was delighted even if her friends were not. "She used to walk around saying, 'I'm an early bloomer, I'm an early bloomer.' Mostly to me and Kim," Lisa remembers. Kristin also took great pleasure from a book on the signs of the zodiac that she found at the library and kept long past the due date. "It told you about the personalities of the different signs," Lisa said. "You'd take it as dogma. You'd say, 'Okay, this is what I will be like when I have a boyfriend.' This was in fifth grade. Kristin was a Leo. I was a Virgo. She was so happy she was a Leo. Leos were the life of the party. I was always a little bit jealous."

Despite all of Kristin's verve, Rosemary often worried about her, as she did about the other children, afraid they wouldn't be strong-minded enough, that they would be "led around by the nose." But Kristin, like her brothers and sister, never hesitated to question authority. With her friends, she was more eager to please, up to a point. But if you passed that point, watch out. In that, Kristin was like her mother. She had too much patience and not enough. As she grew older, she would overlook things she shouldn't, and then blow up over a seemingly trivial matter. If you pushed her too far or accused her falsely, she would make it clear that she did not need to talk to you ever again. Once, in grammar school, she was at a girlfriend's house, jumping up and down on the bed and playing with the girl's pet hamster. Her friend accidentally landed on the hamster, killing it, and told her parents Kristin did it. Kristin did not play and, so far as I know, rarely spoke with the "hamster killer" again. If you did her a worse wrong, she would pursue you relentlessly, as she did a young woman she once spotted wearing earrings from a large costume jewelry collection that had been stolen from her in its entirety. Kristin confronted the suspect repeatedly, complained several times to the girl's mother, and even asked for a room search. It happened in high school, but Kristin was still talking about getting her jewelry back not long before she was killed.

"She kept a lot of things inside her, big things, little things—which she shouldn't have," Lauren Mace said. "Once I got into a big fight with her. She walked in one day, and she was really rude. It came to the point where we had a sitdown. She was shaking because she didn't want to tell me what was bothering her. I said, 'Kristin, you're my friend. What's wrong?' She was really p.o.'d. She finally told me what was bothering her. It wasn't really that much. But she'd kept it to herself. She would also forgive people real easily for things she shouldn't have."

In any case, I never worried about Kristin's independence. Most teenagers pay too much attention to what their friends think. To me, her biggest fault may have been that she took too long in the shower— and you never knew what color her hair was going to be when she emerged. It was, in its natural state, a beautiful chestnut, but she liked to experiment. In one notable episode, the dye didn't take to her hair but turned her neck and scalp green. Classmates at the Museum School teased her about it. One of them, Chris Larkin, asked her if she wore a lot of copper or brass jewelry. Kristin thought that was pretty funny.

2

Kristin's room on Winchester Street was unmistakably hers. We would have recognized it if we had encountered it on another planet. It was in the middle of the house, with windows overlooking a quiet driveway, and it was remarkably neat. Even the canceled checks and bills were in careful order. Circe the snake was curled up comfortably in her tank, nestled against a piece of driftwood Kristin had found on Jekyll Island the summer before.

In the tape player by the windows was a punk tune by a group called Suicidal Tendencies. On the turntable near her futon bed was a recording of Stravinsky's "Rite of Spring." Kristin liked to sit up late, reading and listening to music. Her books, paperbacks mostly, included Alice Walker's *The Color Purple* and Margaret Atwood's *The Handmaid's Tale*, both with strong feminist themes, and Christopher Lasch's *The Minimalist Self*, a provocative criticism of contemporary society, along with favorites by Sinclair Lewis, Dickens, and E. B. White and a book about upper- and middle-caste women in Hindu families in Calcutta.

On a shelf and in a drawer were some photo albums, with pictures going back to her ninth-grade prom at Alice Deal Junior High, showing Kristin smiling brightly in a sleeveless black-fringe evening dress. There were numerous photos of Jason Corkin, a former boyfriend and Boston University student, who had returned to his native New Zealand the previous year, but apparently none of Michael Cartier. The only signs I could find of Cartier were on the pink plaintiff's copies of a Complaint for Protection from Abuse and several Abuse Prevention Orders that Kristin had obtained earlier that month and carefully folded away in a bureau drawer. The court copies, I would discover, had more detail. Her copy of the complaint simply stated that he had "caused me physical harm" on April 16, 1992, and the prevention orders instructed him to stay away from her and "not to abuse" her.

Kristin said in the complaint, which she dated May 11, that she and Cartier had been dating since January 1992, that they were "boyfriend/girlfriend," and that they had been seeing each other "daily" until the relationship ended on April 16. She filled out a box saying he had "placed me in fear of imminent serious physical harm."

I thought back with a frown to the phone calls I'd made to her since then. Brian usually answered, in what I vaguely thought was a suspicious, apprehensive way when he heard a male voice asking for Kristin. "Who's calling?" he would ask. "Her father," I would reply. I should have asked, "Who else did you think it might be?" Perhaps I should have asked Kristin, too, but I'm sure her response would have been reassuring and unenlightening. Children tell their parents what they want them to know, and she was twenty-one, after all. She was taking care of the problem, legally and on her own, as a grown-up woman should.

Rosemary was staring at the floor, lost in thought, grieving for her little girl. "Why didn't she tell us?" she kept asking. "Why didn't she tell us?" I just shook my head. The truth is, I didn't know then and I don't know now. I'm guessing. But I think it's a pretty good guess: She saw no need to call home. It would have been embarrassing. Besides, she told herself, she could handle it. And what if she had told us? What would I have done? Called the police? She'd already called the police. Demanded a court order? She'd already gotten one. Gone up to Boston with a crowbar? Or a gun? Maybe I should have. More likely, I would have asked her, "Kristin, is there anything I can do? Is there anything you want me to do? Do you want to come home?" And she would have said, "No, Dad. I can take care of it." And I would have said, "Fine, I'm sure you can." I had great confidence in her. I had no idea of what I now know are the clear and present dangers posed by men like Michael Cartier.

I went back toward the living room at the front of the house, where Kristin's friends were morosely drifting in and out of the house in awkward succession. There I learned a little more about Cartier, but at that point, for me, a little was a lot. Kristin's friends talked about how jealous he was, how he would come over and talk only to her, how intimidated he was, or pretended to be, in the company of college students.

A tall, handsome young man who had just graduated from BU, Wiley Hyde, stopped by to offer condolences. His story jolted me. Kristin and he had once roomed together on Glenville Avenue in Brighton, along with Lauren, Matt, and others. He came over to Winchester Street quite often. On the afternoon of May 28, just two days before she was killed, he and Kristin were hanging out together. Sometimes they played darts or cards. This time they played Scrabble (Kristin won) and chess (Wiley won), and then they decided to get something to eat.

"We kind of ran out of games," Wiley said. "I said, 'I have a motorcycle here.' It was an old Yamaha cult bike, a seventies bike. Two-stroke load. She said, 'Oh, let me come with you.' There was an extra helmet at the place that one of Lauren's friends had left." Kristin grabbed it and put it on. Hyde was impressed. "She was a great person, a great sport," he said. "She was up for anything. She was one of the guys."[1]

First stop was the Bay Bank branch on Commonwealth Avenue, two doors from Marty's Liquors. Kristin wanted to get some cash from the automatic teller. Wiley wheeled down Harvard from Brookline, then turned left onto Commonwealth "into the horse lane" next to the sidewalk. They passed Marty's and parked. Kristin saw Cartier staring in the liquor store window. "Did you see that?" she asked Hyde as they got off the bike. "Mike was peeking in the window. Like he was trying to see if I was working. What a weirdo!"

Wiley didn't see him. And he didn't think that Cartier saw them.

Cartier had disappeared by the time Kristin got her money, and she and Wiley walked down the sidewalk together, past Marty's, across Harvard, to a Boston Chicken on the corner, just a few doors from Bunratty's. They hemmed and hawed and decided it was too expensive. "We went someplace else," Wiley said, "a Thai place on Brighton Avenue." From there, he brought Kristin back to her apartment on Winchester, and then he went home.

Around 12:30 A.M., he got restless and went over to Bunratty's. He thought he might find Andy Meuse, another old roommate from Glenville Avenue. At that hour, Wiley said, "you can get in for free and still see the bands playing. It's too late to charge you." Besides, he liked to play the pinball machines downstairs. Cartier saw him and went over for a few words. It seems plain now that he had seen Kristin and Wiley together. "He was trying to be the tough guy," Hyde said. "He was definitely being weird." Cartier was "usually straightforward" but not this time. He began an awkward conversation to find out where Hyde lived, asking about a party in the same apartment building that had taken place a week earlier.

"Where is this party?" Cartier asked, as though it were still going on.

"Oh, those guys live right upstairs from me," Hyde told him.

"Oh, where is that?" Cartier asked. "Where do you live?"

Somewhat puzzled, Hyde gave him the address. "I thought it was kind of weird, but I didn't think too much about it," he said. He wondered about it after the shooting.

I was numb when I first talked with Wiley, too dull and dim to appreciate details or even comprehend them. It would be weeks before I contacted him again and pestered him to repeat himself. But I remembered the import of what he had told me: What happened to Kristin was no uncontrollable outburst of passion, no irresistible impulse. It was premeditated murder. Michael Cartier had been stalking her.

Mike Dillon, a clerk at Marty's, came over, still shaken by the horror of what he had seen the day before. He had clocked out at 6 P.M. and just stepped onto the sidewalk when he heard the first shattering noise. Once again, I took in what he had to say in slow, befuddled motion. "It was very loud," he told me. "I looked up immediately. I saw Kristin fall." She dropped instantly to the sidewalk outside the Soap-A-Rama, a combination laundromat, tanning salon, and video rental store, four doors from Marty's. "She was lying on her right side, curled up in kind of a fetal position," Mike said. "I kind of froze in my tracks."

Witnesses said the assailant came at her from behind and shot once. Then he ducked into a nearby alley, between Arbuckle's Restaurant and the Heads Up Salon. Al Silva, a restaurant worker at Arbuckle's, told police he saw the man flee. Silva started toward Kristin to see if he could help her. Suddenly Cartier darted back out of the alley, rushed past Silva, and leaned down over her. He wanted to make sure she was dead.

"He shot her twice more in the left side of the head," Mike Dillon said. "Then I saw him run down the alley again. . . . I had no idea who he was. I was able to give some sort of description, but I was still in shock. I didn't know what to do. I took one of her hands for a second or so, I don't know why. Then I ran back to call the police, but I saw a woman in the flower shop. She was already on the phone."

I nodded, trying to catch every word. But he talked so quickly that would have been impossible. He was still upset, too excited to go slow. In the weeks ahead, I would ask him to repeat himself. Right now, I wanted to see where it happened. There had been a photo in the *Globe* that morning of a policeman at the scene, with Kristin's black leather knapsack in the background next to a dark spot on the sidewalk. I'd grimaced and hurried past it. Now I wanted a better idea of what Mike and Wiley were talking about. James Harn, a thoughtful philosophy major who had been one of Kristin's roommates in the Glenville Avenue apartment, offered to take me, but not without a quizzical look. "You have to do this, don't you?" he said.

The question caught me off guard. Did I need an excuse? Was I being ghoulish? "Yes," I told him after a moment's hesitation, fumbling for a reason. "I'm a reporter. This is what I do." Better to do something than just sit here, I told myself. Keep moving. Keep busy. I asked Rosemary if she wanted to come, but I knew she wouldn't.

I wasn't prepared for what I found: a dark pool of caked blood, the shape of a curled-up body, on a narrow sidewalk outside the video store. It was Kristin's. No one needed to show me where she died. I thought she'd fallen outside the sandwich shop. I thought someone would have washed it away. I thought a thousand things. Harn looked at me as I looked at what was left of my daughter. In a way, I was glad that no one had scrubbed it away. I didn't want Kristin to be forgotten.

She wasn't. In the days ahead, people would come by to lay flowers. Women's groups stopped to put up handmade posters saying "Women, Fight Back" and "Women Unite." A man walked into Gay's flower shop, a few doors closer to Marty's, with a photo of Kristin he'd had enlarged from the newspaper. "He asked if he could put it up," said Gay Sheldon, one of the proprietors. "I told him to lay flowers. People came in here to buy them. I decided we couldn't charge for that. Everyone was touched in a different way." When rain fell on Boston Monday afternoon, it watered a dozen roses and about as many pink and yellow carnations where Kristin had died.

City maintenance crews didn't do anything at first. The proprietor of the video store eventually washed the blood away. "He found it uncomfortable that people were laying flowers there," Sheldon said. Then some of Kristin's friends painted the spot with black paint as sort of a memorial, but it didn't last long. The city could stomach the blood but not black paint. A city crew came by the next day and toned it down to battleship gray. It's fading now, but you can still see it. I may steal up there some night and paint it again.

The walk back to Winchester Street is slightly uphill. It felt like climbing a mountain trail. Rosemary was still in Kristin's room, her tears telling her thoughts. She had always wanted to be an artist herself. When she and I started dating, she was taking art classes at the Layton School of Art in Milwaukee at night. They were long sessions, three hours twice a week, in a modern building overlooking Lake Michigan. It sometimes got quite cold in the classrooms, especially for the models. Rosemary studied painting and drawing for two years, with much more enthusiasm than she was able to muster for most of the academic courses she took at Marquette. Her face glowed when she had a brush in her hand. My favorite painting was an oil portrait she did of an old man in a brown jacket who posed for the students. It's still sitting in the basement, unframed, on top of some boxes from the Watergate cover-up trial. She was still quite good when she had the time for it, especially with oils. She would usually bring a sketchbook with her on summer vacations, and she took a few more art and art history courses at the University of Miami when we lived there and at the University of Maryland after Kristin was born. She had talked with Kristin about opening an art store together, after Kristin graduated. Kristin's friends said she had talked about it, too.

Kristin's work was in the dining room. She had turned it into a studio, and it was scattered with clear signs of the talent that caught the attention of teachers at the School of the Museum of Fine Arts. Wide-banded silver and brass rings, one with a Celtic design, others filigreed with what looked like barbed wire. The nude self-portrait. Some striking sculptures of bound figures. A madonna she had painted for her mother, painstakingly gilded. A curved arc of marble, brindled and polished, looking, as Kristin wrote, "like a wave, curving and sensual."

A reporter for the *Boston Herald,* Sarah Koch, came by the house to talk to Kristin's friends, discovered I was there, and asked to talk with me. I didn't want to, but hell, I was a reporter myself, and the idea of me hiding in my daughter's room didn't seem right. I showed Koch the rings Kristin had made. "She did beautiful work, and I think she would have made a fine artist," I said. "Everything about her was special." I also said I knew little of the troubles she'd had with Cartier, even though I'd talked to her as recently as Friday. But I said, "Kristin did, from all we could tell, the right thing in getting the court order." At that point, I broke down in tears. Koch handled the subject tastefully, under a sidebar the next morning headlined: "A Young Artist's Dreams Brought to an End."

A little later, a reporter from the *Globe,* Don Aucoin, left a message at the flat. I felt obliged to talk to him, too, so I called him back. He'd already spoken with our daughter Helen, so he had a good sense of Kristin's indomitable spirit, her distaste for convention, the punk look she'd adopted in her teens. Helen even mentioned the ankle tattoo

Kristin had gotten that spring. Kristin had told her sister about it in wait-till-you-see-it tones over the phone. "She would act so tough and do this whole punk thing, but she was just so kindhearted," Helen said. "That's how she took this guy in. She saw the best in everyone."

When Aucoin asked me about that, I agreed. "She would see the good side of people, obviously to her detriment," I said. I was determined to keep my composure this time, but once again I lost it as I spoke of my cheerful conversation with Kristin just two days earlier and her last words, "I love you, Dad." I said they would stay with me forever "as fresh as they were when she said them."

Rosemary took a dim view of so much talking in public about Kristin until I reminded her of her distasteful reaction to the coverage in the morning's *Herald*. She'd been alarmed not because of the mistaken ages it gave, but mainly because it was so short and bereft of any insights into what a wonderful person Kristin was. Having said all that, I must admit that I backed off when a TV reporter came knocking at the door. I didn't want to start crying on camera, and by now I knew the only sure way to avoid that was to avoid the camera. I decided to duck all TV requests by laying them off on daughter Helen and son Richard in Washington. They did a great job: angry, plain-spoken, and composed. Unlike their father, they managed to keep their tears to themselves.

It was late afternoon by now: time to go to the morgue. Rosemary didn't want to come, and I didn't want her to. Brian offered to drive me down in his car. He'd been there the night before. Billy Hayes, the director of the funeral home that was going to ship Kristin's body to Washington, met us there. He was congenial and comforting, a perfect fit for what has to be a difficult, often depressing job. He knew just what to say and how to say it. I'd tried to get ready for what I thought was about to happen, reminding myself that I'd been in morgues before. I expected Kristin to be wheeled out on a gurney. I wanted to hug her. But this was different. No doubt it was designed to be as painless as possible. It was remote and unreal.

We were directed to a spartan anteroom with a TV monitor on a high ledge against a wall. It produced a head-and-shoulders view of my little girl, lying dead on a table somewhere else in the building, a sheet pulled up almost to her neck. The attendants had focused the camera so that the least damaged side of her face was showing, but I could still see an awful wound in her forehead. It was hard for me to breathe. I didn't try to hold back the tears. I confirmed into some unseen loudspeaker that it was my daughter, it was Kristin, but the distant, antiseptic atmosphere bothered me. It struck me as Orwellian. I said that I wanted to see her, and not on some black-and-white TV screen. The voice on the other end of the loudspeaker began to give me an argument, when Billy Hayes intervened.

Wait until tomorrow, until he had a chance to take her to his funeral home, he suggested. I could see her then. There was an urgent, compassionate look on his face that told me I didn't know what I was doing. He knew what Kristin looked like at that moment far better than I did. So I agreed. We left with an envelope stuffed with the contents of Kristin's purse. I didn't open it.

By the time Brian drove me back to Brookline, it was after 6 P.M. Detective Dwyer and the other homicide detective on the case, Mark Molloy, were on duty by now. I called Dwyer and told him I would like to have a copy of the police report on the case. He and Molloy offered to meet us at Kristin's flat and give us a ride back to the hotel. The two detectives, faces furrowed by their work, parked on the other side of Winchester Street, signaled their arrival, and waited for us to come out. I put some of Kristin's things, mostly papers, bills, and bank records, into a shopping bag, and we got into the back of the unmarked police sedan. It was a difficult trip, for all of us. What do you say to the parents of a girl who has just been killed by someone who, we would soon learn, had a record as long as your arm? Dwyer was driving. He made it back to our hotel, the Boston Sheraton, in minutes, weaving in and out of heavy traffic like a stock car driver. It was a hell of a ride. I closed my eyes once or twice. There were no sirens. He didn't need them. He put our cabbie to shame.

Back at the hotel, we headed for a cocktail lounge just inside the entrance. I offered them a drink, but they declined. Quite properly, I realized. They were on duty. Dwyer produced the homicide report on

Kristin. Then he showed me a printout of the state's CORI (Criminal Offender Record Information) report on Michael Cartier.

I was stunned. It was three pages stretched out. But all I got was a quick look. I couldn't have a copy. The law in Massachusetts, as it stood then and as it still stands in many states, seemed to care more about the criminal's rights. A convict's privacy might be invaded if the public could find out what a thug he was—how many times he'd been arrested and tried, and on what charges—even after he was found guilty beyond a reasonable doubt. The CORI law was to change in Massachusetts in just a few weeks, but until then, I had no right to obtain the record of my daughter's killer.

The two detectives had seemed gruff at first, but now they became more soft-spoken. "Was she your only child?" Molloy asked. "No," Rosemary said, "we have four other children." Molloy nodded sympathetically. Cartier, he concluded, "was with the wrong girl at the wrong time."

I didn't say anything, but I winced. What was that supposed to mean? I asked Rosemary after they left. I'm sure they were just trying to find something comforting to say, but who could have been "the right girl" for someone like Cartier? Rosemary was too torn with grief to do more than shake her head.

The detectives left us with a final bit of well-meant advice. "Try to put this behind you," they told us. "Don't keep going over what happened. Get on with your lives." Dwyer gave us a set of the police reports on the homicide but not Cartier's "rap sheet." That was confidential. Cartier, they emphasized, was dead. They told us, incorrectly as it turned out, that he left no parents, no relatives who could be located. As far as they were concerned, the case was closed.

The trouble is, Cartier had accessories. In the probation system. In the courts. And perhaps in friends who had a glimmering of what he intended to do. What happened to Kristin was, as one Massachusetts prosecutor would later call it, "almost a primer of how the system can fail."[2]

When we got back to our room, we found we'd missed a number of important calls, including one from Dr. Kessler, the acting medical examiner. I talked to him over the phone later that night. He said Kristin had been shot twice, in the head and face, from a distance of perhaps four to six inches. Either would have been fatal. "There was no skull left," he said. He said, "Maybe Cartier fired three shots," but he could find no evidence of that. He said the forehead wound had been caused by a piece of bone exploding outward and nothing more. I thought the autopsy was wrong then, and I still do. Witnesses heard three shots, and three spent shell casings were found. Kessler suggested that the first shot might have missed and that Kristin just fell to the ground out of fright. I don't think so, not when witnesses said she was unconscious before the last shots were fired. But it's a distinction without a difference. It won't bring Kristin back.

I told Kessler I would like a copy of the autopsy report. "You don't want a copy," he replied. "It's up to you, but remember her as she was, not as she is." I told myself I wouldn't have any trouble doing that, but I wondered. Perplexed, I turned on the TV set to watch the late news. The CBS affiliate, Channel 7, had a report on the shooting that quoted a Brookline police lieutenant about the restraining order Kristin had gotten and a sympathetic friend of Cartier saying that he had been "abused as a kid." Rosemary, I was glad to see, had fallen asleep. Disheartened and exhausted, I turned out the lights.

The Monday morning papers were full of news. "Hub Killer Abused Other Women," the *Boston Herald* said in a front-page headline over a picture of Kristin. "For the second time in a week," the story said, "a Massachusetts woman has died at the hands of a man who, authorities say, should have been in jail.

"Police said yesterday a Brighton man with a history of abusing former girlfriends should have been behind bars the day he murdered a 21-year-old arts student who had tried to get him into professional counseling.

"Convicted felon Michael Cartier, 22, was on probation and under a restraining order when he shot Kristin Lardner in broad daylight . . .

"The latest tragedy echoes last Monday's death of 27-year-old Suzanne Hoeg, who was allegedly killed in front of two of her three children by her husband, Roger, 39. At the time of the slaying, Roger Hoeg was wanted on a warrant of assault and battery and threatening to murder his wife, but Brockton Police failed to execute the warrant despite several opportunities."

I was glad to see the *Herald* had gotten a closer look at Cartier's rap sheet than I had the night before. It didn't mention the rap sheet, of course. It referred to what "court records" showed about a criminal record dating back to 1987, when he was seventeen. But the courts were closed on Sunday when the article was written, and the cases that dealt with Cartier were scattered across the state. Only the CORI report laid it all out in one place.

The story jumped to a two-page spread where it quoted Brookline Police Sgt. Robert G. Simmons, who had helped Kristin get her first court order against Cartier on May 11. She had obtained a permanent order, good for a year, on May 19.

"Simmons said he doesn't know why Cartier didn't end up imprisoned after the restraining order was issued May 19. At the time, court records show, Cartier was on probation from several prior criminal offenses and should have been forced to surrender based on the issuance of the restraining order, which constituted a violation of his probation. 'The way the law is written, he should have been back in the can,' Simmons said."

A related story dealt with Massachusetts' enactment of a tough "anti-stalking" bill two weeks earlier, on May 18, and was headlined: " 'Anti-Stalking' Law Difficult to Enforce." It pointed out that Cartier could have been jailed under the new law if Kristin had told police he was bothering her after she got her restraining order on May 19. As it turned out, he was stalking her. The new law carries a minimum one-year sentence for those who repeatedly follow or threaten a woman in violation of a restraining order. The story also quoted Massachusetts Attorney General Scott L. Harshbarger about the difficulties of enforcing the law. Harshbarger said, "A key dilemma confronting women is their fear of 'escalating' the danger by turning to law enforcement to protect them."

"There's a tremendously disheartening cycle in which these

women are trapped," he said. "Once you make an arrest, you raise the stakes and the victim really needs to be supported. Otherwise, these guys' macho ego, often in combination with drugs, alcohol, passion and jealousy, make them very dangerous individuals."

At that point, almost twenty states had enacted laws against stalking.[3] California was the first to make it a crime, spurred in 1990 by the murder the year before of actress Rebecca Schaeffer and a fan's chronic harassment of comedian David Letterman. Since then, the laws have spread like brushfire. Forty-eight states and the District of Columbia have prohibited stalking, with a sometimes bewildering variety of definitions and penalties. But enforcement is another matter. Many prosecutors and police don't like the law their legislatures have given them, partly because of complaints about constitutionality, partly because the enforcers are more comfortable with other laws that have been on the books for years, partly because stalking is most often defined as a misdemeanor, something that is usually penalized with nothing more than a slap on the wrist. The criminal justice system tells itself that it has more important crimes to worry about.

The trouble is that it often has those bigger crimes to worry about—crimes like Kristin's murder—because it dismissed the smaller ones as unworthy of serious attention. Perhaps the biggest flaw in our criminal justice system today is its inattention to supposedly minor crime, its failure to deal with the deviant behavior that disrupts communities and is the first step toward clearly serious crimes of violence.[4] The system today resembles one of those tightfisted, supposedly outmoded medical insurance companies that tell you to come back when you have cancer. The "preventive medicine" it grudgingly pays for, which it calls probation, is the routine prescription for any first offender. It is usually a hoax, a placebo that makes society feel better while doing nothing to the criminal except convincing him that he has nothing to worry about.

As one St. Louis prosecutor told the *Post,* the "fraud" in the criminal justice system is that virtually no one convicted of a misdemeanor does jail time. Misdemeanors, of course, include assaults, much domestic violence, property destruction, and the like. And a "misdemeanor" assault can be quite vicious.[5] The point is that long before an arrest for murder or life-threatening violence, many criminals go through a juvenile court system where the likelihood of punishment is very low. Then, in many states,[6] these same people enter the adult system with records expunged. When they get arrested as adults, they get put on probation, which, as Massachusetts Governor William Weld has observed, "is not taken seriously by the criminal element."[7] The perpetrators become convinced they can get away with their criminal conduct. If they do eventually wind up in state prison, most of them will by then be violent or repeat offenders, responsible for dozens of crimes they were never charged with as well as the ones they were convicted of committing.[8]

But I'm getting ahead of myself. I knew very little of that then. I'd been covering court cases and criminal investigations, among other assignments, for more than thirty years when my daughter was killed. Most of them were high-profile cases: Watergate cover-up defendants in Washington; Mafia figures in New York and Kansas City; Teamster officials in Chicago; contract killers in Cleveland; Ku Klux Klan murderers in Georgia; Robert Kennedy's assassin in Los Angeles; former White House aide Oliver North and other Iran-contra defendants in Washington again. Except for the Iran-contra cases, those defendants were all convicted and went to prison as they deserved. It wasn't until Kristin was murdered that I began paying closer attention to the supposedly routine violence that police, prosecutors, and judges see every day. It wasn't until then that I realized how hard it is to be put behind bars. What surprised me was not the number of people in prison and jail, but the number of those who weren't.

Across the country, according to the latest Justice Department study, 59 percent of the 4.8 million people convicted of a crime and under active correctional supervision in 1992 were on probation, and another 13.8 percent were on parole.[9] To put it more simply, almost three out of every four people serving a prison sentence on any given day in this country are walking the streets, eating at McDonald's with us, taking the bus with us, living much closer to us than we think. Even more chilling is the fact that in 1993, 42 percent of the 2,716 inmates on death rows across the country were on probation, parole, or pretrial release at the time they had killed, and 66 percent of them had one or more previous felony convictions.[10]

The *Globe* that morning ran its story about Kristin across the top of the front page, again questioning the fact that Cartier had not been arrested, especially since he was on probation for beating up a previous girlfriend and since he had violated the court orders to stay away from Kristin well before the shooting. "Legal Procedures Examined after Slaying in Allston—Critics Say Grounds for Arrest Existed," the headline said over a photo of Kristin smiling so happily it was painful to look at. The article had more detail about Cartier's criminal record and fresh insights into what kind of a person he was. Rose Ryan had decided to speak up. Upset by the weekend news reports, she called up Channel 4 (WBZ-TV) and then talked to the newspapers. "Do you want to know what he's really like?" she said she asked them. "I'll tell you." Rose was indignant. She recalled thinking, "Here was this nameless friend telling the *Globe* he was really in love with her. I wanted people to know he was a nut to begin with. He had a total disregard for the law."[11]

Rose had dated Cartier between August 1990 and February 1991. She had been planning to get a restraining order before Cartier attacked her, but she didn't actually obtain one until two days later. He attacked her at a subway stop, lunging at her with a pair of scissors and punching her in the face. She said Cartier was a violent, moody person who had threatened to kill her on numerous occasions. He was also quite manipulative. "He would do whatever he could to make [his girlfriends] feel guilty," she said. "He would play games with our heads." When she read about Kristin, she said, "All I could think of was this could have been me who was dead."[12]

There were more details, too many to fathom at the time. We were too grief stricken to go much past the headlines, too preoccupied with funeral arrangements to grapple with the injustice that had taken place. We were due at Billy Hayes's funeral home in West Newton. He told us not to come before noon, to give him a chance to make her presentable, "but if you want to see your daughter," he said, "you can."

The damage to her forehead was still prominent. Hayes whispered that it looked like an exit wound to him.

An old friend and college roommate of mine, Peter Mitchell, vice chancellor of the University of Massachusetts Board of Regents, drove us out. He was shaken, too. He and his wife, Lou, had stayed in touch with Kristin for the four years she had been in Boston and just a few days earlier had tried to reach her to invite her to dinner at their house. They were out of town the weekend she was killed and were stunned to find her cheerful voice on the answering machine when they got back.

Kristin was lying in an inner room. Rosemary could see the foot of her casket from the first room we entered, and then sat down and would go no farther. I approached and knelt down by Kristin's side. I hadn't seen her in weeks. "Oh no, oh no," Rosemary kept repeating from the other room. I was drained and almost speechless. Stupidly, I hoped she might stir. "Kristin?" I murmured. We did not stay long.

Before heading for the airport, we stopped in Brookline again. The check I'd sent Kristin for June was in the mailbox, a bleak reminder of that last, happy conversation. "Have you sent me my check?" she'd asked me. "It's in the mail," I assured her. I put it in the box outside the *Post* building on L Street a few minutes after I hung up. It was postmarked on the afternoon of May 30, around the time she was getting off work.

Reflecting a sensitivity to the issue not found in many other cities, the Boston papers kept digging into what had happened with daily, often front-page stories about Cartier's explosive temper, the other young women he'd terrorized, the permissive officials who let him stay out of jail, the judges who didn't bother to ask about his criminal record when Kristin asked for help. I saw some of the stories, but Rosemary and I were still in a daze, wondering where *we* had gone wrong. What kind of society makes us think that way? Why do we tend to blame everyone and everything but the person who committed the crime? Whatever the answer, it's time to stop. The era of excuses should be over, but it isn't. When are we going to stop saying, "She asked for it"? When are we going to stop hearing, "He couldn't help it"?

Rose Ryan kept running into that mindset after Kristin was killed. She said, "People kept asking me, 'Why did you stay with him?' not 'Why did he do this?' The attitude was, 'You seem to be intelligent, how did that happen?' I mean, do you have to be stupid to have somebody punch you out? But that's the attitude. That's why you don't want to tell anybody, because you're embarrassed. I remember one of the TV interviewers kept asking me over and over again, 'Don't you think Kristin could have done more? Don't you think she could have called more often?' And I said no. I argued with him about it. He kept asking me, wanting me to say, 'Well, maybe if she had done this or that, she'd be okay.' I wouldn't tell him what he wanted to hear."

3

Kristin could get along with anyone. Well, almost anyone. She had her limits. Once when a boy from high school dropped his pants in front of her, she knocked out one of his front teeth. She was compassionate, and strong-minded, too. In Boston, she showed up for a baby-sitting assignment and found herself accidentally locked out. She got a neighbor to help her break in.

"She was so strong. She didn't take anything from anyone," said Amber Lynch, a close friend who graduated from Boston University that last spring. "She didn't back down from anything. You could tell that basically from her art, the way she dressed, the opinions she had. If you said something stupid, she'd tell you."

So what did she see in Michael Cartier? Was she attracted to him because he was disturbed and misunderstood? Because he could protect her? Because of his bad-boy allure? I don't know. In high school, friends say, she had generally poor taste in boyfriends, although there weren't that many of them. She had been raised to be assertive and independent. She was also soft and lonely. The road to the young man who killed her was paved with low expectations.

Some of that may have come from growing up in a home where both parents worked and where she often had to fend for herself. Some of it may have come from the stubborn notion that she wasn't very good-looking. Some of it may have come from experiences in high school, where she seemed to lose some of the self-confidence she assuredly had at Lafayette Elementary. Adolescence is hard on everyone, but it works more harm on girls than it does on boys.[1]

Unlike her older sister and brothers, all of whom went to private school at one point or another, Kristin remained a D.C. public school student until she went off to college. She took pride in being a city girl. Outwardly, not much harm befell her, unless you counted her taste for rock music, lots of jewelry, and funky clothes from Value Village.

For my part, I wasn't keen on the public schools beyond Lafayette. I remembered Ed's first year at Deal Junior High when another boy hit him in science class, with two teachers looking on. The boy, who had been talking loudly, grew enraged when Ed told him to keep quiet. When I called the principal the next day, he referred me to the assistant principal, who vaguely recalled sending a boy home for the day for hitting someone in science class, but he didn't know who was hit and didn't care. "I don't necessarily have to have [the name of the boy who was hit]," he told me. "None of this is necessarily geared to right or wrong." I was appalled.

The principal was a bit more forthcoming. He said he'd been working at controlling the level of "random, uncontrolled violence" at the school, especially among new-arriving seventh graders, and was optimistic about long-term results. But he allowed that, "We still have difficulties teaching the boys that girls are not objects of play."

It was a line that quickly became a classic in the Lardner house. But when Kristin's turn came, she was not to be dissuaded. She wanted to go to Deal. She didn't like the uniforms and rigorous rules of the Catholic girls' schools that Helen had attended and grumbled about. She didn't want to go to private school with the "snobs" from the suburbs. Finally, and most important, all her friends were going to Deal. Case closed.

At Deal and later Woodrow Wilson High School, Kristin enjoyed her friends and her freedom. Looking back on it now, it's easy to say she had too much of it. I didn't see it that way then. We let her go to rock concerts and performances of all sorts of cacophonous music and hang out on Connecticut Avenue with youngsters who seemed to be pioneering in grunge. We didn't know who all her friends were. She brought home only those she thought would pass muster. Her taste in clothing and hairstyles made it difficult to be picky. I remember seeing a terribly gaudy crowd of youngsters in punk leathers at the bus stop on Connecticut Avenue on my way home from work one night and then being stunned to realize that one of them was Kristin. When I got home, I twitted Rosemary about a favorite insult from our childhood: "Your mother wears army boots." Now our daughter did.

We figured she'd grow up. Part of my complacency stemmed from the fact that I'd gone through high school in New York in roughly the same way, or thought I had—both parents working, hanging out in front of a candy store close to home or playing pool in a walkup parlor on Third Avenue near school. Our worries at the time were focused on Charlie, almost four years older, who drifted from one high school to another before finally settling down. Kristin was, by contrast, a pillar of reliability.

"I was in the 'dumb class' at Wilson, she was in the 'smart class,'" Charlie says. "They totally denied that [having a so-called track system], but it was blatant. They said it was just 'the luck of the draw.' The teachers in my classes weren't as good. The students were totally disruptive. I think Kristin liked it at Wilson because she could wear her Mohawk and all that stuff."

The Mohawk was something else her mother and I didn't know about. Kristin would spike it up with the help of her girlfriends when she got to school and undo it before she got home. She was a practicing nonconformist. I guess she did it for the reasons most teenagers do such things: to get attention, to shock people, to have some fun, to "express herself." It was also a lot of work.

All we knew was that Kristin had shaved one side of her head close. That was bothersome enough. "Kristin and I quarreled about things like that all the time," Rosemary remembers. "At home, she combed it down the other side to give it a 'sculpted' look. One side would be short and the other, long."

During tenth grade, it turned into a Mohawk in the girls' rooms at Wilson. "It used to take two cans of Super Hold Aqua Net at the beginning," said Eleanor Ross, one of Kristin's best friends. "That was just to get it up. It wouldn't last through the whole day. It'd take half an hour to get it up. Kristin's hands used to get white from the spray." After a while, Eleanor gave up. Jennifer Ficke, another close friend, took over the coiffure.

"We did it just about every day [in tenth grade] at Wilson," Jennifer remembers. "It was fun. Everything we did together was fun. I think of Kristin as my guardian angel now."

The hijinks included playing hooky together. "We used to cut classes a lot," Jennifer said. "Sometimes we walked to the zoo or Rock Creek Park. We'd go on picnics. Or we'd go to my house and stay all day. Once we got on a bus, and then we saw my mom get on. We got off in a hurry. She didn't catch us. That was a funny one."

The girls took in a lot of movies, too. "We were on this kick," Jennifer said. "We went to every scary movie we could possibly find. I especially remember *The Dorm That Dripped Blood.* And we used to recite lines to each other from different shows. We'd rent them when we stayed at each other's house."

They had a wonderful time on the overnights. "She was a very sensitive young woman, particularly articulate for her age," Jennifer's mother, Sandi Sokol, said. "If I had to choose another daughter, or adopt one, I'd pick Kristin. She was always very up, very spirited. She just captivated me."

Cutting classes at Wilson was easier than it had been at Deal. At Deal, students needed an excuse to go off campus. "I have no idea how we got away with it," Jennifer said. "Somehow we did. I know I practiced my mom's signature a lot." They did get caught once at Wilson. The principal was driving around looking for people who were cutting assembly. "This was when we were seniors," Jennifer said. "He kept us in his office for two hours."

The same principal kept students and parents sitting in the rain at outdoor graduation ceremonies in 1988 for a drawn-out program that featured a fiery talk from Mayor Marion Barry, who drove onto the field, quite late, in his chauffeured limousine. He kept talking and talking, with lines liberally borrowed from Jesse Jackson. "Up with hope, down with dope." There was much sniggering among the students. They suspected the mayor was high on something himself.

Despite the truancy and other distractions, Kristin was a good student at both Deal and Wilson. The schools didn't demand that much effort, but Kristin did what was required, busying herself at home most nights. "She had a great social life, but she was one of the few people who did her homework," said another close friend, Chris Dupre. "At Wilson, you could get away with a lot." Jennifer agreed. "You could study the night before and do just fine," she said.

After school, Kristin, Eleanor, and Jennifer would hang out with other friends outside a Baskin-Robbins ice cream store on Connecticut Avenue. The boys, Kevin VanFlandern, Mark Arden, Matt Miles, and Mike Myers, called themselves the Mercenaries—no girls allowed. "We called ourselves the Beefcake Bikers," Eleanor said. "It lasted about a week. It was a big joke in retaliation for their stupid name."[2]

Kevin was one of Kristin's first boyfriends. It lasted just a week. "She finally dumped me," he says with a grin. "We went out to dinner a couple of times that week. But it's very uncomfortable dating someone when you're just good friends. We finally realized it was silly. This was when we were at Deal. That's when we became good friends. At Lafayette I knew her mainly as Charlie Lardner's little sister."

Kristin was "Charlie Lardner's little sister" to a large number of people. To others, she was Helen's little sister, Eddie's little sister, or Dickie's little sister. To Kristin, that must have been a bit tedious at times, but I never heard her complain about it. Brothers and sisters always have fights from time to time, but they were proud of each other, and the older they got, the more they liked each other's company. One of Kristin's big worries, just before she was killed, was that she might not be able to get to Jekyll Island that summer because of the new job she'd gotten.

By the time Kristin started at Deal in the fall of 1982, the three oldest children had either graduated from college or were getting close. Helen graduated from Xavier University in Cincinnati in 1980, Edmund, from Yale in 1981, and Richard, from Marquette in 1983. As resident "big brother," Charlie took it upon himself to keep track of

Kristin. A student of the world, not to mention Lafayette, Holy Trinity, Gonzaga, Wilson, and Emerson, he knew a lot of people. They reported back to him, as concerned citizens.

"She was hitchhiking all over the place," he says. On the way to school in the morning, she would station herself at the Metrobus stop with a hand-made sign saying "Wilson or Bust" that she waved at passing motorists, hoping someone would give her a ride before the bus came along. "She'd hitch to Georgetown and back, Bethesda and back, all over," Charlie says. "This was when she was in her punk rock mode. People I know would keep coming up to me at parties and tell me about it. She'd hitch a ride, they'd ask her her name, and they'd say, 'Oh, you're Charlie Lardner's sister?' Then they'd come up to me and say, 'Hey man, I just gave your sister a ride. That's dangerous. She shouldn't be out there like that.' I'd say, 'I know. It's a good thing she gets picked up by people I know. It's a good thing I know so many people.'" Charlie scolded her. "I told her not to do it," he says. "She kept on."

As Charlie says, it's a good thing he knew so many people. But he couldn't know everybody or everything. After all, she didn't even tell him about the Mohawk. He found out about that by accident when he got a job pumping gas at the Connecticut Avenue Exxon, across the street and up the block from the Baskin-Robbins store. He saw the Mohawk first. Then he saw it was his sister.

Chris Dupre wasn't a regular on the Connecticut Avenue sidewalk. But he often used to go down to Georgetown or Dupont Circle to take in the scene with her on weekends and summer evenings. They'd sit around smoking, looking cool, playing rebels without a cause. She liked to wander around the shops at Georgetown Park and hang out at places like Roy Rogers and Burger King. "We'd buy a small order of French fries and hang out for three hours," said Melissa Klein, a close friend in high school. Kristin often popped into Commander Salamander to try out its black nail polish and blue hair spray. Another favorite was the Smash, a place that sold punk rock records, posters, and T-shirts. "A mecca for urchins," Chris said of the Smash.

Another reason for going to Georgetown was Andy Armstrong,

Kristin's first steady boyfriend. She met him in the fall of 1985 when she was fifteen, a sophomore at Wilson, but she never brought him home. Photos in one of the albums she kept suggest one reason he never materialized. He had what he now calls "the stupidest haircut in Washington." He is a slender young man, six foot two, with a long nose and dark hair, which was dyed yellow and teased into long, tricolored spires of red, green, and yellow sticking out all over his head. He called them his liberty spikes. He wore a leather jacket with metal studs on the collar and shoulders, and he was smitten the first time he saw Kristin at the uptown apartment of Adam Lief, the manager of the Baskin-Robbins store. Kristin and her friends often collected at Lief's place.

Kristin's interest was sparked at least in part by Andy's status as someone who knew and traveled with a number of local punk rock bands. He would set up tables at their concerts and sell T-shirts, pins, and other mementos. He was a high school dropout, but he wasn't dumb. Today he owns a small screenprint company in the Washington area, making all sorts of T-shirts, including some fashioned on the horror movies he and Kristin liked to watch. Back then, he cashed in on the punk rock circuit. "I'd get in free, drink free, and come back with a few hundred dollars in my pocket," he said.

Armstrong also worked at Electromax in Georgetown, a spot where Kristin and other teenagers often wandered in to get their photos taken for "official IDs" or just to look around. It was also a "head shop," with a wide variety of drug paraphernalia for sale. But not all the customers understood the rules. The store's wares were supposed to be "harmless," so if you wanted to buy something, you couldn't mention drugs. You could ask for a pipe, you could order papers to roll your own cigarettes, but if you mentioned cocaine or marijuana as the reason for your purchase, the clerks were supposed to tell you, no sale.

"Some customers didn't understand these fine points," Armstrong said. "They thought we were fucking with them." There was one in particular who got very angry and banged Armstrong's head with a tobacco jar, then pulled a gun. The injured clerk retreated into a back room, blood running down the back of his neck, until he thought the customer had departed. Armstrong then strolled out, saw friends on the sidewalk, and began regaling them with the story. "Suddenly, the guy comes out of the record store next door to us. This is around 12:30 or 1:30 in the afternoon. There was not a cop to be seen. He pulls out his gun again. Everybody starts to surround him. He says, 'I'm gonna get my boys,' and walks off. Then my boss says, 'I'm going to follow him. I want him arrested.' I say, 'No, don't do that.' The guy sees he's being followed and comes back. He punches me in the mouth. I run into the record store. I'm bleeding all over. Then we hear a banging. The guy's butting his gun against the window. In this day and age, I would have been shot. But he goes away. Then the ambulance comes. The cops come. The newsies come."

Parents, even when one of them was a "newsie," didn't think of afternoons in Georgetown being like that, unless perhaps they were wealthy enough to live in Georgetown. When Kristin said she wanted to go down there with friends, we just told her to have a good time and be back for dinner. Sometimes we asked what friends, but she always had an acceptable litany she could recite. Kim Thompson, Melissa Klein, or Jennifer Ficke often used to make the trek with her.

On schooldays, Kristin didn't even have to ask. With both parents working, there was nobody home until evening. Quite often, she took a Metrobus after class and went down to Georgetown to see Andy.

"She would take this horrendously long bus ride," he said. "I would take my break from work. And we'd go walking. We walked around a lot on the canal path. She used to call me Andy Panda all the time. . . . We just had this storybook, fantasy romance. 'I love you.' 'I love you, too.' It was great. I spoiled her rotten. I did the corniest things."

One afternoon, before Kristin arrived, Armstrong went next door to an arcade game store where a friend of his was fixing a coin-operated machine that had a claw in it for retrieving stuffed animals and other prizes. Andy saw some stuffed hearts in the machine and told his friend he wanted three of them. He drew an eyeball on one, a "U" on another, and left the third blank. Then he hid them along the towpath so he could discover them for Kristin when they went for their walk. "She got a big kick out of that," he said. "It was a little kid romance, but it was real intense. Something about her blew my mind."

A handsome gray cat jumped onto the table as I spoke with Armstrong at his shop. He looked at it and smiled. Its name was Squeegee. "That's another thing Kristin did," he said. "I always hated cats. Your daughter turned me on to them. I've got a lot of them."

A couple of times, Andy came uptown to hang out with Kristin and her friends on Connecticut Avenue, but it made him uncomfortable. He was five years older. More often, their weekend dates consisted of renting a video and watching it at his apartment on P Street.

"We used to watch a lot of silly B-movies," he said. "Some of it was H. G. Lewis's stuff. He was one of the greatest worst directors of all time. He made horror movies on no budget. I used to repeat the lines from them all the time. It drove Kristin crazy. We'd rent the videos, laugh, and neck. It was great. She had to be home by a certain hour, and she always wanted to take the bus, but it was a terribly long ride. I'd give her $6, and she'd take a taxi."

Sometimes he took her to concerts at places like the 9:30 Club and the Safari Club for "all ages" shows. If you were under eighteen, you could go in, but the doorkeepers stamped your hands so you couldn't drink. Armstrong said Kristin went to the shows more often with friends like Kim Thompson than she did with him. Once he took Kristin to Philadelphia for a two-day tour with a band called Government Issue. Where did Rosemary and I think she was? Overnighting at a friend's house, of course. I'm sure we had the phone number, just in case.

By then, Kristin had her Mohawk. Andy didn't like it, either, but there it was. "We'd been going together for three or four months when she shaved her head," he said. "I got annoyed. I said, 'You're just acting like one of these trendy wanna-bes.' She'd go off when I said that. 'What are you saying?' she'd ask me."

Kristin spiked it up for the trip to Philadelphia. "We all went up in a van with the band for the show at a place called the Electric Banana," Andy remembers. It was an "all ages" program, and Kristin helped him sell T-shirts. "She had her hair up. I had my hair up. We were the ugliest couple you ever saw, the punk rock Mohawk couple. Some guy working on a fanzine took a photo of us and put it in his fanzine. I got a copy of it later. It was a really horrible picture, xeroxed from a dark black-and-white photo."

They dated for about nine months. The closest Andy came to the front door was Christmas morning 1985, when a friend of his drove him by to toss a gift onto the front porch. It was a stuffed animal, a goose, with a button he'd made. It said: "For Kristin, A Christmas Goose." She loved stuffed animals.

When Armstrong got back from an out-of-town trip flush with cash, he took Kristin to dinner, usually at a Chinese restaurant that called itself McHuang's. There's a hair salon there now.

Eventually, the glow wore off. "She wanted to see all the shows," Andy said. "I'd seen them. She wanted to be at 'the scene.' For me, it had worn off. Things started getting pretty nasty. We got to be like an old, noisy couple. We kind of took each other for granted."

Through it all, he said, Kristin never drank or took drugs. "I can honest to God state that on a stack of Bibles," he said. He said he saw her try pot just once, after they had stopped dating. Other friends say she'd tried marijuana before that, too. It was easy to get, in George-town, at Wilson, and even at the Lafayette playground. The Lafayette school song used to have a line that said, "Hail to Lafayette, high on the hill." There were a lot of giggles over that. "All the kids got high on the hill," Kim Thompson said.

Kristin broke up with Andy in the summer of 1986. He was going to take her to dinner at McHuang's, but they never went. "This isn't working out," she told him. He saw her several times after that and tried to get her back, but she'd made up her mind. Once Armstrong made up a T-shirt for a band called the Angry Samoans with tiny letters at the bottom, "KISLY," for "Kristin, I still love you." Kristin figured it out right away, but she wouldn't budge.

"I think she outgrew him," Kim Thompson said. "For her, he represented teenage rebellion, the way he looked and acted."

Besides the Mohawk, which I never saw, Kristin also experimented with a nose ring and a wide variety of hair colors, which she couldn't hide. I banned the nose ring whenever she was home, but it seemed to me that all I could do about the hair colors was give them unenthusiastic reviews and hope that natural beauty would eventually prevail. I tried all sorts of ploys. "Kristin, you're going to be bald by the time you're forty. . . . How much longer are you going to be in that shower? . . . Kristin, goddammit, get out of that shower—there's no hot water left for the dishes."

Even some of her friends expressed their dismay. "Why do you put all that crap in your hair?" Chris Dupre asked her one day. "It's really beautiful when you leave it alone."

Kristin just shrugged. She was doing her own thing, determined to carve out her own identity. In a way she was rebelling against being a girl, or at least against what society still expects of "a young lady." Kristin didn't want to be "sweet," or quiet or submissive. Her friends admired her for that, even if it sometimes mortified her parents. Parishioners used to look quizzically at Kristin, and then at me or Rosemary, as they filed past this young girl in the back of church at Sunday mass, slouched against a wall in leather jacket and pointed boots. One day, Rosemary was waiting with Kristin for the next train at the Metro station at Friendship Heights when commuters began staring, first at this young girl with purple hair and torn fishnet stockings and then at the mother she evidently belonged to.

Teenagers are frequently embarrassed by their parents, but occasionally it works the other way. Either way it usually ends in fond memories. Cosmetics aside, Kristin was a girl we were proud of. She was doing well in school—not as well as she could have but well enough. She did the dishes and other chores around the house with a minimum of grumbling. She could be sullen, even depressed at times, but a lighthearted joke would shake her out of it in seconds. She was solid, dependable, lively, and fascinating. She could hold forth on subjects from politics and photography to sorcery and Celtic gods. She could develop and print her own pictures. She could tell your fortune with tarot cards. She gobbled up books on mythology and witchcraft and historical romance and practically memorized *Gone with the Wind*. Her bedroom ceiling still glows at night with fluorescent constellations, moons, shooting stars, and planets that she applied with painstaking precision. Laughter came easily to her, and she was always ready for a conversation about art, religion, philosophy, or music. As she got older, she loved to go out with friends until all hours of the morning, to talk great themes and think big thoughts. "I don't really remember any time we had together when we didn't have a good time," said Bekky Elstad, a close friend from Boston University.

"She liked to speculate on where we were, where we were going, what it all means," said Miraval Suarez, a close friend of Kristin and Charlie's. "We used to read Nostradamus and do tarot cards together. You can ask questions of tarot cards: Where am I going? Am I going to find a new job? Do I like this guy? It's like a journey through life. She liked the Ouija board, too. And she had this book she bought in Boston called *The Necronomicon.* It had passages on secret worlds and how to get there, with something in the beginning that warned, 'Don't repeat these incantations aloud.' I think her interest in all these things came through her art. Anyway, they were fun to read about and imagine. She got into so many different things; she became a really unique person."

"She was very articulate; she could keep you in stitches," Chris Dupre said. "We used to watch the news together and discuss politics. We were all sort of on the liberal side. Reagan was president then, and we weren't too happy with his administration."

Kristin's first year at Deal was devoted to drawing horses and devouring books such as the illustrated edition of Edgar Allan Poe that I bought her for Christmas. When *Gone with the Wind* ended a local theater run, she persuaded one of the attendants to give her a huge cardboard cutout depicting Clark Gable as Rhett Butler embracing Vivien Leigh as Scarlett O'Hara, and she set it up in her bedroom, leaving little room for anything else.

In her second year, she became an avid music fan, committed to all the works of Duran Duran and especially its keyboard player, Nick Rhodes. She even sent him a birthday card. The high point came on April 2, 1994, when the so-called "masters of fop rock" played to a sellout crowd at the Capital Centre, Kristin, Kim, Lisa, and another friend among them. They screamed for everybody and everything, even the guy who came out to scrub the stage on his hands and knees, but as the *Post* reported the next morning, "nothing could prepare the naked ear for the sheer sonic blast of the scream that greeted Duran Duran" as they charged onto the stage. The girls brought hand-made posters, signed with their names and an address, and saying "We love you from Washington."

"We put the posters on the stage," Lisa remembers. "We were hoping they would write us."

After a few songs, it seemed clear that Nick Rhodes set off many of the loudest screams, and I have no doubt that Kristin had something to do with that. Kim's father brought the girls to the show, but the sounds were no match for the NCAA basketball championship game that night. He went off with a hotdog vendor to watch it on TV. It was a big night for D.C.; Georgetown won, beating Houston 84–75, so everybody came home happy.

Now a certified teenager, Kristin began smoking cigarettes when her parents weren't around and curling her hair, trying different hairstyles. But she still trudged to Monday night religion class at Blessed Sacrament Church often enough to receive confirmation in March 1984. She also spent a memorable Saturday working as a volunteer at Martha's Table, a shelter where poor and homeless people, especially children, could get something to eat. Kristin helped clean the sleeping areas, sweep the floors, and wash the windows. But most important, she helped make tuna sandwiches for the children. All of them were under twelve, she told me. She was disturbed to realize that this was probably all most of them would eat that day but glad to have had a part in helping them, even in a small way.

Her last year at Deal, 1984–85, was more mischievous. She cut classes more often, cultivated horror movies, acquired new favorites in music (David Bowie, the Ramones, U2, Bronski Beat, Depeche Mode, and General Public). "That was the year we started getting into punk," Kim Thompson remembers. "It was real high-energy, anti–Top 40 music. The lyrics were anti-authoritarian types of things." Kristin began paying more attention to boys. Jennifer was an enthusiastic co-conspirator, delighted, as she told Kristin, at how many people they kept meeting " 'cause we're so damned cute." Kristin at least was still playing the field. Friends wished her luck with "Adam," and warned her of "Josh." She graded some of the boys in her yearbook. "Nice legs," she wrote next to the picture of one young man. "Great voice," she said of another. "Gross" and "Spaz!" she wrote of several others.

Summertime that year brought what struck some friends, and perhaps Kristin, as detention. For the first time in years, Rosemary and I decided to go somewhere besides Jekyll. We picked Prince Edward Island in Canada and told Kristin we wanted her to come along. The other children weren't interested. All but Charlie had moved out, and he had a summer job to excuse him. We rented a Ford Taurus and dragged Kristin with us.

It was the best vacation we ever had together. She'd just turned fifteen and had started summer classes at the Corcoran Art School. She had talked of becoming a botanist or a veterinarian, but now she was interested in photography. I bought her a Pentax that required her to figure out everything, including the F stops, and she took to it like a natural. She even used that camera for the portfolio she put together to get into art school three years later. But it wasn't the pictures that made the trip unforgettable, at least not for me. It was the first, and last, vacation we'd ever taken with just one child in tow.

If Kristin had any regrets, she kept them to herself. She was great company. We commiserated with one another over a miserable Chinese restaurant in the forlorn city of St. John, found we all liked the MacKenzie brothers, and got up at midnight together to watch the tides of the Bay of Fundy rush into a dry creek bed with the roar of a freight train. On Prince Edward, I took her fishing, hopping aboard a dayboat that hurried us into the Gulf of St. Lawrence. Years of frustration on the bridge and piers at Jekyll Island washed away. She hauled in the first keepers she'd ever successfully hooked, mackerel and cod, and was almost as delighted as I was when the French Canadian crewmen filleted them for us. Rosemary can't stand fish, for reasons rooted in Wisconsin, but she cooked them for us. We ate every bit. The next day, I found a rough-hewn nine-hole golf course, with a barn for a clubhouse, overlooking the Northumberland Strait. We'd brought some golf clubs with us that the boys always used. This time, Kristin used them. Once she made sure I didn't care how many balls we lost, she socked them all over the lot and sometimes straight up to the green. She was so pleased when we finished the course that we went back the next morning for another round.

On other days, we bought fresh-caught lobster right off the boats and visited virtually every shop in Charlottetown. Frequently, we stopped the car so that Kristin could try out her Pentax on friendly cows, picturesque churches, and breathtaking views of the sea. But the biggest hit was the home of Anne of Green Gables, on the north side of the island. Kristin was fascinated to find there was a real story, a real place, behind the books. We bought the whole series for her, and she read every page, mostly in the back seat of the car, before we got home. By then, she *was* Anne of Green Gables and having the time of her life. But once was enough. The next year she wanted very much to go back to Jekyll Island with her brothers and sister.

She started dating Andy Armstrong regularly in the fall and, with other friends at least, developed a taste for marijuana. Once in a while she tried other drugs, too: hallucinogenic mushrooms at one party, a designer drug called Ecstasy at another. I suppose most teenagers experiment with drugs, just as their parents did with liquor, sometimes to excess.[3] Drugs and violence were often part of the mix at the nightclubs she patronized. "It's every parent's nightmare," Chris Dupre said of the punk rock scene. "When you're young, the pure aggression appeals to you. So does the repeated theme of rebellion. There's wild-looking people, usually a lot of drinking, and trivial fighting and yelling. Some people take it too far."

A flyer on slam dancing that Kristin tucked away in a photo album gives some of the flavor. "DO YOU WANT <u>YOUR</u> FRIENDS HURT?" it asks. "That's what's happening, because slamming at shows has become increasingly violent over the past few months, to the point where going into the pit is risking extreme injury! At the June 6 DRI/BMB/Rhythm Pigs show, there were multiple casualties including bloody noses, a smashed-in face, and a broken rib. This is really unnecessary. Pit slamming is supposed to be *fun,* not dangerous."

The flyer offered several photos, including one of a youngster with a smashed-in face, along with some advice and concluding observations. The advice: "Take off spikes and armbands before going into the pit. Obviously, these things could hurt people." The concluding observations: "The pit is a *collective*. Everyone shares the same space and the right to be safe in that space. If we can't even reach a non-violent level with 20–50 people who slam, there's no hope for the D.C. scene, and forget about this country."

That's the way the kids see it, I guess: roughhousing that doesn't get out of hand, sort of a friendly violence. Dozens of people should be able to bang into one another and just have a great time. Maybe so. It sounds like teenage utopia to me. Like a professional hockey game where nobody ever loses his temper.

Kristin had her favorite rock groups. One of the first was the Dead Kennedys. The name made me flinch, but I couldn't escape the tapes, and some of the wry lyrics stuck with me. The lead singer, Jello Biafra, was politically active on the West Coast, and I can remember one satirical tune about Jerry Brown called "California Über Alles" that went: "Carter power will soon go away. I will be fuehrer one day." Another loud number that both Kristin and Charlie played incessantly was "Kill, Kill, Kill the Poor."

"Mozart, it wasn't," Rosemary says. She's right about that, but Mom and Dad were a captive audience. Sometimes I found myself nodding, especially at the all-time young Lardner household favorite: the Ramones' "I Wanna Be Sedated."

The Dead Kennedys were just one of the groups billed at a big show she attended that November in the WUST Radio Music Hall at 9th and V Streets NW. Government Issue, a local group, and Morally Bankrupt also played. The roster of musical groups that filled her ears that first year at Wilson could have made a chapter for Mencken: "Madhouse . . . Marginal Man . . . F.E.A.R. . . . Dag Nasty . . . Dain Bramage." Some of those have a vaguely familiar ring, but I'm sure she never mentioned the F.U.'s or Teenage Sluts from Hell, and I doubt she ever heard them play. They had their gigs in Trenton, New Jersey.

Kristin liked to collect the flyers. But I suspect she made the "alternative anti-military parade" on Dupont Circle for Armed Forces Day in May 1986, featuring Beefeater, 11th Hour, Mourning Glories, and many more. Marchers were encouraged to bring "pogo sticks, roller skates, silly string, Twinkies, and whatever props you particularly enjoy." That would have appealed to Kristin. She paid attention to politics. The next spring, she took part in a protest outside the South African Embassy, spending four hours on the picket line.

There were other adventures on the way to college. Rides on Charlie's motorcycle at 100 mph, flying off to Italy at age sixteen for vacation with a friend and her parents and having her bottom pinched in Rome, learning to shoot in the woods of West Virginia. Sometimes, of course, things went awry. One day, while she was still at Deal, she called Kevin VanFlandern in a panic. She had come across an old black powder gun—fully loaded, I'm distressed to report—in a drawer in Charlie's room. It was an antique that belonged to one of his friends, a .36 caliber pocket Navy with a cap and a ball.

"What a neat-looking cap pistol," Kristin thought. She took it out of the drawer, turned, and pulled the trigger. Flames more than a foot long belched out.

"Kevin," she said over the phone, "come over. Right away. I shot it off by accident. There's a big hole in the floor."

"Relax," Kevin told her. "It's not that big a deal. Your parents probably won't even notice."

"I'm not worried about my parents," she told him. "It's Charlie. He'll kill me."

Kevin calmed her down. When they finished talking, Kristin got busy expunging the evidence. She sprayed all the Lysol she could find. She opened the windows. Maybe she even turned on a fan.

Charlie didn't notice a thing, at first. But eventually he opened the drawer and took the gun out. Something was wrong. One of the cylinders was empty. He shook his head. Couldn't figure it out. But not too long after that, he happened to be walking across the floor in his bare feet and picked up a big splinter in the middle of the room. Bing!

A light went off in his head. He went to the drawer, took the gun out, turned slowly, and pointed it down at the floor. The hole was right there.

"Hey, do you know what happened here?" he asked Kristin when she got home.

She confessed. Charlie yelled at her, as though she should have known the gun was loaded. "You could have killed the kitty," he told Kristin. "What if T.C. [full name, TurboCat] had been there?" I'm sure Kristin would have aimed it in another direction. In any case, she was right in not worrying about what her parents might say. We didn't find out about it until a few months ago.

Another boy Kristin liked was Matt Miles, a good friend of Kevin's who also hung out with the group on Connecticut Avenue, but they never dated. One day, Matt did something that bothered her, and Kristin, playing sorceress, put a hex on him. "He was working at a construction site with some buddies that day," Kevin said. "He ended up falling two floors and getting all beat. Kristin was really upset about that. She called me, told me she'd almost killed him. . . . I'm not sure how seriously she took the hex, though."

Kristin was sweet sixteen when she had the showdown on Wisconsin Avenue with the young man who dropped his pants in front of her. It was a Friday night outside Amaryllis, a store that sold vintage clothing that Kristin greatly admired. She once bought a pink silk organza gown there, out of her own earnings, to wear to her senior prom, but it was so full of torn seams that Rosemary had to skip her secretarial job for two days to make it wearable. That night she was doing some window shopping with Jennifer Ficke and another friend, Elisa Arden. Three boys came along, including one who was quite drunk. He told the girls they were "ugly" and pulled down his pants.

By coincidence, a friend of Charlie's who was working with him at a lock store on Capitol Hill, Mark Novak, had taken some lock strikes and made a set of brass knuckles as a recent present for Kristin, just in case she should ever find herself in a difficult situation. Kristin put them on, wound up, and hit the boy right in the mouth. Then the girls ran off, worried that the trio would be coming after them. "We ran all the way home," Jennifer said.

As soon as Kristin got in the house, she told Charlie what had happened, unaware of the extent of the damage she'd inflicted. The next morning, he enlisted a friend and went looking for the errant young man to pre-empt any more nastiness. They found him in a playground in his neighborhood. Charlie laughed as soon as the boy opened his mouth, displaying a missing front tooth. "All right then," Charlie said as he left to inform his sister that no further action was needed.

Kristin was still annoyed. Mark Novak was delighted. "It was just a chance thing," he said. "I'd given it to her just a couple of days before." He'd made a set for Charlie, too, but after that, the standing joke among their friends was that Charlie would never use them, but Kristin sure would.

Kristin broke up with Andy Armstrong around the start of junior year. Friends say he never physically abused her, but he treated her shabbily at the end. He says he'd started drinking because of the breakup and sometimes shouted at her when he saw her around Dupont Circle. "I was angry," he says. "I started being belligerent towards her. I remember getting into a shouting match with her at Burger King."

"Kristin had a bad impression of herself. You could tell that by the guys she went out with," Kevin VanFlandern said. But that may be a bit of overstatement. Kristin didn't have that many boyfriends, even counting Kevin. And in Boston, she found somebody everyone liked. His name was Jason Corkin and he was from New Zealand. "Jason was an exception," Kevin said. "He really liked her. He cared for her a lot." He also looked like a "bad boy" even if he wasn't.

"She always went for the bad-boy type," Eleanor Ross says. "She said 'nice guys' liked her, but she didn't like them. It's not that she liked being insulted, but she didn't expect much. She had a self-confidence problem . . . about her looks and her personality."

Thinking it makes it so, I always preached at home. I tried to encourage the children to realize they could do anything they wanted and make a success of it. All they had to do was believe in themselves.

But the proposition has a bad side to it. If you're convinced you're not going to win, you won't. I often told Kristin what a beautiful, talented, can-do-anything person she was. But she was skeptical. After all, who's a teenager to believe on matters like that? Her father?

"She was popular. Everyone liked her," Chris Dupre says. "She didn't have to feel insecure with anyone, but she did with boyfriends. She was very insecure in those relationships. Kristin would either fall for somebody I didn't think was right for her, or she would go with someone she didn't really like but didn't want to tell him. She always seemed to go for the strongest type, the hard-edged type, not the most clean-cut. She used to call me up and say, 'I wonder if he likes me,' whoever that happened to be. 'What should I do?' Then she'd turn that into an hour-and-a-half argument. That's what I liked about Jason. When she was around Jason, she was no different than when she was around us."

4

We left Kristin in a coffin by her grave on Thursday, June 4, after a funeral mass at Blessed Sacrament Church in Washington that underscored the injustice of what had happened. Our son Richard choked back tears to read from Ecclesiastes. Our pastor, Monsignor Thomas Duffy, gave a remarkably eloquent sermon, recalling Kristin's confirmation at the church and talking about the "pure evil" that had struck her down in Boston. I'm afraid I had daydreamed through a lot of Father Duffy's sermons in the past, but this time he had my undivided attention. To talk about murder and violence in the language of love does nothing but invite more of it.

The week after the burial, I called Leonard Downie, executive editor at the *Post,* and told him I wanted to go back to Boston to poke around a bit. It seemed clear to me by then that the justice system had failed Kristin. And I could see that the defenses were going up. That had been plain since Monday evening, June 1, when we got back home to find messages waiting from the *Boston Globe.* Boston probation officials were telling the *Globe* that if they had been aware of the restraining order Kristin got against Cartier, they would have moved to revoke his probation. But police in Brookline, a separate jurisdiction, were contending that nothing could have been done to prevent the murder. They told the *Globe* that since access to an individual's criminal record is restricted by law, they were unaware of Cartier's background.[1]

"Everything was done right by the numbers," Brookline Police Lt. Edward Merrick told the *Globe.* "The system did not fail this young lady."[2]

The excuses were beginning to trip over one another, as they often do when something has gone wrong. One thing I'd learned early in my career was that anyone on probation is supposed to stay out of trouble. As the standard line from the Commonwealth's probation form said: "You must obey local, state or federal laws or court order." Michael Cartier hadn't done that. Yet he was still free to stalk and finally murder my daughter. And the public was being told: "The system did not fail this young lady."

Count on it: it is failing us all. And it will continue to fail us unless we stop winking at its shortcomings. The public safety is the first duty of government, but our tolerance of crime, particularly violent crime, seems to know no bounds. We shrug it off until it happens to us. And when society is confronted with too much of it to ignore, it blames itself more than the perpetrators. It talks of long-range solutions, of saving the next generation with the same kind of social programs that failed to save the present one. We look for excuses to do anything but hold people accountable for their conduct. In the process, we normalize criminal behavior. Instead of being outraged by it, we learn to live with it. As Senator Daniel P. Moynihan has observed, "The amount of deviant behavior in American society has increased beyond levels that we are capable of acknowledging. So we have redefined deviancy so as to exempt much conduct previously stigmatized. That is what has happened to urban violence. Because there is so much of it, we have come to see it as normal."[3]

When I spoke with Len Downie, I wasn't at all sure of what I was going to do if he let me do it. But I was sure of the limitations of daily journalism. Reporters generally work very hard to tell the truth, but they can tell only a thin slice of it at a time. There is rarely room tomorrow for what they found out that day. There is almost never room for what they want to say, much less for what they know.

All I could tell Len was that I had a half-baked idea of finding out more about Kristin's murder and perhaps writing about it. I think I have the reputation of being a fairly hard-nosed reporter, but I told him

I wasn't at all sure I'd be able to do it. Len didn't hesitate for a second. He told me to go. I left the following week.

One of my first stops was the courthouse in Brookline, a patrician-looking, leaky brick building, where Kristin had gotten her restraining orders against Cartier. When I stepped into the clerk's office on the main floor, I was, at first, impressed. On the counter to the left was a rack full of free brochures and other literature on the state's domestic abuse law, battered women's shelters, counseling services, hotlines, and mediation programs. The pamphlets, I soon discovered, reflected a newfound sensitivity in Brookline District Court. "Those weren't there before Kristin was killed," one of the women in the office whispered to me on a return visit.

I was trying to get an understanding on that first trip of what Kristin had reported to the police and the courts, and when. Some of the early news stories cited dates that didn't seem quite right. As a reporter, I've always tried to be especially attentive to when things happen. Finding out when can be crucial to understanding how and why. As I was waiting for some of the court records, Lt. George Finnegan of the Brookline Police Department came in and introduced himself. I'd already spoken with him over the phone and arranged to meet him there.

A tough-minded cop, with eighteen years on the force, he had the face of a choir boy under a shock of white hair, and he could probably charm a confession out of a stone. He remembered Kristin quite well. He had been the police liaison officer—sometimes called the police prosecutor—handling complaints at the courthouse on May 12, 1992, when paperwork accusing Cartier of beating her up, stealing from her, intimidating her, and violating the domestic abuse law came to Finnegan's attention. Later in the day, Kristin turned up in the main courtroom to obtain a temporary restraining order, telling Cartier to stay away from her. The decree replaced an emergency order Kristin had gotten the night before.

The case bothered Finnegan. He had a niece who was an art student and a daughter in graduate school. He walked up to Kristin outside the courthouse.

"I had this gut feeling," he said. "A lot of these [restraining] orders involve divorce cases. The husband takes them out against the wife or the wife takes them out against the husband. A lot of them are frivolous.[4] But in this case, my alarm system went off. I asked her if he had a gun. She said, 'He may.' "

Finnegan told her to call the Brookline police if she saw him hanging around. He said he cautioned her not to dial 911. She lived so close to the line between Brookline and Boston that dialing 911 might give her Boston police, who were unfamiliar with the case.

"Was she scared?" I asked Finnegan, not knowing that he'd already told the *Brookline Citizen* that she was "petrified."

"I'd say yes," Finnegan told me. "I asked her if she'd considered relocating." Kristin told him she couldn't. Graduation from the Museum School was a year away. "She was concerned about finishing up school," Finnegan said.

Finnegan narrowed his baby blue eyes at me. He said I should try to find out how Cartier got his gun. "You're a reporter, aren't you?" he said. I was shamefaced. I looked away, either up or down or sideways. I couldn't look at him. Here I was, a big-deal reporter for the *Washington Post,* and I didn't have a clue about what had been happening to my own daughter. It was as if Finnegan had been waiting for me to come by, expecting me to do something about this.

"I'm supposed to be," I mumbled. "I'm supposed to be."

I think it was then that I resolved to keep working on that half-baked idea until something came of it.

The story about Kristin's murder had died down by now, but I still had a lot of reading to do. The Massachusetts media had kept at it for several days after we left for the funeral. Our daughter Helen had managed to get some of the Boston papers from an out-of-town newsstand. Now I had time to read them closely and track down others. Individually, they showed one shortcoming after another in the authorities' handling of Michael Cartier. Collectively, they amounted to a chilling failure of law and order, all the more frightening because such failures are commonplace.

The *Herald* disclosed that Cartier had been allowed to avoid a six-month prison term by attending weekly therapy sessions at Boston Municipal Court even as he was abusing Kristin. Meanwhile, the *Globe* reported that the Brookline judge who granted Kristin a temporary restraining order on May 12 was sorry that he had been unaware of Cartier's criminal record and of the fact that he was on probation. Judges in domestic abuse cases in Massachusetts did not routinely check a defendant's criminal record when a woman applied for a restraining order. In most states, they still don't. It is an inexcusable failure, part of a dangerous pretense that domestic violence is a civil matter and that restraining orders should not be permitted to intrude on a batterer's privacy. When contacted by the *Herald,* the judge, Lawrence G. Shubow, was even more critical of the lapse than he had been in his remarks to the *Globe.* "If we do it [criminal background checks] for minor traffic violations, we can do it for 209A's [restraining orders]," he said.[5]

There was, of course, no law *against* such checks. Not every batterer has a record, either. People who abuse their partners, friends, or relatives wear Hickey-Freeman suits as well as leather jackets. They drive Cadillacs as well as motorcycles. Some even wear police badges. Some beat up their parents. Some are gay or lesbian. A few are women. Most are men. And when their victims muster up enough courage to bring their attackers to court, it's very likely there is a much more frightening backdrop to the filing than the petitions suggest. Until Kristin was killed, any thug in Massachusetts accused under the domestic abuse law of beating up his wife or girlfriend, or ex-wife or ex-girlfriend, could saunter into court without much fear that his criminal record would catch up with him. That is still true in most of these United States.

Kristin felt strongly about such matters. I got a hint of that when I returned to her flat in Brookline to go over her papers and records and make some phone calls. One of the flyers she had tucked away in her photo album was a striking ocher and red poster that she'd probably picked up in Dupont Circle when she was in high school. It was put out by the Revolutionary Communist Party USA for International Women's Day on March 8, 1986, but for Kristin, it was important for the message, not the messenger.

"Break the Chains!" it said. "To Be A Woman In This Or Any

Other Present-Day Country Is To Be In A Constant State Of Suppressed Rage." Then it added, as though men were speaking:

" 'She has a big mouth . . . made me beat her up. It's *her* fault!'

" 'She was asking for it being out there on the street at midnight.'

" 'His old lady messed with him. He had her committed.'

"NO MORE!" the poster continued. "ESCAPE!"

Kristin tried.

Walking about Kristin's flat was depressing and comforting all at once. There was much more of her there than at the funeral. She was there with me, in the paintings, sculpture, and jewelry in the dining room, in the essays in her bedroom. I'd never seen them before she was killed. They were full of determination, talent, anger, and anguish. Kristin knew pain, and it showed in her art. It's painful to keep secrets but difficult to share them. For Kristin, art was the perfect medium. There were hanging clay figures of a man and a woman, each bound in black thread from head to toe, with the female holding her arms up defensively and the male flexing his, fists clenched. A prostrate woman in green clay, her long hair flung forward on the ground. A square plaster cast, roped in like a boxing ring and studded with upright nails, sitting atop another plaster square in which there was a small recessed cell, cushioned with white feathers and containing a small figure. There was the madonna she had painted for her mother, gilding it with delicate and expensive sheets of gold leaf, and the angry self-portrait showing the large leg bruise where Cartier had kicked her.

"It felt as though she was telling her secrets to the world," she wrote of her art in an essay she left behind. "Why would anyone want to know them anyway? But making things was all she wanted to do. . . . She always had questions, but never any answers, just frustration and confusion, and a need to get out whatever lay inside of her, hoping to be meaningful."

Kristin began thinking of becoming an artist midway through high school, taking art, graphics, and photography courses at the Corcoran on weekends and in the summers. She was encouraged when an art teacher at Wilson, Sandra Williams, decided two of her paintings were good enough to go on display at a little makeshift gallery there, and even more when Mrs. Williams wrote a warm letter of recommendation saying that "her talents far surpass her years." In senior year she scrambled to produce a portfolio for interviews at Boston University's School for the Arts and other art schools, and I took her to Boston in March of 1988 to look around. We took a water taxi across the harbor, explored Back Bay, ate deep-dish pizza, and discovered the great art treasures of the Isabella Gardner Museum. I probably had a better time than Kristin. It was my first trip to Boston that didn't involve a reporting assignment. She was anxious about being accepted. We were both impressed by the skillful work in the student sculptures and paintings on display at the art schools, and Kristin wondered if she would ever be able to match them. Of course, she also applied to other schools in other cities. In the end, she was accepted at BU, the Savannah (Georgia) College of Art, and the Chicago Art Institute. I'm afraid I showed my bias by taking her only to Boston. Both Rosemary and I wanted her to go to a university where she could take another major in case she changed her mind. And we thought Boston with its zillions of students would be more congenial. So did Kristin. She wanted to go to art school but not one that offered only studio courses.

So was it a good decision to go there? My philosophy teachers would have said yes. There is no need to repent an honest decision simply because of "the unpredictable interference of contingent causes."[6] I repent nonetheless. If only we hadn't sent her to Boston. . . . If only she'd stayed home the night she met him. . . . If only she had asked for help. . . . If only Cartier's probation had been revoked. . . . If only he'd been sent back to jail for six months. . . . The chain of circumstances that put Kristin on Commonwealth Avenue that day, as I was about to find out, would make any parent shudder. Any break in that chain would have kept her alive. Life and death are a series of accidents. Some are wonderful. Some are inevitable. Some are inexcusable.

Arrival on the Boston University campus in early September 1988 was inauspicious. We drove up in a rented station wagon that took hours to unload. Rosemary and I attended a no-nonsense orientation talk by BU President John Silber, who knew what parents wanted to hear about rules, regulations, and the enforcement thereof. We left Kristin at the end of a busy day sitting unhappily in a dimly lit dormitory room, teary-eyed because BU beadledom had yet to designate a roommate for her and anxious to keep Mom and Dad with her a little longer.

The gloom didn't last any longer than it does for most students. It was soon dispelled by classes and new friends. One of the introductory courses she'd taken at the Corcoran had convinced her that graphics would be her niche, but the campus visits and art displays the previous spring opened her eyes and made her anxious to explore other possibilities.

"I want to experiment and grow," she wrote in a statement of purpose. "I want to find out all the different things that are the foundation of art. I think my first year in college will be spent finding out where my best talents lie. . . . It's like trying on 100 perfumes until you find the one that matches your chemistry. Your perfect scent. I want college to help me find that and take what in me is raw and shape it, so that I can truly call myself an artist."

She was determined to make a difference, too. "I don't want to be an artist just because I enjoy it," she said. "There are other reasons. One reason is that through art, I can show things to people in a new way, maybe by taking something ordinary and doing something new with it. Or when you see something in a certain way you just can't put into words. What you see you can illustrate. You can paint it. You can draw it. You can sculpt it. You can photograph it. That always gives me a feeling of satisfaction.

"Another reason is that art is lasting. Maybe, in a hundred years, someone will see a work that I created and know what I was feeling when I made it. That person wouldn't need to translate it because art has no language barriers. Great art is timeless and universal."

Settling in had its difficulties, especially when it turned out that students couldn't cash checks at the BU student union anymore because too many bounced. Kristin had a checking account with the *Washington Post* credit union, but the only way she could cash those in

Boston was to use the write-it-to-a-friend trick and have friends deposit them in their Boston bank accounts and give her back real money. Her first roommate turned out to be from Detroit, a major in theater arts. "She's really sweet," Kristin wrote. "We're total opposites, but we get along great." She was also delighted to find a friend on the eighth floor—Kristin was on ten—who had a TV and a VCR, loved horror movies, and had a complete *Friday the 13th* collection and many others, not to mention Nintendo. "I'm psyched!" Kristin said in a postscript for Charlie. "I watched *Friday the 13th Part III* last night and one of the victims looks like my sculpture teacher."

It was a busy semester and it went quickly. Mira Suarez and some other friends drove up for a surprise visit over Veterans Day weekend. They found Kristin hungry and working hard. She couldn't goof off as she did in high school. One of her electives was "Religion and Culture," and the teacher knew how to instill fear in the freshmen. Kristin did her first paper on a fierce Indian deity named Mahakala, but before the professor passed the papers back, he kept telling the class how those who got F's could make it up. Kristin was sweating until she saw she got a B-minus. "Hoo-rah!" she said. "God, college is so hard." She did a painting of Mira for one of her art classes and was delighted when the teacher told her how much he liked it. She was discovering the joy of learning, especially when she wasn't hungry. We'd signed her up for fourteen meals a week, but her schedule kept her from using her meal ticket for anything but dinner. Do colleges plan it that way? "School's been cool lately," she said just before Christmas. "Send food."

Kristin spent two years at BU, but one year on the tenth floor of Claflin Hall was enough of dormitory life. Claflin is one of three thirteen-story buildings on the west campus, overlooking Nickerson Field. Just waiting for an elevator could be tiresome. Kristin probably would have moved off campus for sophomore year anyway, but her thoughts of leaving were fortified early in second semester with a stern letter from the Office of the Dean of Students. I was perforce annoyed about it at the time, but I still can't help laughing about the fact that Kristin wouldn't have been caught if she hadn't been taking so much time in the shower.

"Dear Ms. Lardner," the letter began. "The Office of Residence Life has reported that you have been found in violation of the Code of Student Responsibilities. On February 17, 1989 at approximately 9:00 P.M., you produced a Boston University I.D. with unauthorized information—a false birthdate—added to the card.

"As a result of this misconduct you are hereby placed on Residence Probation through December 1989. Any further misconduct on your part during this period will result in the imposition of additional disciplinary sanctions."

What happened was that someone in authority had decided to have a fire drill that night while Kristin was taking a shower. The alarm bells went off, but the shower spigots did not. Kristin didn't discover what was up until long minutes after everyone else had evacuated the building. Hair wet, she got dressed and rushed downstairs, only to be told to show her ID because she was late. She produced it without thinking. As far as she was concerned, what happened after that was simply proof of the excesses of the "fascist" Silber administration.

By the time I drove Kristin home that summer, in another rented station wagon sagging near the ground with all her belongings, she and several friends had found an apartment in Allston at 26 Glenville Avenue, a short ride on the "T"—Boston's trolley and subway system—from BU. She was looking forward to having her own place, but it was a memorable trip for the music as well. Kristin was by now into "heavy metal," and she decided to play some of it on the tape deck for my edification. I may have asked what it was like. She may have volunteered it. Either way, it was a mistake. Beyond the noxious twangs of one particular number, all I could hear was somebody saying "fuck . . . fuck . . . fuck . . . fuck." I was, to put it mildly, perplexed. Maybe Kristin was, too. I guess I could have ignored it, but it didn't seem to me that that was what a parent should do. We spent much of the next hour or so—I think it may have taken us all the way from New Haven to the Throgs Neck Bridge over Long Island Sound—talking about whether that was really music and why she liked it.

Kristin was glad to get home. "Ohmigod," she told her friends, "I'll never take another road trip with Dad."

Actually, we drove back in September 1989 to move her into Allston. It was a good trip. We didn't play any heavy metal. We listened to the car radio, and Kristin played a tape she'd made of Creedence Clearwater Revival. We both liked Creedence, especially "Bad Moon Rising." Sitting in Kristin's room in Brookline, I saw it again in a cardboard box full of records at the edge of her bed, somewhere between the Beatles' *Abbey Road* and the works of a group called Megadeth. I never dreamed how sorrowful and haunting the lyrics would turn out to be: "Don't go round tonight. It's bound to take your life. I see a bad moon on the rise."

Lt. Finnegan had suggested that I try to find out how Cartier got his gun. First I wanted to find out more about what happened that day and what led up to it. Who was Michael Cartier, and why had he been stalking my daughter?

Marty's had been closed that Sunday when we first arrived in Boston. It was three weeks later when I went there again. It's a big store, a supermarket of beers, wines, liquors, and a potpourri of other items advertised from the windows overlooking Harvard Avenue on one side and Commonwealth on the other: "Gourmet Deli . . . Coffee . . . Cookbooks . . . Dart and Billiard Supplies . . . Boxed Cigars . . . Braun Coffee Makers . . . Henkel Knives." Most of the clerks were college students, working to help pay the bills. Kristin hadn't been working there long, but everyone remembered how enthusiastic and diligent she was. She began as a part-time cashier on April 27. It was her first job outside of the college work-study program in months, and she was counting on it to make the summer affordable while she was taking more classes at Tufts for academic credits.

But with Cartier skulking about, throwing hard stares in her direction, it could be discouraging. He was a customer at Marty's, known in the store as Castle Mike or Castleneck because of a hand-sized tattoo on his neck with turrets and parapets rising over the collar line to the back of his right ear. Bunratty's, the nightclub where he hung out and worked as a bouncer, was just across the street, halfway up the block on the east side of Harvard. One afternoon, Kristin stamped back into Marty's after a short-lived break.

"I can't go out because of men!" she told Lauren. "I went out one way and saw Mike staring at me from the doorway at Bunratty's. Then I went around the corner to Commonwealth, and here were all these bums on the sidewalk, yelling at me. I can't even go out of the store without being harassed."

Kristin was too tough-minded to think of that as violence. She knew it was outrageous. She knew it was wrong. But she was more alarmed about the more tangible, physical violence that millions of American women suffer every year.[7] Kristin may not have known the statistics, but she knew the problem.

"What is a monster?" she asked in a paper she wrote at BU for a course called "Women and the Masculine Ideal." She wasn't satisfied with the dictionary definitions she'd found. All of them described a monster as a being, animal, or infant that was "physically deformed or abnormal" or that inspired "horror or disgust." "The obvious emphasis on appearance or deformity of appearance is typical of contemporary society," Kristin wrote. "It is abnormal physique or ugliness which 'inspires horror or disgust.' Centuries of history of the human race have imposed standards of beauty set by the select few which undermine the self-confidence and ambition of those individuals who stand apart from the norm. Ugliness and deformity are not socially acceptable. Therefore it is not surprising that a good-looking rapist and murderer, such as Ted Bundy, could go for years undetected, one of the crowd, normal."

The paper was on the monster in Mary Shelley's *Frankenstein,* a creature who Kristin observed was "agile, strong, intelligent, sensitive, and eloquent." But he was never given a chance. He was ugly, repulsive, hateful. "The creature became bitter and began to kill, [taking] revenge against the man who created him and the human race, which rejected him. This is when he became a monster . . .

"Society," Kristin continued, "creates its monsters in the same manner. Underprivileged and abused children grow up in this country desperately trying to fit in. They may be retarded, disfigured, or maybe just black. Many begin using hard drugs when very young. They grow up angry, and when they take their revenge against society, society feels justified in handing them over to prison wardens, our brutal surrogates, or taking their lives."

Revenge against society, however, was one thing. Raping women was another. "It is a universal feeling that rapists are monsters," Kristin said. "Crimes of sexual violence are one of the most horrifying. Rapists use the penis as a weapon to completely destroy a woman's mind and soul. A woman who has been brutally raped loses all self-confidence and self-respect. Rapists take what should be a woman's giving act, and ridicule her with it. This society seems to encourage an attitude of male domination. Women are seen as sluts who always want sex."

Frankenstein's creation became a monster because of the way he looked and because society never gave him a chance at humanity. A real monster, Kristin concluded, was "any being who has no sense of humanity." Ugliness and deformity are inconsequential. "The rapists and murderers are the real monsters . . . twisted beings without humanity."

Kristin wrote that in May 1990, almost two years before she met Michael Cartier. She had read *Frankenstein* from cover to cover when she was in high school. She knew her Gothic novels. But her insights suggested more than book-learning. I don't know whether she drew them from general observation, or from the way men treated girls she knew, or from something that happened to her as well. But the paper was just one illustration of how strongly she felt about violence against women. She saw that society was complicit in it, creating twisted images of women and then disassociating itself from what happens to them by denouncing their attackers as monsters.

"Just as Frankenstein hated the monster he brought to life, so society hates the monsters it creates," Kristin said. "Society, like Frankenstein, is so egotistic that it refuses to see its own deficiencies."

Kristin didn't make the monster who killed her. She tried to help him. She saw "a sense of humanity" in him. But the demons that drove Michael Cartier were firmly planted long before she met him. To hear his mother tell it, he was "born that way."

Kristin met him at a nightclub called Axis in early February 1992, shortly after her return from Christmas vacation. Like so much in life, it was a completely accidental encounter. He wouldn't have been there but for the leniency of the courts. Kristin had been planning to stay home that night. Tickets for Axis were $5 a head, and she didn't have any money, which was often the case before another slender check from home arrived in the mail.

Lauren urged her to come. Her new boyfriend, Brian Fazekas, had a friend playing in the band that night. "I'll pay," Lauren told her.

It didn't take long for Kristin to notice Cartier. She'd seen him a few days earlier, at Bunratty's. With a scar under his left eye and tattoos on his left arm, right arm, and left hand, not to mention the castle on his neck, he stood out in a crowd. Unfortunately, Kristin liked tattoos. She decided they were fashionable long before they were. She'd been thinking of getting one of her own when she was still in high school, somewhere in between the time they were deemed subversive and the time they became accessories for rich kids.

"When done correctly, tattoos are beautiful," Kristin wrote in a journal she started as a senior at Wilson. "Many of my friends have tattoos. A skinhead I know named Steve has about 10 of them [including] a huge dragon which starts on his chest, goes down across his stomach, around his side and ends on his back. . . . Some people think tattoos are ugly and disgusting. However, they would probably appreciate the same artwork if it was on paper. I think this makes them hypocrites. I hope to get a tattoo soon."

Kristin could see the tattoos on Cartier. What she couldn't see was that he preyed on women. He had been released from jail just before Christmas after serving consecutive terms, one for attacking Rose Ryan with a pair of scissors in a downtown subway station and one for violating probation in another case by virtue of that attack. He had just gotten a job at Bunratty's as a part-time bouncer. Kristin had noticed him there on January 29 when she went there with Lauren and Brian. Seeing Cartier at Axis the next week, she wangled an introduction. At twenty-two, he was tall and solid, a six-footer with dark brown hair and blue eyes.

"Isn't he cute?" she asked Lauren.

Lauren said no.

Cartier could be sweet, even charming. He knew how to play on a girl's sympathy and make her think she was the only one in the world who understood him. He was slyly manipulative and clearly disturbed. Once he talked about killing his mother, and he fantasized about seeing her dismembered by wild animals. When he was five or six, he ripped a pet rabbit's legs out of their sockets. When he was twenty-one, while dating Rose Ryan, he tortured and killed a kitten. In a bizarre 1989 incident at an Andover restaurant, he injected a syringe of blood into a ketchup bottle. He had all the earmarks of a violently abusive personality, someone desperately in need of being in charge, in control. To his girlfriends, he could be appallingly brutal. He wasn't "born that way," but something went wrong very early in his life and kept going wrong.

5

Eleven months older than Kristin, Michael Cartier was born in Newburyport, Massachusetts, on August 20, 1969. His mother, Penny, was seventeen; his father, Gene, nineteen. They weren't ready for marriage, or a baby. Their infant son was a problem from the start. He was struck with a fever not long after he was born. It still isn't clear what it was, rheumatic fever maybe. The doctors didn't think he would pull through. "He was real hot," Gene Cartier said. "He almost died. We had to get him baptized right away."

Gene Cartier left when his son was six months old. His young wife didn't appreciate being left in the lurch. Whatever happened to young Michael remains clouded by parental disclaimers and a seal of confidentiality that still surrounds official records, even after his death. I don't know what people that policy protects, other than those who don't deserve to be protected, officials included, but such is the state of the law, at least in Massachusetts. But it seems clear that baby boy Cartier was the principal casualty of the breakup.

"She couldn't handle him," Gene Cartier says of his ex-wife. "He had a mind of his own. He was a little boy, but he grew up fast. He needed a disciplinary structure. I wasn't there to give it to him. . . . He turned into a behavior problem. I was the same way as a kid."

A traveling amusement-park worker, Gene Cartier returned for a while, but it was only "a year or so" before the couple split up again, probably when Michael was three or four. By then, the little boy had developed a habit of trying to pour too much into too little. He would try to make his own breakfast, throwing a whole box of Cheerios and a bottle of milk into a tiny bowl. Gene Cartier said he tried to see his son as often as he could, even when he and his wife were separated. Michael was always climbing the fence, trying to run away. "I don't know why," Gene Cartier said. "I could never understand why."

Loud and shrill, Penny Cartier said she couldn't understand it, either. But whatever the reason, she will tell you, it wasn't her fault. "I'm not going to take the blame for it," she told me a few weeks after Kristin's murder. "He was a problem from the day he was born."

I came across Mrs. Cartier by chance. A Boston reporter I'd called on another subject offered me what was thought to be her number, without having tried it. When I dialed it, a young woman answered and said Penny Cartier wasn't home. She offered to take a message. I gave her my name and said I was Kristin Lardner's father.

"Wait a minute," she said, putting down the phone. She walked away but spoke to someone in a voice loud enough to hear: "You're not going to fucking believe this. There's a Mr. Lardner on the phone. Kristin Lardner's father."

Penny Cartier came on the line. I told her I was in the Boston area, trying to find out more about what had happened. I had to bite my lips several times. The only interviewing "technique" that I have as a journalist is that I always try to be sympathetic and understanding. Never argue. Never lecture. Never shout. That was never more difficult than it was in talking with Penny Cartier.

She said there had been a lot of lies in the papers. She said she hadn't "abandoned" him, no matter what other people said. In fact, they were just repeating what Michael had told them. No matter. Penny Cartier insisted it wasn't so. She was still seething over an article that had appeared weeks earlier in the *Boston Herald,* quoting the director of a state-supported boarding school in Jamaica Plain where his mother had left him at age seven.

"He was an abused child, abused at an early age," Octavia Ossola, director of the Knight child center at the New England Home had told the *Herald.* "This might very well be an example of a youngster who had so many difficulties at such an early age . . . that even with treatment it was not sufficient to overcome his difficulties."[1]

"He was a problem child," Penny Cartier said. "He was put there because I called the school and asked for help. Sending him there probably made him a bigger problem. . . . For me to be blamed for this, that's just bull. . . . I don't know what made him that way. . . . I didn't beat him, abuse him, sexually molest him, nothing."

At some point in Michael Cartier's early years, according to his father, Penny Cartier took up with a fellow named John. "I didn't care for the guy," Gene Cartier said. "He took off on her, left her pregnant. He was a Golden Gloves champ, a professional boxer." How he treated little Michael, I don't know, but Michael grew up feeling unloved, unwanted, rejected. He responded aggressively.

"He'd squirt the hose in people's windows," Penny Cartier remembered. "He'd take a bottle away from his sister. He'd light matches behind a gas stove. He was born that way. His father says he took after him. I couldn't handle him."

I don't think he was born that way. Differences in temperament do have a significant genetic basis,[2] but basically, Kristin was right. Real monsters aren't born. They're made.[3] But the making can begin at a terribly early age. One of the most frightening lessons of Michael Cartier's short and brutish life is how fruitless it was to think he could be rehabilitated after he came to the attention of the criminal justice system. Criminal behavior is set much earlier in life than job-training programs and midnight basketball leagues and most other anticrime programs are designed to address.[4] Many of those efforts are worth undertaking on their own merits, but if we are looking for ways to reduce crime, especially violent crime, we need to begin much sooner.

For Michael Cartier, the breaking point came in first grade. "That's when we found out he needed professional help," Gene Cartier said. "He wanted to beat up his teacher." Of course, "none of this had anything to do with what he did to Kristin," Penny Cartier asserted. "Michael's childhood had nothing to do with anything."

In fact, Cartier's story is a close-up of violence in the making, a graphic example of what President Clinton was talking about in his

1994 State of the Union speech when he said tougher penalties for violent crime are only part of the cure. As Clinton said at one point, "We can't renew the country when children are having children and the fathers walk away as if the kids don't amount to anything."

Even more troubling is the fact that Michael Cartier, for one, did not go ignored by the Commonwealth of Massachusetts. He was no footloose street urchin, left to fend for himself. He grew up as a ward of the state, provided with extensive treatment and therapy. Life with mother ended at age seven when Penny Cartier took the boy to the New England Home's residential treatment center for troubled children. "I imagine he was angry," Gene Cartier said of his son. "His dad wasn't around. That was my fault. But she didn't dump him. She sought professional help. She was a single parent, and she couldn't help this very active kid."

What all that overlooks is how much Cartier hated his mother. The particulars of what made him so hostile remain hidden. The authorities to whom he was entrusted say they are still restricted in what they can say. But they are quite emphatic about the grave damage that was done by the time they got him.

By Penny Cartier's account, it was everyone's fault but hers. Her ex-husband: "I blame him for everything." The state schools: "They did him no good." Even Kristin: "They say she aggravated him to the point . . ."

I nearly jumped out of my hotel room chair when she said that. I was lucky I was on the phone. I grimaced. I counted to ten. Expletives deleted ran through my head. Shut up, I told myself. You want to hear what she has to say. Don't lecture. Don't argue. Don't shout. Let her talk. I waited. Long seconds passed.

Penny Cartier never finished the sentence. Perhaps she remembered who was on the other end of the line. Her next words were safe and unctuous. "But who can say that you get aggravated to the point that you kill somebody?" she asked.

So what went wrong?

"The system messed up with Michael," she said. "He was a bad boy. He was not a killer."

Reporters, no matter how sympathetic, have to dispute false

statements. "Oh, yes, he was," I said as softly as I could. "He killed Kristin."

She ignored the point. It plainly didn't matter. It had no relevance. "I blame the Harbor School [the institution that inherited Cartier after he got too old for the New England Home] for letting him leave that school before he was ready," she said. "He got into the wrong crowd."

I decided to ask about something else that was in the back of my mind. I'd heard about a daughter, Melissa, Michael Cartier's half sister. Where was she? Mrs. Cartier—she still uses her first husband's last name—didn't appreciate the question. "My daughter lives with her mother," she said in huffy tones.

That must have been the young woman who answered the phone and said, "You're not going to fucking believe this . . ."

Michael Cartier often told people that his mother abandoned him when he was a child, that she never loved him. What happened to make him say such things?

"What about his father, who left him when he was six months old?" Penny Cartier responded. "Who walked him to the hospital to get him baptized because I was afraid he was so sick he was going to die? I'm not going to take the blame for it. He was a problem from the day he was born."

Octavia Ossola scoffed at that when I talked to her. "She was a problem from the day he was born," Ossola said. "This young man suffered the kinds of abuse and indignities and abandonments that are pretty tough for people to recover from." Adults can sometimes cope with such traumatic experiences. It's much harder for children. Cartier's mother rejected him. Kristin paid the price.

"With Michael, even though there was a fair amount of treatment," Ossola said, "I think that the rejection he experienced from his mother and the hatred he experienced there spilled over in the way he dealt with people, and especially women."

At the New England Home, the boy was regarded as bright and likable. Teachers and social workers rooted for him. They had an idea of the baggage he brought with him. They knew what he had done to his pet rabbit, tearings its legs out of their sockets. Penny Cartier had told them about that. They kept a special eye on the Home's mascot, a well-fed beagle named Tammy. But Tammy was big enough to take care of herself. The staff wanted Michael to succeed. His child-care worker, Tom Walsh, the man who took care of him in the residence hall and put him to bed at night, found him engaging, and interesting to talk to. "He was somebody that you actually thought you could reach," Walsh said. "You could almost trust him. Of course, he'd completely blow your trust off, but they all did." In some ways, Cartier seemed like an average boy, making models with his roommate, Alan, and chattering on with preteen bravado about girls. "You'd hear them talking and you'd think they'd been in the navy," Walsh said. "They'd talk about women's breasts and, you know, the whole nine yards. Meanwhile, they didn't have a clue. One time [when they were about twelve], I went in and had to explain sex to Michael and Alan. At first, they thought I was kidding. They both sounded like six-year-old girls going, 'oooooh.' "

"People at the Home felt a good deal of empathy for him, because it was reasonably easy to want things to be better for him," Ossola said. But they got no help from Mrs. Cartier. "His mom could not say, 'Yeah, I did it, let me fix it,' " Ossola said.

Rich DeAngelis, one of Cartier's probation officers, was familiar with the problem. "That's the worst childhood I've ever seen," he said after the shooting. "This just didn't happen in the last couple of years."

"Michael was someone I did not want to be around," his mother said.

That much was made brutally clear to the boy while he was at the New England Home. Officials there said Mrs. Cartier would invite Michael to visit her at her home in Lowell "at her convenience" and sometimes stand him up when he arrived. A social worker would drive him out and "the mother would be nowhere to be found," Ossola remembers. The rejections tore Cartier apart. "Time after time, Michael lost complete control and was brought back to the agency," Ossola said. "Time after time, it was 'I want you to come, I want you to come,' and then she wouldn't be there." One of the social workers, Chip Wilder, will never forget one devastating trip when the boy was about ten. Mrs.

Cartier wasn't there when they arrived so they waited, with Michael growing "more and more anxious and restless and agitated," Wilder said. They went to get something to eat and returned to wait some more. Wilder told him, "Well, maybe she just forgot."

Michael went wild. "He started throwing rocks at the house," Wilder said. "He was just enraged. . . . I remember him getting on top of the car and swearing and threatening his mother. I didn't know what else he was going to do." Wilder finally managed to get him back into the car for the tense ride back to Boston, only to get a flat tire that mangled one of the rear wheels. Wilder was worried that if he stopped, Michael would jump out and run away, but the flat left him with no choice. He made an emergency call to the New England Home, and a night staffer drove out to pick them up.

For the next visit, Wilder was so uneasy that he asked Tom Walsh to come along. Mrs. Cartier was there this time, but it was, as usual, a stiff, strained get-together. "He never really seemed comfortable there," Wilder said. "I remember definitely the lack of any warmth." Cartier's mother didn't even give him a hug. On the ride back, Wilder turned to Walsh and said, "It was almost like she wasn't there."

"She wasn't too fond of him," Gene Cartier said. "He reminded her too much of me."

Michael was encouraged by the staff to think his mother wanted to see him, but that didn't help much. Once, in expectation of another visit, he climbed out a third-floor window to brood on the roof of the New England Home's dining room. "He had gone out there because he was very angry and very anxious about going on this visit," Wilder said. "He stayed out there until two of the staff went out and talked him into coming back in." Wilder said episodes of rage and self-endangering behavior occurred frequently, throughout his stay at the Home. "It didn't take," Wilder said of the treatment Cartier got. "Nothing took for him."

The boy had a terrible temper, Gene Cartier allowed. "He had a problem with [his temper] because he thought his mother had abandoned him. He used to run away. He was driving her crazy. So she put him in a school. . . . She did not dump him. If anyone was at fault, it was me." He tried to visit the boy at the New England Home but was turned away.

"They said, 'We don't think it would be good for you to see him,'" Gene Cartier said. "They took over. The system took over. The system failed."

Some children are so disabled emotionally that they are always going to need treatment, Ossola said. And there are some whose relationships with their parents constantly defeat them. There is no way for those children to escape the feeling that they are the bad seeds. "Maybe all of us have to do better in figuring who are the kids who are potentially dangerous and who are the ones who have hope," Ossola said. "But what to do with those who are dangerous, I don't know."

Cartier stayed at the New England Home until 1981, when he was twelve. He spent some time in foster homes, but they didn't work out. One foster family looked particularly promising; it was well known, Wilder said, for being able to "tolerate anything in terms of behavior." The family found Michael too disruptive. In October 1982, the Massachusetts Department of Social Services sent him to the Harbor School in Amesbury, Massachusetts, a treatment center for disturbed teenagers. He stayed there almost four years and then was turned over to his father, by then a facilities maintenance mechanic in Lawrence.

Penny Cartier said she wanted to take him home with her, but Harbor School authorities wouldn't hear of it. She was miffed that they let his father have him. "I washed my hands of the whole mess," she said. "They said my [second] marriage wouldn't be able to survive him," she said. "But they were willing to let my [first] husband take him. . . . The [boarding] schools did him no good. The biggest injustice was they let him go back to live with his father in Lawrence. He got in with the wrong crowd. I wouldn't even acknowledge the people he hung around with."

Cartier was typical of teenagers the Harbor School takes on. At first, there were temper tantrums and a lot of what school officials call "impulsive behavior." He got into fights. But gradually he seemed to settle down a bit. He struck the staff as shrewd and reasonably intelligent even though he didn't do particularly well on achievement tests. He wasn't particularly artistic, but he liked art class and was good at some sports.

"He liked basketball," said Art DiMauro, executive director of the Harbor School. "He stayed away from football. He started out being very difficult with his peers. By the time he left, he was a leader, someone the kids looked to in a positive way."

The Harbor School staff found Cartier "quite endearing" before he left. He made friends. One of his teachers thought of him as a kid with a sense of humor and an ability to reach out and connect with the adults around him. "It wasn't all manipulative and superficial," DiMauro said. "He could sustain it."

No one at the school considered giving him back to his mother or thought she wanted him. She was "something of a lost cause," DiMauro said. "There was a terrific amount of unhappiness associated with her memory."

Cartier remained bitter about his mother for the rest of his life. "I know he hated her," said Kara Boettger, a young woman who dated him years later. He told her he wanted to get a tattoo on his arm of his mother hanging from a tree with wild animals ripping at her body.

Penny Cartier didn't seem surprised when I told her this. In fact, she said, after he turned eighteen, "He asked my daughter if she wanted him to kill me." "That's Michael's psychological problem," Penny Cartier said of the tattoo fantasy. "It had nothing to do with me. . . . I have nothing to feel guilty about. . . . Michael's life was a piece of cake compared to others."

As I spoke with Mrs. Cartier, an eerie realization came over me. I was talking to the person who made my daughter's killer what he was. Of course, Michael Cartier was responsible for her murder. It was planned and premeditated. I don't believe in irresistible impulses or uncontrollable urges that absolve us from whatever we do. The psychologists and psychiatrists who are called as courtroom experts to testify so knowledgeably about such compulsions are really preaching a doctrine of nonaccountability, a rule of law that says there is no law. Michael Cartier didn't "have" to kill my daughter. But when he did, he was really striking out at the woman he was afraid to kill. Throughout his life, Cartier had sent out repeated signals of how troubled he was. Too often, the danger signs went unnoticed, in large part, I think, because Mrs. Cartier's creation, unlike Dr. Frankenstein's, was quite good-looking. Even Kristin, who had seen the hypocrisy of defining monsters in terms of their abnormal physique or ugliness, had been fooled.

Gene Cartier tried to make amends as his son grew older. At times, he drank too much, but he was trying to stabilize his life. The staff at the Harbor School found him guarded and mistrustful at first, but he grew warmer and kept up his visits. "It took a lot of work for me to get Michael back," he said. "I had to go there every week. It took about six months of talking with people there before they would even consider giving him back to me."

In June 1986, Michael was released to his father, who was living with his second wife, Trudy. He was sixteen, with no particular ambitions for the future. At that age, DiMauro said, many teenagers are thinking of what they want to do, whether it's becoming a cop, a doctor, or a ballplayer, but Cartier was "somewhat immature" in that regard. "That's typical of the kids we see," DiMauro said. "They're not very well equipped to look to the future in positive terms."

An informal review of the records of those who were Harbor School students around this time showed that about a third of them had a very hard time after they got out, and about a third of those, roughly 10 percent, "didn't make it at all," DiMauro said. "Michael was obviously one of those."

Cartier entered Lawrence High School in September 1986 and was put in a special class to determine the right grade level for him. He was seventeen, but he wasn't up to speed.

In Washington, D.C., Kristin was beginning her junior year at Wilson; she'd just returned from a trip to Europe with a girlfriend and her parents. She signed up for the yearbook staff, joined the Art Club, and began a succession of weekend jobs, first behind the deli counter of a restaurant in Friendship Heights and then as a cashier at a greeting card shop in Georgetown. She became a fan of Goth music, sort of an intellectual punk style from England, where it was called "doom rock," but as always, she read more than she listened. Goth fans wore black and had to read nineteenth-century Gothic literature to understand the music. More books for Kristin to devour. *Wuthering Heights* became one of her favorites, with all its "perverted passion and passionate perversity," as Charlotte Brontë once described the setting. Kristin must have felt a special kinship with author Emily Brontë, the fifth child in a literary family, fond of nature and animals, dissatisfied with organized religion. They even shared a somber imagination and a taste for outdated clothes. Kristin's sense of being an artist was very much like Charlotte Brontë's description of her sister's creative gift: "Something that at times strangely wills and works for itself. . . . Be the work grim or glorious, dread or divine, you have little choice left but quiescent adoption."[5]

At Lawrence High, special class was held in a different building from the regular high school, and Cartier spent the entire year there. The next year, at age eighteen, school officials classified him as a sophomore. He didn't like it. He couldn't keep up. It's not clear whether he even attended many classes.

"I guess he got disappointed or disgusted," his father said. "He was a little bit older than the others. He worked at it for a while. Finally, he just got aggravated. He was really frustrated. He said the hell with it."

Even before he dropped out, Cartier and the police were getting to know one another. By the end of his second semester at Lawrence High, he was facing the first of nearly twenty criminal charges that he piled up in courthouses from Lawrence to Brighton over a four-year period. He was arrested in Merrimac on May 10, 1987, for putting stolen license tags on an uninsured, unregistered, uninspected motor vehicle and driving it without a license. Brought before a judge in Amesbury District Court, he was fined $525 and put on probation for three months.

Before that probation was up, he was arrested again for getting into a noisy brawl on South Broadway in Lawrence, on August 30, 1987. The case was continued. He got into another fight on September 12, this time with employees of the White Hen Pantry. He was taken into custody and released on his own recognizance. Nobody bothered to see if there were any outstanding warrants for his arrest. One had been issued the day before, up in Amesbury, when he failed to pay his fines for the "auto violations."

The two disorderly conduct cases were consolidated, and on November 10, 1987, Cartier appeared in Lawrence District Court and was put on probation again, this time for six months, on condition that he undergo alcoholic counseling.

Cartier still hadn't paid his fines in Amesbury, and the warrant for his arrest was still outstanding, but no one paid any attention to it. Under the state's antiquated and dysfunctional system of paper warrants, it probably wouldn't have mattered if it had been noticed. The judge presiding over the disorderly conduct cases in Lawrence would have had to have the actual warrant in his hands to stop Cartier from going out the door. The needed piece of paper was apparently sitting on someone's desk in Amesbury. The law was reformed in December 1994, but as Governor Weld said in signing the new measure: "In the past, and I can tell you this from personal experience, defendants have been defaulting on warrants almost with impunity."[6]

Under the new system, court clerks must enter warrants into a computer when defendants default in criminal cases, and police are permitted for the first time to make arrests based on the electronic warrants. The law also requires court and police personnel to determine whether there are any outstanding warrants against an individual before allowing him to be released on bail. Much of the impetus for the reform came from Suffolk County Sheriff Robert Rufo, who pointed out the absurdity of a system that prevented drivers from getting their licenses renewed if they had an outstanding parking ticket but routinely permitted criminal defendants to go free when there were warrants out for their arrest.

"We were tougher on traffic violations than we were on violent crimes," said Charles McDonald, spokesman for the state Executive Office of Public Safety.[7]

Cartier was unlucky this time. He was picked up on the Amesbury warrant just before Christmas 1987 and tossed into the Lawrence House of Correction, a dilapidated building that has since closed down. He was jailed from December 23, 1987, to January 9, 1988, reducing his fines at the rate of $3 a day. At that rate, he would have had to stay behind bars almost six months, but he knocked his debt down by about $50 and paid the rest. He listed his occupation as a "roofer."

Apparently, he'd already dropped out of high school. He moved on to a string of jobs, keeping none of them for very long. At first he worked stripping furniture for a shop that did refinishing work, but then he was laid off. He found another job with a man who did housepainting, siding, and roofing jobs, but it wasn't steady employment.

Cartier had no run-ins with police for a few months after getting out of the Lawrence jail, but he celebrated his nineteenth birthday that 1988 summer by getting arrested for trespassing at a local variety store.

He was released on his own recognizance, which left him free the next month to become a felon by burglarizing a Lawrence meat and grocery store. On September 10, 1988, he broke into Nader's Market on South Broadway through the front door, forced open the cash register, and helped himself to $100 in bills, $20 in change, 1,500 scratch lottery tickets worth $1,050, and about 19 packs of cigarettes valued at just $30. He had told police the month before that he was a painter. Now he said he was unemployed. A district court judge decided he was indigent and appointed a lawyer for him.

Charged with breaking and entering in the nighttime, grand larceny, and malicious destruction of property worth more than $250—all felonies—Cartier was released on a personal recognizance bond of $5,000, which meant he didn't have to put up any money up front.

Eight days later, on September 23, 1988, he was arrested again on a felony charge for breaking the glass door of another South Broadway store, causing more than $250 in damages. By now, he had another job, pumping gas at a Sunoco station. The judge who arraigned him this time, the third judge to greet him over a six-week period, found him sort of indigent—able to contribute $100 for the costs of his court-appointed lawyer.

Once again, he was released on his own recognizance. He didn't have a track record for violence—yet. Under Massachusetts law, then and now, the only justification for detaining a defendant before trial rather than releasing him on bond or his own recognizance was risk of flight, the danger that the suspect wouldn't show up for court proceedings. Governor Weld was working strenuously to change that rule when Kristin was killed. He had, and has, a compelling argument: the danger a defendant poses to other individuals or the community at large should also be grounds for denying bail. Why should the courts be more concerned about a defendant's fleeing the jurisdiction than they are about his or her propensity for violence? Congress changed that rule for the federal courts in 1984, but the Massachusetts legislature is heavily populated by defense lawyers who make a living representing criminal defendants.

Anger over Kristin's murder and the other victims of "domestic violence" in Massachusetts that year gave impetus to Weld's bail reform proposal. The governor was almost as indignant as I was when he read in the Boston papers the defensive claims of various police and court officials that nothing could have stopped Michael Cartier. By then, of course, Cartier had a track record for violence. "If the law was different, the guy would very probably have been in jail and wouldn't have been able to shoot her last Saturday," Weld told reporters the next week after meeting with House and Senate leaders on his proposal. "It's just ludicrous that state government is not responding with legislation that would protect these women."[8]

Weld's plan had provisions that would have applied directly to Kristin's case. Under it, a person who had violated a restraining order could be detained at a police station until a court hearing was held. The bill would also have provided for a temporary detention of up to five days so that a case involving a potentially violent person could be investigated for the court's consideration. Even a cursory investigation of Cartier would have shown that he was out on probation for attacking

Rose Ryan, and that he had a suspended, six-month jail sentence coming to him if he got into trouble again.

What were the police saying? "Everything was done right by the numbers," Lt. Edward Merrick had told the *Globe.* "The system did not fail this young lady."[9] And the courts? "Right now there is a lot of scapegoating on the courts," said Dorchester District Court Judge E. Sydney Hanlon. "But if someone makes up his mind to commit murder, the courts can't stop him."[10] And the Massachusetts Bar Association? Its chief spokesman seemed more concerned about inconvenience to the courts than about the dangers their inattention might pose to the public. Governor Weld's proposal would overwhelm the already clogged court system because it would require judges to determine the dangerousness of defendants, said state bar association president Daniel C. Crane. "The courts as they are currently organized are not capable of implementing that change."[11]

A former prosecutor and once high-ranking Justice Department official, Weld was outraged. "The Brookline police said this guy was absolutely crackers, that nothing was going to stop him until he killed somebody," the governor told reporters. "Well, if they're behind bars and disarmed, that stops them."[12] Even before Kristin's death, he had declared "the epidemic of domestic violence" a public safety emergency in the state. Kristin was the nineteenth of the women and children to be killed in such bloodshed that year in Massachusetts.

"I'm not sure society has faced up to the extent to which people are walking time bombs, people who constitute a danger to themselves and others," Weld said. "I think there are quite a lot of them out there. My solution is to lock 'em up and throw away the key. They're not crackers in the sense of being mentally ill. They can control their actions. They should be confined. There is a lot of evidence of a nil rate of success in psychological treatment."[13]

Weld's bail reform measure was enacted in 1992, but without certain constitutional safeguards that his proposal had included. It was subsequently declared unconstitutional by the Massachusetts Supreme Court but was repaired in light of the ruling and enacted in 1994. Passage came after the May 1994 murder of a Massachusetts woman,

Donna Bianchi, allegedly killed by her estranged husband while he was free on bail on earlier charges of having assaulted her. Lieutenant Governor Paul Cellucci predicted at the signing ceremonies that "this law is going to save lives and help protect dozens of battered women and innocent children throughout Massachusetts." It affects, among others, defendants accused of violating restraining orders.[14]

Penny Cartier blamed her son's growing troubles on the company he kept. He became a skinhead. "I wouldn't even acknowledge the people he hung around with," she said. "I don't want to be around someone who shaves their head, who gets arrested for breaking and entering."

There were other problems, too. On November 27, 1988, he was severely injured in a head-on auto accident in Methuen. There were three other teenagers riding with Cartier when their car veered out of control and smashed into a car coming the other way. Michael was sitting in the front seat on the passenger side, and he got the worst of it. His legs and a hip were broken. A head wound left his brain exposed. The impact made one of his eyes crooked.

The accident put him in the hospital for a long time, and it delayed disposition of the two felony cases against him until the next summer. Apparently, the judge felt sorry for him. John F. Sapienza, the Lawrence police officer who nabbed him for the grocery store burglary, said the court was presented with "a lengthy medical history saying that [Cartier] was going to be incapable of doing much of anything but collecting welfare. So I think the court took pity on him."[15]

Almost everyone felt sorry for Michael Cartier until it was too late.

On July 8, 1989, Cartier was sentenced to six months in the Lawrence House of Correction for the break-in at Nader's Market. He was given a concurrent term of thirty days for malicious destruction at the second store. But all the jail time was suspended. He was put on probation again, this time for a year.

Officer Sapienza had his misgivings. There was something about Cartier that bothered him. "He had a skinhead background and the attitude to go with it," Sapienza said. "He never really was combative or disrespectful towards [the police]. But if he was around, you could just seem to sense that he was trouble, bad news. I have no other way of saying it except that he was one of those people you could feel that when he was around, there was going to be a problem."

Perhaps the judge should have read his local newspaper more closely. By the time Cartier showed up in court, he was having what appeared to be a perky recovery. In June 1989, less than a month before the sentencing, he enjoyed brief notoriety as a self-proclaimed skinhead, lumbering into the newsroom of the *Lawrence Eagle-Tribune* with four stubble-headed friends to complain of the bad press and "neo-Nazi" labels skinheads usually got. The "crew" was delighted to see heads turn as they made their way into a conference room in their de rigueur flight jackets, Doc Martens boots, and loud suspenders. Completely bald from the accident, Cartier cut an especially striking figure, walking on crutches and shooting cold stares. Under his jacket, he was wearing a T-shirt that said "Fuck Racism." In fact, he disliked blacks intensely, but that isn't the message he wanted to convey on this youthful propaganda mission.

"We are not racists," Cartier assured columnist Kathie Neff.[16] He said newspapers were being unfair to his kind by portraying them as "white supremacists with shaved heads." Another member of the crew, Tim McKernan, seventeen, of Framingham, agreed. "People just see us with the uniform and think we're Nazis," he said.

So why take all that grief? Why be a skinhead, especially when the crew conceded that many skinhead groups, like the Providence Nazis, were anti-Semitic or racist? The answers, boiled down, were simple enough. They felt isolated, estranged. They needed to belong to something, to protect one another, to feel wanted, to be the center of attention, Cartier most of all. His parents had turned their backs on him, he said. He grew up in boarding schools. He even saw some virtue in being a ward of the taxpayers.

"The state supported me all my life, with free doctors and dentists and everything," he said. "My parents never had anything to do with that because they got rid of me. This is my way of saying thanks." Being a skinhead appealed to him because of "the unity, the brotherhood, the all for one" of it.[17]

Neff looked at him. She noticed one of his eyes was crooked, but she noticed something else about both of them. They registered no emotion whatever. "Not someone I'd like to meet in a dark parking garage," she told herself.

Yet he seemed so sincere, so earnest, so childlike that she gave him her home phone so that he could call her and give her the numbers of other skinheads she could talk to. Should she have been able to pick him out as a potential killer? Neff wondered after he shot Kristin. Probably not, not when she realized that on the day she learned of Kristin's murder, she also found out that a friend would not be reporting to work because her husband had beaten her the night before. Not when she remembered that the ex-husband of another close friend was awaiting trial, accused of shooting that friend and two other women. Not when she thought of still another friend who had recently left her abusive husband, and then gone back to him.[18]

None of those women was crazy, Neff wrote. They were all "accomplished, educated, professional women—much as Kristin Lardner was on her way to becoming—who made a bad choice in love, as virtually every woman has at some time in her life.

"They are women who bought—at least for a time—that ancient folk 'wisdom' that it is women who are responsible for the emotional health of the planet, women who are the caretakers, women who can 'rescue' damaged men from the horrors of their past. They are women like me and like you."[19]

6

Within a year of the accident, Cartier moved to the Boston area, leaving his father, his new stepmother, Kimberly, and a baby half brother, Justin, of whom he was quite fond. The accident produced what seems to have been a magic purse for him. He told friends he had a big insurance settlement coming and would get periodic advances on it from his lawyer. Gene Cartier said his son got a final settlement of $17,000 and "went through $14,000" of it before he shot Kristin and killed himself.

Michael seems to have done his best to hide the income from snoopy creditors. He owed a considerable amount in hospital bills. When the final settlement came through, his father said, Michael didn't have the proper ID for his own bank account. Gene Cartier opened an account in his name and gave Michael an ATM card for it. "He did what he wanted to do with it," Gene Cartier said. "It was his money."

According to his parents, something else happened after the accident. His terrible temper got worse.

Rose Ryan could tell you about that. She knew how brutal Cartier could be to women. When Kristin's murder was reported on TV—the newscaster described the killing as "another case of domestic violence"—she said to a friend, "That sounds like Mike." It was. Hearing the newscaster say his name, she remembers, "I almost dropped."[1]

She was seventeen when she met him at a party in Boston in the summer of 1990. An honors graduate of East Lynn High School, set to enter Suffolk University that fall, she was a striking girl with brown hair and brown eyes, just like Kristin. She was 5'5", 120 pounds. Kristin was 5'7", 114 pounds. A coincidence? I don't think so. His mother, Penny, had brown hair and brown eyes. She was about 5'5". When I asked Gene Cartier how much she weighed when they got married, he replied: "She was built. She had a fine figure. I understand what you're saying."[2]

"He was really my first boyfriend," Rose said. "I was supposed to work that summer and save my money." She got off to a good start. She got a job at a breakfast shop in Swampscott, and she found an apartment for herself in a nearby building that was sort of like a dorm for working women under thirty—dinners included, no men allowed. The arrangement didn't last. Rose became enthralled with Boston and all the fun it offered. Cartier used to take her to the nightclubs, introduce her to the bands, and buy her drinks. And he had to see her every day. He didn't want a girlfriend he could date just on weekends. He wanted her with him all the time.

"Control" is the word for it, although Rose didn't realize it at the time. Batterers like Cartier can't stand the idea of "their woman" having any sort of independence, an existence of their own. They're afraid they wouldn't be real men if they weren't in charge. As Sarah M. Buel, a Massachusetts prosecutor and once thoroughly battered woman, describes her life with her abusive husband:

"We lived in a second-floor apartment, and I wasn't allowed to raise the shade in the kitchen," she recalled at a 1993 domestic violence conference in San Francisco.[3] "We didn't argue about it. I never raised the shade. I was told not to listen to the radio. We didn't argue about it. I didn't listen to the radio." Her then-husband let her read the *New York Daily News* but not the *New York Times,* lest she get too smart. "Batterers are terrified that you are going to get too smart. It's a huge issue with them . . ."

Caught up with the scene in Boston, and Cartier's attentions, Ryan quit her job, and with it, her plans for starting college in the fall.

"At first," she said of their relationship, "everything was fine." Cartier made a good first impression on her parents, too. He knew how to behave when he was supposed to.

Even so, there were disconcerting signs. Rose remembers a birthday party for Cartier's two-year-old half brother, Justin, at Gene and Kimberly Cartier's home in Lawrence. It was then, Rose said, that she discovered Mike "was weirder than I realized."

"There were a lot of children there, young kids," Rose said. They were in one room, with Rose and Mike. The parents were in another room. Cartier was very careful with Justin, but he began roughhousing with the other children, twisting their arms backwards and throwing them around the room. Sometimes, one would run in and tell the mother, "Mike's hurting me." Cartier would follow, laughing and saying they were just playing. A couple of the parents kept their children in the kitchen after that, but most didn't realize what was going on. "He was hurting little kids," Rose said.

Then there was the story of the spider web tattoo. Rose never knew whether Cartier was making it up or not. But he had a spider web tattooed on his elbow, and he told her that it was a symbol for having killed someone. He said that he was walking home late at night over some bridge in Lawrence when he encountered a woman who was known as a prostitute or who he knew was a prostitute. By the account he gave Rose, "She said she wanted to jump off and kill herself. He said he talked to her for a minute. And then when she turned around, he pushed her off the bridge and ran home. They said it was a suicide. He told that to other people, too, because [after Cartier killed himself], they said, yeah, he told them the same thing." Perhaps Cartier was just trying to build a tough-guy legend for himself. A check of the *Lawrence Eagle-Tribune* files shows no report of a "suicide" such as the one he described. Officer Sapienza adds that a spider web tattoo is "common with bikers. It doesn't necessarily mean that you've killed anybody."

Cartier became violent with Rose about two to three months after they started dating. They were on the Boston Common together, in the fall of 1990. Cartier started "kidding around" and put her in one of the big municipal barrels in the park. Rose got angry, especially when a woman police officer came by on horseback and admonished her as though she had jumped into it by herself. "Hey, get out of that barrel," she ordered Ryan.

Mortified, Rose scrambled out, falling down at one point, and then walking off. She had had more than enough of Michael Cartier that day. "I'm not going with you," she told him.

Cartier was furious. "You're coming with me," he told her. Rose refused. He got angrier. "I came here all the way to meet you. You've got to come with me," he told her, punching her in the back of the head.

Rose was shocked. No man had ever hit her before, including her father and five brothers. She kept walking, determined to get to the train station about two miles away. "You'd better stop," Cartier told her. The policewoman on horseback, having protected the trash barrel, had disappeared, but there were bystanders everywhere.

"Oh really?" Rose said angrily. "What are you going to do, Mike? Hit me again?"

Cartier didn't hesitate. "Okay," he said, and punched her in the side of the head. Tears ran down her face. Then Cartier started yelling at her because she was making a scene. People were starting to look at her because she was crying. Still no one asked if she needed any help. That was what aggravated her the most. "Every time something happened, it was in public and nobody stopped to help." As far as Cartier was concerned, it wasn't his fault. She asked for it.

With everyone staring as though there were something wrong with her, Rose sat down, sobbing. He ended the scene with "his usual thing," breaking into tears and telling her, "Oh, why do I always hurt the people I love? What can I do? My mother didn't love me. I need your help."

Batterers are often encouraged to think that way: it isn't their fault. Their therapists frequently foster the idea. One survey of fifty-nine so-called battering prevention programs found that 90 percent listed "increased self-esteem" as one of their main treatment goals. Only 14 percent mentioned "having the abuser take responsibility for his violence."[4] Counseling a batterer about his unmet childhood needs, his insecurity and dependency won't necessarily stop his violence if he continues to get what he wants by being violent. Violence, like alcohol or drug abuse, "is self-perpetuating unless directly confronted. It cannot be interpreted away."[5] Even programs that try to confront it directly, like Common Purpose in Massachusetts, have few success stories to tell. Many of its clients attend the sessions because it is the only way to stay out of jail, "like a class of teenagers trapped in after-school detention."[6] In group discussions, they "don't hesitate to answer when asked why they hit their wives during any given incident; it was because it worked. It was the fastest and surest way to get the control they felt entitled to."[7]

Men who beat women typically try to excuse their actions by saying they just "lost control."[8] What they're really doing is keeping control under the guise of losing it. Sarah Buel says, "They know exactly what they're doing. They don't beat up the boss who yells at them for being late for work. They don't beat up the cop who gives them a traffic ticket."[9] But when they get home, they say they just can't help themselves. It ought to be an unacceptable dodge, at least in a society where violent assault is supposed to be taken seriously, but it has been ratified in too many police stations and courtrooms to count. Indeed, Buel may be overlooking the lawlessness of many batterers. Those who come to the attention of the justice system, simply by way of civil restraining orders, are not even outwardly ordinary citizens, according to several recent studies. Most of them are criminals. And many of them beat up other people, too. But their wives and girlfriends, and ex-wives and ex-girlfriends, suffer the most.

Cartier was a familiar face on the Boston Common, partly because of his career as a freelance nightclub bouncer, partly because he used to panhandle for money there. The clubs he worked in when he was dating Rose usually paid him off with T-shirts, free drinks, and free admissions for friends. He had other sources of income, such as his magic purse, enough, acquaintances said, to give him access to drugs like cocaine and heroin. Whatever the secrets of his success, he scraped up enough money to share a Commonwealth Avenue apartment with a Museum School student named Kara Boettger. They met during a show at a club called the Rat (the Rathskeller on Kenmore Square), dated a few times, decided they didn't like each other very much, and then settled down in a strained truce.

Kara Boettger moved up to Boston from her home in Connecticut at the end of August or beginning of September 1990. "He was much nicer—well, just say nice—then," she remembers. "But he had varied mood swings. He liked to do things his way."

They became friends when he was still being "nice." Boettger was looking for help in finding an apartment. He needed a place to stay. "We dated and ended up getting an apartment together," she said.

The lease they signed kept them together for a month or two. A mutual distaste was apparent well before that. "He didn't like me very much," Boettger said. Cartier liked to play his music loud. Boettger would tell him to turn it down. Fortunately for her, Cartier wasn't around that much. He had other interests.

"He was high at times," Boettger said. "Not a lot, but once in a while. The only thing I know is that I was told he was doing drugs, and he said he was doing drugs . . . cocaine and heroin."

Cartier had been seeing another young woman, someone named Deb, and he wanted to stay with her, but he was stuck with the lease he'd co-signed with Boettger. He told Rose Ryan the reason he could afford it was his claim for damages from the car accident. It was supposedly still in the process of settlement. His lawyer kept assuring him, "You're gonna get money." So every once in a while, he told Rose, the lawyer would give him $1,000 or $500, just to shut him up.

Cartier beat up Deb, too. Rose found that out after she'd been pummeled herself. She met another girl who told her how Mike had given her flowers to take to Deb. Deb wouldn't accept them, and the girl remembered thinking, "What a rotten thing she is." But later she found out that Cartier was beating Deb up. Deb "changed her phone number and everything," Rose was told. "She didn't press charges against him."

Those discoveries, Rose says, were "towards the end." At the start, she was mesmerized. Cartier had her feeling sorry for him. No one else loved him. She was the only one he could turn to. She had been encouraging him to get a GED. He said he couldn't do it without her. She told him she'd help him study for it.

"So if I left him, or if I told somebody about what was going on, then I was kind of betraying him," she said. "It was my fault. He just had me in a mindset of guilt, basically."

The guilt trips didn't stop there, of course. He would tell Rose he never had a real Christmas, that he never had anything. But when she tried to make up for it, he would make her feel guilty about that. "I'd go crazy," she said. "I'd buy him things, but anything I did, it wasn't good enough. I guess maybe it was because he had no real self-esteem. So he tried to degrade me."

When Cartier was going with Kristin, he downgraded her art. So, too, with Rose's scholastic accomplishments. She was an honors student. He boasted that he was smarter, because "he knew how to survive in the streets, and that was what really counted." He told her that going to school was a waste of time. He took credit for all the new friends she was making, from street vendors to college students whose parents, as Rose put it, were "basically paying for everything so that they had the time to hang around with us and do nothing or just go to concerts" at various nightclubs.

"You only know all these people because of me," Cartier chided her. "I'm the center of attention here. These really aren't your friends. They're my friends."

When she put off college to make him happy, she told herself she could always start the next year. But the next year, when it came time again to go, she was too scared, "afraid to go into Boston" and find Cartier breathing down her neck.

When he was in jail for attacking her, Rose used to tell her friends how scared she was that he was going to get out and come after her. "And they'd go, 'Oh, you don't think he'd actually do anything to you, do you? He's been in jail. That'll smarten him up.' "

Soon after they started dating, Rose spent a few days at the Cartier-Boettger apartment at 1298 Commonwealth Avenue while she looked for a job. She happened to mention that she missed her cat. Cartier went out and brought back a little gray kitten, but he left it alone all day without a litter box. The kitten looked around and did what it needed to do on Cartier's jacket.

"He threw the cat in the shower and turned the hot water on and kept it under the hot water," Ryan recalled in a wooden monotone. "And he shaved all its hair off with a man's shaving razor."

The kitten spent most of the rest of its wretched life under a bed. It never had a name. Perhaps Rose didn't want to make it her cat because she felt Cartier would be that much meaner to it. She didn't want to become too fond of it.

On the night of October 4, 1990, Cartier went on a rampage. Rose had just gotten a new mountain bike. Cartier borrowed it to keep an appointment with a therapist. He told Rose he was in counseling because of his emotional problems. He told her he had to go to court once "for throwing a rock through a window or something like that." She didn't realize what kind of a record he had.

On the way back, he went drinking and damaged the bike. Rose was waiting for him when he came in with two drinking buddies, and she got angry when she saw what he'd done to her new bike. She left the apartment without telling anyone. Cartier was irate when he found out she was gone.

"When I came back, the police were in the hallway," Rose said. "They asked me what I was doing there. I said, 'I live here.' They said, 'Get out. This guy's crazy.' They were taking him out in handcuffs."

Cartier had taken a sledgehammer and smashed through the bedroom wall into a neighbor's apartment. And he killed the kitten, hurling it through a closed fourth-floor window.

Kara Boettger came back a bit later than Rose. She'd gone to dinner with friends. "When I came home, the door was open and it was trashed," she said. "I was told that Mike and two other guys were drunk. Mike lost it."

"He was always telling me he had to be careful," Kara Boettger said. " 'Because I can't be arrested,' he said."

Cartier, it would seem, had reason to worry. The number one condition of his probations was that he was to "obey local, state or federal laws or court order." He had six months coming to him for the burglary in Lawrence. And now he was charged, once again, with breaking and entering in the nighttime with intent to commit a felony, malicious destruction of private property worth more than $250, and, of course, cruelty to animals.

The killing of the kitten was a clear tipoff of what he was capable of. According to experts, it is one of the strongest signals of danger.[10] Immanuel Kant once said, "We can judge the heart of a man by his treatment of animals."[11] Cartier probably knew of the connections that could be made. He was angry that the dead kitten had been traced to him. Its small, battered body had landed in an alley where anybody could have left it. The police who answered the call from the neighbor next door didn't know about it. Cartier accused Rose of telling authorities, but she hadn't. All she knew was that the cat was missing. Someone else in the building apparently heard the noise and called the Society for the Prevention of Cruelty to Animals the next morning.

Peter F. Caulfield, an investigator for the SPCA, arrived for a closer look. Years later he could still remember the case. The caller had said the kitten was lying next to a white Honda parked in back of the building. "I couldn't find it anywhere," he said, "but then I noticed two dumpsters. Something told me to look in there. I jumped onto one of them and lo and behold, the cat was on top. I don't think it landed there. Some neighbors must have noticed it. They probably picked it up and put it in the dumpster."

It didn't take long for Caulfield to trace it to Cartier. Someone from the building management company said there was a litter box in the apartment. One of the windows was smashed. Caulfield left his business card with Rose. "She was still afraid of him," he remembers.[12]

"He really scared me that night," Rose said. "Besides being his usual nutty self, he was just—I never saw him that bad before. So I snuck out. Actually one of his friends—I was staying in my room and they were in the next room—and one of his friends came in and said, 'You better get out of here before he hurts you.' "

For now, Rose stood by him. She went to his arraignment the next day in Brighton District Court. He hadn't been charged with animal cruelty yet. As Rose recalls it, a woman judge was presiding that day, and "it was like she felt sorry for him, like 'He needs help and we're going to get him help.' She asked him why he trashed the apartment. He said, 'I don't know, I don't remember doing it.' "

Rose didn't believe that. Cartier knew just what he was doing. "Everything in the apartment that was mine was ripped apart," she said, "and all his things were fine."

Cartier pleaded not guilty. A court psychologist or psychiatrist, Rose can't remember what his name was, spoke with him for a few minutes before he left the courthouse. "Mike was laughing and joking with him," Rose said. The doctor came over and talked to Rose briefly, too. He asked her if she was afraid of Cartier. She wanted to say yes, but she didn't. She was afraid to say she was afraid. "He just said, 'Okay. Keep an eye out for him. Don't let him get in any more trouble.' "

A couple of days later, Mike offered her more details about the kitten. He laughed about it. "I had to throw it out the window twice," he told her. The window didn't break the first time, so he picked the kitten up and threw it harder. That time it went through.

Its jaw was broken when Caulfield found it. Its spleen and liver were ruptured, and it suffered an acute pulmonary hemorrhage. The autopsy doesn't say whether it was male or female. "It was so young it was hard to tell, but I think it was a boy," Rose said. It had also showed signs of earlier damage: a systemic infection of the heart, lungs, and liver.

"I don't really remember it," Cartier insisted to Rose, even while recalling the details. "I didn't know what I was doing." He had been convincing himself of that.

"As long as you tell yourself something didn't happen, then it didn't happen," he told her. "As long as you pretend it didn't happen, as long as we keep telling ourselves it didn't happen, then it really didn't happen."

The animal-cruelty charge, a misdemeanor, was filed on October 25. Cartier pleaded not guilty, of course, and asked for a jury trial in Boston Municipal Court downtown on that and the two felony counts.

Kara Boettger was evicted, even though she did her best to distance herself from Cartier. The week after the incident, before she was told to leave, she went to district court in Brighton and got a restraining order telling him to stay away from the apartment. He ignored it and, she said, "broke in several times." Cartier defiantly turned up in court at one point, when she got either the temporary restraining order or the permanent one. "He started yelling at me, and I started yelling at him," Boettger said. "He said he didn't do anything wrong. He said it was all my fault."

In her initial request for a restraining order, Boettger had asked the court to "immediately send him to jail for violating his probation." She didn't know the details, but Cartier had told her he had "broken some windows somewhere and then there was this other thing for putting something in someone's food. I know he was on probation for that."

The "something in someone's food" happened on August 29, 1989, at a Brigham's ice cream and sandwich shop in Andover. Cartier and some of his skinhead friends, one of them a diabetic, were sitting in one of the booths. The diabetic, a student at Phillips Academy there, had some hypodermic needles with him.

"Here, let me have one of those," Cartier said. He stuck it in his arm, drew blood, and squirted it onto the wall and ceiling. Someone sitting in another booth told police Cartier then emptied the rest into a ketchup bottle. The crew laughed and left the sauce for the next customer. The witness called the police.

Andover police hurried over to Brigham's, picked up the ketchup bottle for a lab report, and caught up with the skinheads in the town park. Detective Donald H. Pattullo said Cartier admitted doing it.[13] Cartier was always deferential when he had to be.

"He was friendly. Polite," Pattullo remembered. "He was older than the other kids." Cartier told him that he just wanted to find out how it felt to stick a needle in his arm. He said he didn't think about what might happen if somebody used the ketchup.

"He apologized in regard to what happened. A hundred other kids who come through here, they wouldn't tell you if your pants were on fire. . . . He never gave me any trouble. I remember talking to him again later. We had him upstairs in the booking room for something, I don't remember what, but we didn't arrest him. I remember him saying he'd just gotten out of jail. He said he was living in Boston."

Cartier was charged with illegally contaminating food, a felony carrying a maximum of five years in prison, and unlawful possession of a hypodermic needle, a misdemeanor. He was found guilty on June 15, 1990, and given probation on top of probation. Evidently, no one thought of sending him to jail, even for the six months he had coming to him for the 1988 burglary. That might have smacked of real punishment.

It wasn't until a few weeks after Kristin's death that I was permitted, officially, to discover these things. Until mid-1992 when changes in the CORI law took effect, criminal records, even of recent convictions, were kept from the public in Massachusetts, on the grounds that disclosure would somehow be an invasion of a defendant's privacy. The individual court records of this or that offense were public—if you knew where to go and what to ask for—but the master list of offenses, the record showing what courts had records, was not.[14] Criminal histories are still kept secret in many jurisdictions on the same misguided basis, even after adjudication of the charges. What the public and, more important, new and potential victims need to know doesn't count. A Virginia woman who wrote the *Washington Post* in November 1992 reported:

"Off and on for three years in the late 80s, I was stalked because I'd turned down a date. The lengths to which I had to go to get help were unbelievable; even in the end, I think no one took me seriously. Or, like the Alexandria police, they felt that my stalker's rights took precedence over mine. And only near the end did I discover that this 'harmless' man had a police record and a history of stalking other women. No one thought I needed to know those things at first."

If Cartier's burgeoning record bothered the prosecutor or the judge who handled the rampage at his apartment, there is no sign of it. In January 1991, Cartier, facing not only revocation of his double probation but also imposition of the suspended six-month jail sentence, plea-bargained his way to probation again, pleading guilty to malicious destruction. The charges of burglary and cruelty to animals were dismissed. Even so, he was now a convicted felon four times over.[15] The court put him back on the street.

Caulfield was disappointed to see the cruelty charge dropped. No one consulted him about it. "The case went downtown," he said. "They were supposed to tell me when it came up, but they never did." The criminal justice system as well as social service agencies have long ignored the link between cruelty to animals and other forms of violent or antisocial behavior.[16]

Instead of a jury trial, Cartier and his court-appointed lawyer struck a deal with prosecutors in Boston Municipal Court, the downtown equivalent of Brighton District Court. Malicious destruction of property worth more than $250 is a felony in Massachusetts, but if it's sent to district court, or Boston Municipal Court, it's treated as a misdemeanor, limited to a two-and-a-half-year sentence.[17]

Kara Boettger was surprised that Cartier got off so lightly, especially after all his talk about how disastrous arrest would be. For Cartier, it simply underscored the hypocrisy of the system and how easy it was to wiggle loose.

"I thought he was going to jail because he violated probation," Boettger said. So did Cartier. "But after the January hearing, he told me, 'Oh yeah. Nothing happened. They slapped my wrist.'"

The case was settled in Boston Municipal Court on January 11, 1991. As part of the deal, Cartier was ordered "to stay in the mental health program." The implication was that treatment had been required as part of an earlier sentence, but there is no record of that. The Lawrence district court judge who handled the incident in Andover had referred him to Bridge Over Troubled Waters, a statewide program for street kids that used roaming vans and buses. Its staff, in turn, had referred him to a Tri-City Mental Health Center in the Malden area, where he attended occasional "therapy sessions." Cartier probably initiated the referral himself. The free services comported with his idea of getting through life at state expense. He had told Rose Ryan that his mental health counselor was trying to get him into a program that would give him a subsidized apartment on the grounds that he was mentally unstable and unable to work.

Bridge Over Troubled Waters had a place near the Boston Common that offered free meals. Cartier took Rose there once with a couple of friends. "You just have to listen to their bullshit or whatever, and say yes to everything," he explained. Rose accompanied him to the mental health center one day, too. His female counselor there, he boasted, was afraid of him.

"He told [the counselor] that some guy he thought was gay approached him as he was walking home one time and he fantasized about taking the guy up on a roof and pushing him off," Rose said. The counselor looked shocked and wondered why he would hate gay people. "I think she's a lesbian," Cartier concluded.

Despite his freedom, Cartier was getting worse. Rose Ryan had had her fill of him, and she made that clear. They broke up after a party in January at a friend's place in Allston.

Whenever they went out, Rose said, "he wanted me to only talk to him. He wanted me to be really quiet. I was quiet anyway, because I didn't know anybody. And he used to buy me big clothes. For Christmas, he bought me a dress down to the floor. He'd say, 'I don't want anybody else to know how pretty you are.' " For her part, Rose couldn't do anything right. One morning, she got up at 5 A.M., lugged groceries to Boston, snuck into his house while he was still asleep, and cooked him breakfast.

"I didn't cook it right," she said. "He could cook it better. The eggs were wrong. And as we went along, I didn't tell anybody what was happening because I was embarrassed . . . and of course, I felt guilty."

Rose reached her breaking point at the January party. It was about 1 A.M. Mike decided he wanted to go get a pizza. Rose didn't want one, but he talked her into going along. She was upset because he had already sworn at her in front of some friends. When he got the pizza, she refused to eat it.

"He said, 'I bought this pizza for you, you'd better eat it.' I said, 'I'm not eating it.' So we walked out of the pizza place, and we were walking back to the party. He said, 'Well, where are you going?' I said, 'Back to the party, where else?' "

Cartier backhanded her in the face so hard she fell to the ground. "Before I had a chance to get up—he was wearing steel-toe boots, Doc Martens steel-toe boots—he started kicking me. He started kicking me in the head and shoulders. I'm laying on the ground, trying to block myself off, screaming, and then he finally said—after I don't know how long—'You'd better get up or I'll kill you.' " Ryan picked herself up. She noticed a few people on nearby porches. No one said a word. The memory of that silence still makes her angry. "It wasn't like nobody saw it," she recalled bitterly. "Somebody must have seen it."

When Ryan started walking away, Cartier summoned her back. "You'd better come with me," he warned. "I'll kill you if you don't." They got back to the building where the party was, but Cartier kept going. Puzzled, Ryan asked, "Aren't we going back to the party?" There was a bridge up ahead. "I'm going to throw you off the bridge," Cartier announced.

Rose dropped to the ground and refused to get up. Cartier started dragging her, when "a whole bunch of guys" from the party came outside. Rose didn't say anything, but they could see she was crying. All they said was, "Hey, Mike. How you doing?" Then they walked off. After all, it was "his girlfriend," just as it had been "his kitten."

The ordeal wasn't over yet. Cartier made Rose spend the night at the apartment where the party had been. He'd been mooching space there himself. She plunked herself down in a chair and said she wasn't going to sleep.

"He opened all the windows and took all the blankets away and shut me in the room so it would be really cold." When she got up early the next morning to go home to Lynn, Cartier said, "Don't I get a kiss goodbye?"

Cartier's ferocity had been carefully controlled, in keeping with social conventions about how one's girlfriend should look, especially if she should complain that her boyfriend had just beat her up. "His reasoning was, 'You don't have any bruises on you,'" Rose said. "'Cause he'd kicked me in the head, and I have long hair, so you couldn't see it. There weren't any bruises on my face or anything."

Rose refused to see him again, but Cartier wouldn't take no for an answer. He began stalking her by telephone, calling her parents' house at all hours of the night and hanging up. On one occasion, Ryan said, Cartier stayed on the line and asked Mrs. Ryan where Rose was. All Mrs. Ryan knew was that they had broken up. "I don't know," she told Cartier. "She doesn't want to talk to you."

"Well," he told her, "you better hope Rose doesn't see me any-where, because she'll regret it."

Her parents were confused. Why would he say that? They didn't know the details. She'd been beaten by Cartier more than ten times. But "in my family," Rose said, "nobody talks. I used to write poetry about it. Just to get it out." Besides, what was she supposed to tell her father? "Gee, Dad, I'm dating a guy who beats me up"? Her father had been angry with her for going to Boston so much anyway.

"My parents are homebodies," Rose said, "and they think Boston is this big, bad place. My dad would always tell me, 'You're going to get in trouble if you go there.' I couldn't tell him because then it's 'See, I told you so.' "

Without Rose, Cartier grew despondent. After his eviction in Oc-tober, he shuffled from one friend's place to another and spent nights in doorways when he couldn't find anything else. He began talking of suicide.

On January 18, 1991, a week after his case was settled, he was brought to the emergency room of St. Elizabeth Hospital in Brighton on a Section 12, a Massachusetts law authorizing emergency restraint of dangerous persons. He was taken there because he'd been threatening to kill himself and he'd taken an overdose of some sort. The hospital sent him to the Massachusetts Mental Health Center, where he spent four days before he was released.

Rose Ryan is convinced it was a ruse to get her back. He acted only when she walked out on him and told him she didn't want to see him anymore. Rose said, "He wrote me this note saying, basically, 'It's your fault that I did this, and I can't live without you, and all this.' " He also told everyone in the place where he was staying that morning that he was going to kill himself.

What Cartier did was gobble down all the pills he could find, aspirin and things like that. Then he hurriedly called his caseworker and told her: "I just took all these pills, what should I do?" She told him to go to a hospital and get his stomach pumped. So he did.

For a few days the ploy worked. Rose returned. "I felt that if I didn't stay with him, he was going to kill himself, and I had to help him, and all this," she says. "Now that I look at it, it's obvious that it was just staged to get any attention, to get me to stay with him." The reunion didn't last long. Rose left for good sometime in February 1991. By now, she was working at her sister Tina's company in Salem and living with her parents in Lynn.

At loose ends, Cartier kept looking for her. Even after their breakup, she continued to go into Boston to see other friends. Despite what Cartier had told her, there were people who really liked her. She got a shock one day in March. She was riding on the subway with a girlfriend when Cartier materialized.

"You know," he told her, "I have a gun."

"He said it to scare me," Rose said. "I asked him where he got it, but he didn't say. He said he got it to protect himself."

Rose didn't believe that. As he had in January, Cartier was threatening to kill her. It was a tedious but frightening refrain, one that could be recited to the letter by countless women. "He told me that if I go out with anyone else, forget it, because he's going to kill me," Rose remembers. "And anybody I go out with, he's going to threaten them so they're not going to want to see me. Basically, I was his girlfriend. I couldn't see anybody else, and that was it. One minute he'd call me up and say, 'Oh, I'm sorry,' and get upset and cry. And if that didn't work, he'd get mean. Just to get a reaction out of me."

Cartier spotted Rose again on April 14, 1991, as she was walking to catch the T on Commonwealth at Harvard, just half a block south of Bunratty's. Suddenly she noticed him walking behind her. Then he started talking to her, or at her.

"Oh, I know why you broke up with me," he said.

"Just leave me alone," Rose told him. "Just leave me alone."

He hit her in the back of the head. She kept walking and got on the train. Cartier got on, too, and sat down next to her. "I'm gonna follow you home," he told her.

She jumped off at Park Street, an underground stop, hoping to find a policeman, but it was getting close to 8:45 P.M., well past rush hour. The only person she saw was a man in an MBTA (Massachusetts Bay Transit Authority) uniform.

"Can you please help me?" she asked him. "This guy is following me. Can you please kick him out of the subway so I can get home safely?"

"What do you mean?" he asked her. "I don't see anybody."

Cartier had ducked around a corner. Rose pointed to where he was. "See, he's right there," she told the driver. Cartier came strolling forward. "She's my girlfriend," he assured the MBTA man. "She doesn't know what she's saying."

"Oh, I'm lying, am I?" Rose shot back.

The driver said, "Well, I didn't see it. I can't do anything." But he did tell Cartier to "get out of here." Cartier disappeared around a corner again and got on the next train when Rose did, without her seeing him. She got off at the Government Center station to transfer to another line when she realized he was right behind her. Just as she turned around, he grabbed her hair and accosted her with a pair of scissors. He later claimed he was just trying to cut her hair. Says Rose: "He was coming at my face." She ducked the scissors, and Cartier punched her in the mouth. He hit her so hard she had to go to a dentist.

Once again, Rose recalls with chagrin, "There were throngs of people standing there, and nobody did anything. He ran off, and I was standing there screaming, 'I need a police officer! Where are the police? Somebody help me!'"

At last someone did. A man came by and told her to follow him, the police were upstairs. She found some Transit Authority officers at the top of a staircase and told them what had happened. They put out an alert for Cartier, based on Ryan's description, and helped her home. But they grew a bit chilly when they asked Rose if this had ever happened before and she told them yes. "Oh?" she remembers one of them saying. "He's beat you up before?" Their attitude changed. They still did what they were supposed to do, but they weren't as concerned. They also asked her something that has bothered her ever since.

"One officer said to me—this just goes to show that the police know the system doesn't work—he said to me: 'Don't you have any brothers? Why don't you have one of them beat him up?'"

The officer was trying to be helpful. Kristin's friends and brothers had the same idea, most of them after the fact, but some before. Kristin dissuaded at least one friend who learned about the beating before she was killed. "I wanted to go up, bring some friends with me, kick his ass," Chris Dupre said. "She said, 'No, no, I've already filed a police report.' " She was taking care of it legally. But the justice system didn't take care of her or innumerable other women who looked to it after being severely beaten by their male partners or ex-partners. The danger is plain. If the system can't help them, they, or someone they know, may take the law into their own hands. The chairman of the Senate Judiciary Committee, Senator Joseph Biden, brought up that prospect at a 1993 hearing that dealt in part with Kristin's murder. Unless the system starts dealing effectively with "domestic violence," Biden said, "I would think we would see arise a vigilante approach to this problem." If his daughter were threatened, he said, "I suspect I would think about either myself [taking care of the problem] or hiring someone else to take care of my problem. I shouldn't even say that publicly, but, seriously, I would think that thought would have to cross people's minds."[18]

Rose Ryan was in no position to be a vigilante. That night, she waited for her father to get home from a late shift to tell him how the boy she'd been dating had beat her, kicked her in the head, and, just a few hours earlier, come at her with a pair of scissors and punched her in the face. She didn't want to do it, but she told her mother and her mother insisted. Her father came home around 11:30 P.M., and she told him what Cartier had been doing to her.

"He looked at me and smiled and said, 'Well, it's your fault. You kept bugging him. You shouldn't have gone to Boston.'

"I couldn't believe it," Rose said. "Here's my own father telling me that it's my fault."

And what about her brothers?

"They made fun of me, asking me how long did it take before he started hitting you? Ha, ha. It was a joke. So I didn't talk about it, because I was ashamed."

7

The high-ceilinged courtroom in Brighton has a huge, wide-barred cell built into a side wall.[1] On busy days, it is a page from Dickens, crowded with yelling, cursing prisoners waiting for their cases to be called.

Michael Cartier turned up in the cell on April 29, 1991, finally arrested for violating probation. He'd attacked Rose Ryan at the Government Center subway station fifteen days earlier, but that wasn't why he was in court. Rose and her older sister Tina were already after him. Alarmed over his constant threats, they had contacted one of his probation officers, Tom Casey, who worked out of the Brighton courthouse. He was supervising Cartier for the October rampage. The case had been settled in Boston Municipal Court on January 11, but it was not until January 22 that the paperwork was sent back to Brighton, where the crimes had been committed.

That was the day Cartier was released from the Massachusetts Mental Health Center, presumably no longer a danger to himself or others. Casey talked to him on the phone the next day and set up an appointment for January 30.

"He didn't show," said David Noonan, chief probation officer in Brighton and Casey's supervisor. Cartier made a show of trying to contact Casey the next day—during Casey's lunch hour. A typical trick, probation officers say. Cartier had joined that footloose legion of convicted criminals on our streets, from petty offenders on their way up the ladder to seasoned felons who know the ropes. They know how to play the game. They know they can count on being released at any and every stage after arrest—on bond, on their own recognizance, for rehabilitation, for counseling, for supervision by probation and parole officers too busy to do any real supervising.

At the outset, Cartier's supervision was tighter than most. Tom Casey knows his business. Cartier called Casey February 1 and was told to come in February 6. He said he had to turn himself in on February 8 in Lawrence District Court, where he was on probation for the ketchup incident and had the six-month suspended sentence awaiting him for the 1988 break-in. Cartier said he expected to get six months. Casey set up another appointment for February 22. Once again, Cartier failed to show up. He called a few days later to say that his surrender hearing in Lawrence had been postponed until early March.

"He'd never show up at the reported times," Casey said. "It was always a day late. He'd pop up behind you. Sort of a surprise."

Probation officers have to be patient people, especially with the postponements and continuances that afflict the criminal justice system, almost like a narcotic that it needs to get from one day to the next. The delays usually benefit the defendants. In mid-March, Cartier came in to see Casey and told him his surrender hearing in Lawrence had been put off again, until July. He also said he was seeing a social worker and undergoing therapy at the Tri-City Mental Health Center in the Malden area, where he had yet another probation officer, Rich DeAngelis, in addition to Casey in Brighton and Paul Dube in Lawrence.

A bit suspicious by now, Casey told him, "If you're in therapy, I want proof." Cartier mailed in a letter from his social worker, Caroline May, on March 25.

"Tommy was going to transfer the case to the probation office in Malden, where they had a regular address for him," Noonan said. "So you wouldn't have three probation officers doing the job."

Cartier may have been pursuing mental illness as a career goal, with a subsidized apartment and no work required as the perceived rewards. He seems to have started treatment at the Tri-City Center in 1990 after the blood-squirting episode in Andover.

"He was the one that initiated the Tri-City thing," DeAngelis said. "It was never a term of probation. I forget if I told him to go down there, but he was doing it on his own. The kid was screwed up from a long time ago. He looked weird and he was weird. He dressed like a skinhead. But he denied being one."

The Tri-City Mental Health Center refuses to say anything about its treatment of Cartier. His social worker, Caroline May, told me that Massachusetts law concerning confidentiality "means that I can't even say someone was a client of mine." Whose privacy was she protecting, I wondered. Cartier had been dead for two years when I called her. She said she was sorry, but that was the policy. She had checked with her boss. It was a roadblock that I ran into several times, from lawyers and court officials as well as social workers. The "right to privacy" in Massachusetts extends even into the grave. Too often it provides the living with a pat excuse to brush aside legitimate questions, an easy way to avoid accountability.

According to one official, who predictably asked not to be named, Cartier was treated at the center for about a year, starting in May 1990. But what they thought of him remains a secret.

Tom Casey knew he had a problem the day after the Tri-City letter arrived. On March 26, 1991, Rose Ryan's older sister, Tina Tucker, called to report that Cartier had been threatening to kill Rose. Rose called the next day herself and told Casey that "the subject had threatened to kill her with a gun in one or two weeks."

Just contacting Casey had been no easy matter for the two sisters. For most citizens, the courts are a foreign and intimidating land. It takes persistence to find your way around. I've been in more than I can count. Every one is different. Every one has its own customs and cubbyholes and often confusing, sometimes crotchety ways of doing business. Some, to be sure, can be quite friendly, but most of them expect you to find your own way. After all, there are just so many hours in a day. Documents need to be filed, transcripts made, papers shuffled.

Tina, who is sixteen years older than Rose, said, "The reason I helped her was every time Rose called, they would put her off and hang up on her." It was still a hassle. At one point, Tina said, "I was on the phone for two hours just trying to get somebody to listen." Eventually,

they learned that Cartier had "two or three different probation officers." Finally a secretary in the district attorney's office told them the
name of the man in Lawrence, who gave them the name of the man in
Brighton. After what seemed like "a million phone calls," Rose said,
they got through to Casey.

The probation officer listened carefully. The Ryan sisters were be-
side themselves with fear. Rose had started working at her sister's company in Salem, and Cartier found out about it. He had started calling
her at work, telling her he was going to kill her.

Casey told Rose to go to district court in Lynn, where she was
living at the time, and get a restraining order against Cartier. Massachusetts is one of a minority of states where a girlfriend or boyfriend
can do that without having to allege and establish intimate relationships, cohabitation, children in common, or the like.[2] In jurisdictions
like the District of Columbia, even in cases where physical abuse has
plainly occurred, a judge can pronounce himself required to ask a
woman if she has "had sex" with the defendant before giving her a protective order.[3] In one D.C. Superior Court case, in October of 1993, a
woman pregnant with the child of the man she was fearful of was told
by a court clerk that she couldn't get a restraining order because the
couple did not yet have a child together.[4]

Ryan got her restraining order in Lynn on April 16, 1991, two
days after the attack at Government Center, but that didn't stop Cartier. He had no fixed address where he could be served or arrested.[5] But
he knew where Rose was. When he called her again at her parents'
house, she told him, "You can't call me. I have a restraining order that
says you can't call me, you can't come near me." Cartier laughed at her.
"Oh, that's just a piece of paper," he told her. "By the way, what's my
address?" He laughed again, and then he hung up.

Tina Tucker said the phone also kept ringing at the engineering
and machine shop she owned with her husband. "He was breaking the
restraining order by calling constantly . . . telling her he was going to
kill her . . . getting her all upset," Tucker said.

Tom Casey had already brought Cartier's earlier threats to the attention of his own district court judge in Brighton, Albert H. Burns.

On March 28, Casey told the judge how scared Rose was. Burns authorized issuance of an arrest warrant that day, accusing Cartier of violating his probation in the apartment trashing by threatening criminal violence against his ex-girlfriend. Casey told the Ryan sisters to be ready to testify. If they would do that, he assured them, "we'll get him off the streets."

It took a month before Cartier was picked up. He had tracked Rose down in the meantime. In Massachusetts, "probation warrants have to be served by the police, who don't take them seriously enough," one probation official told me. "Often they just sit at the station house waiting to be served. Changes of address make people hard to find. Probationers know all this. They know they can skip court appearances with impunity." Meanwhile, they're free to commit new crimes, and many do. In some jurisdictions, they don't even have to be released on probation before they find new victims. In the District of Columbia alone in 1993, more than seven hundred individuals serving time for everything from misdemeanors to murder walked out of the halfway houses where they were lodged and didn't come back. Weeks often went by before the D.C. Corrections Department got around to obtaining arrest warrants. The escapees, of course, often went back to the work they knew best. An average of three to five defendants who appeared in D.C. Superior Court each week to face new charges were turning out to be escapees. Yet checks by court officials failed to find any warrant or other record of their escape status in the Washington area computer system.[6]

In many jurisdictions, according to John Firman, research director of the International Association of Chiefs of Police, outstanding felony warrants often aren't enforced even when a suspect is picked up. "You've touched on a very sensitive area in law enforcement," Firman told me recently. An informal IACP survey in August 1994 of ten of the biggest police departments in the country showed that the number of outstanding felony warrants numbered from a low of 2,000 to a high of 28,000. Often, police try to address the problem by inactivating older warrants and setting mileage limits on how far they will travel to bring a suspect back. Constantly short on money and personnel, they don't want to send officers on long trips to pick someone up when that would leave them with fewer officers cruising the streets at home.[7]

"Say some department calls from fifty to a hundred miles away and says, 'We have your guy,' " Firman explained. "The department might say, 'Fine, but we don't want him.' What they're saying is, 'You can ignore that warrant because we're not coming to get him.' They weigh the seriousness of the offense against their financial resources. If they're misdemeanor warrants, in all likelihood, the suspects are not going to be picked up."[8]

Women who have been beaten within an inch of their life should remember that. What happened to them was, all too often, just a misdemeanor. The system doesn't work, but it works for them least of all. It is a house of cards held up by mostly well-intentioned people who work very hard to keep it from collapsing. It is a system that is hard put to take even felonies seriously. The offenders know that, even if the public doesn't. In Chicago, the Cook County jail has been so over-crowded that suspects sent there by a state court have been promptly released, even though the charge may be a serious felony. The sheriff would rather do that than risk the ire of a federal court that had ordered him not to let the population get too high.

"The offenders know the system," said Firman, who used to work at the Illinois Criminal Justice Authority. "They know what level of offense they have to commit before they get stuck in jail. They're fear-less about committing certain crimes. The scary thing is that [the cut-off level] had been bumped up all the way to felony offenses, even some pretty aggravated felony offenses. . . . A state judge might say, 'No bond, you're going to jail, you're a dangerous person.' It doesn't matter. The people at the jail will say, 'We don't care what the judge said, we have a federal problem.' It boils down to which court is more powerful. That is a threat to the public."[9]

On April 2, 1991, while Boston police were ostensibly looking for Cartier for violating probation, he turned up at the Massachusetts Men-tal Health Center on another Section 12, this time for talking about killing Rose Ryan. A Bridge Over Troubled Waters van brought him there. He denied making the threats and was released the next day. No one seems to have checked to see if there was a warrant out for his arrest.

Another warrant was issued April 19 for his attack on Rose Ryan at Government Center. He was finally picked up ten days later and delivered to Brighton District Court. Tom Casey was determined to have him locked up. The Ryan sisters were petrified. He gave Cartier a "surrender notice" as soon as he showed up. Since Casey knew that Cartier had spent four days at the Massachusetts Mental Health Center in January, he also arranged for a visiting court-appointed psychiatrist, Dr. Michael Annunziata, to check him out.

"We used to have a doctor from the court clinic here every day," Casey said. "Now we have social workers who come only twice a week."

Annunziata examined Cartier in the huge, noisy cell that opens into the courtroom.[10] Court officials call it the cage, and it is sometimes crammed with fifteen to twenty prisoners. The sixty-nine-year-old courthouse has individual cells downstairs but no funds for guards to watch them. "They should be kept down there and brought up one at a time," Noonan said.

The psychiatrist found that Cartier had "no acute mental disorder, no suicidal or homicidal ideas, plans or intents." Annunziata's report noted that Cartier was being treated by the Tri-City clinic and was taking 300 milligrams of lithium a day to control depression. (Other records show Cartier had earlier acknowledged having taken LSD, marijuana, cocaine, and hashish. Asked on a probation office questionnaire about "mental illness," he checked "yes.")

"He was very quiet," Casey remembers. "Sullen and withdrawn. It was obvious he had problems, deeper than I could ever get to. He was sort of sad. He said, 'Gee, I've got no place to live. I'm just staying in doorways. I got thrown out.' . . . I asked him about the sledgehammer. He said, 'I was drunk.' He denied substance abuse, other than five or six beers on a weekend. That and lithium can put you out."

Cartier was less subdued in talking with the other prisoners waiting for their cases to come up. "I noticed he was very friendly to the other prisoners in the cell," Casey said. "Joking and laughing. Prison time didn't seem to bother him at all."

A visiting judge from West Roxbury, Robert P. Zemian, ordered Cartier held on $200 bond and set the probation violation charge down for a full hearing later in the week before Judge Burns, on May 2. For the record, Zemian noted that there was another warrant outstanding for Cartier at Boston Municipal Court for the attack on Rose Ryan. Casey called the Ryan sisters after the session and urged them to come down to Brighton and testify. "If you come here in person and testify," he told them, "we'll get him off the streets."

When the Ryan sisters arrived in court on May 2, they found themselves no more than five feet from Cartier, who was cursing at them from the cage like a lost, vengeful soul.

"Soon as he saw me," Tina Tucker said, "he said, 'I know who you are. I'm going to kill you, too,' all these filthy words, calling me everything he could." To Rose, Cartier said in contemptuous tones, "How's your face?" The cell was full of other defendants, "a bunch of them, all screaming and yelling."

Perplexed by the tangle of charges confronting Cartier, Judge Burns postponed the case for a week. The Ryan sisters wanted to complain about the attack at Government Center and to inform the court about the restraining order. Authorities in Lawrence, alerted by Casey, were preparing to charge him with violating probation in the two cases against him there. "Straighten this out," Burns told the prosecutor on duty. "I've got three pages full of charges against this guy, and I've got two people here [the Ryan sisters] for something else." Burns ordered Cartier held without bond and sent him back to the Nashua Street lockup.

As Rose and Tina were leaving, Casey said he would call to make sure they came back for the next week. "This guy is on prescribed drugs, too. He's really a lunatic. I've dealt with him before, and I'm afraid of him," he told them.

The two sisters were careful to stay away from the cage on their next trip. Casey brought them into the courtroom through another door. They sat behind the police officers waiting in the front row for their cases to come up. Some of them remembered the women from the week before and invited them to sit down.

Cartier's court-appointed lawyer, a woman from the public defender's office, did her best to protect her client. She tried to prevent the Ryan sisters from testifying, on the grounds that what they had to say had nothing to do with his violating probation on the malicious destruction conviction. Tina kept pleading, "Your Honor, please, give us two minutes." The judge decided to listen. Tina told him about the restraining order, about Cartier's frightening phone calls, his threats in the courtroom, his taunting Rose about her sore face.

Judge Burns looked at Cartier's lawyer and said, "He's punching this girl in the face and beating her up and you don't think that's breaking his restraining order? You don't think that's breaking probation?" He slammed the gavel down.

The lawyer was embarrassed. She came over to Rose and told her, "Tell him anything you want."

Cartier kept popping up, yelling, "I have a right to speak," but at length Burns told him he was getting three months at the House of Correction on Deer Island for violating probation. "That's it," the judge informed him. "It's over." Cartier kept protesting, saying, "I never got the restraining order."

The judge obtained a copy from Rose, signed it, had it stamped with a court seal, and served it on Cartier in the courtroom. "I'm putting it on record that he has it now," the judge announced.

On Deer Island, Cartier was assigned to a special unit for medical observation in light of his troubled history. He was brought back to Boston Municipal Court on June 20, 1991, to be tried for his attack on Rose Ryan at Government Center. Under the law then on the books, he was entitled to "two bites at the apple."[11] He could get a trial before a judge in the municipal court, and if he didn't like the verdict, he could demand a jury trial. This was his first bite.

Rose Ryan arrived at the dreary building with a statement from her dentist saying she'd sustained a bruised face and nerve damage to her front teeth. She found the designated courtroom, took the witness stand, and began testifying under the assumption that the court would want the truth, the whole truth. She started by explaining, "Michael had been calling me at home and harassing me, and he threatened to kill me . . ."

Cartier's lawyer, an energetic assistant public defender named Wayne R. Murphy, interrupted and told her to stick to what happened at the subway station on April 14. Defendants are by and large entitled to be tried in a vacuum, lest any prejudicial information from the real world intrude.[12] He'd already talked with Cartier several times and knew there wasn't much of a defense. Murphy figured that the best he could do was get Ryan under oath and see if anything she had to say could be used to Cartier's advantage at a jury trial.

They got no help from Rose. She was on the stand for little more than a minute, giving a thumbnail sketch of what was really a double assault. She told the court how Cartier had harassed her and punched her before she got on the T, followed her onto the train, and finally attacked her from behind at the Government Center station.

"I had to go down a flight of steps to catch the Blue Line," she said, "but it was dark. I didn't know if there was anybody who was going to be down there. So I turned around and walked back. And he grabbed me by the hair and came at me with a pair of scissors. I shoved him away and he punched me in the face. . . . I reported it to the police." She concluded in a firm, clear voice by reciting what her dentist had to say.[13]

There were no openings for his client there, Murphy could see. "No questions on the facts," he announced. The judge, Peter Donovan, pronounced Cartier guilty moments later. Murphy proceeded to emphasize the lack of any other assault or assault and battery charges on Cartier's burgeoning record.

"This is a case where the complainant and Mr. Cartier knew each other and at some point in time, had a relationship," Murphy said, as though that somehow made his client less culpable. "Mr. Cartier also tells me that he has a history of alcohol and drug abuse, and this may have something to do with this state of facts."

Murphy chose his words carefully. He was telling the court what Cartier told him. Deep down, Murphy didn't know what to make of him. The lawyer didn't see any clear signs of addiction to either drinking or drugs. If he had to guess, he would have said it was a mental problem. "Troubled, that's the best word [for him]," Murphy said later. "He had a lot of baggage. . . . He seemed to be on a different plane, mentally, than a lot of my clients. Not a higher or a lower plane, just different. It was almost a bit eerie dealing with him. The facts of the case were obviously disturbing. If he had no record at all, everybody in the system would still have a right to be concerned about him." And he did have a record. "I've represented people charged with murder, rape, and robbery," Murphy said, "but I never had a guy who had been charged with contaminating a food substance or with cruelty to animals. It's just one more indication this guy was troubled. It's scary."[14]

A public defender working out of Dedham, Massachusetts, when I spoke with him, Murphy was uncomfortable in talking about Cartier at all and adamant about not imparting anything Cartier might have said to him, not just about the facts of the case, but anything under the sun. Apparently, even the time of day is covered by the attorney-client privilege in Massachusetts. "In Massachusetts, the attorney-client privilege is forever," Murphy declared. "The client needs to be the one who waives it. And [Cartier] can't."

I thought of all the lawyers, including some from Massachusetts, who had been much less reticent with me over the years. I couldn't believe that they had been violating the attorney-client privilege. I'm sure they would have taken great umbrage at any such suggestion. But I could tell I was up against a stone wall. Murphy was trying to be helpful, but he didn't want to step across what he understood to be a very clear line. I shook my head in disbelief and moved on. Time and again I heard doors slamming shut, mental tapes being erased, with the final shot from Cartier's gun.

In the courtroom that June day in 1991, Murphy left his client smiling on at least one point. Murphy told the judge that Cartier would have "no problem" in staying away from Ryan during any probationary period, but "he asks that she be told to stay away from him as well."

It was a typical abuser's ploy, one that Cartier would try against

Kristin also, an effort to assure himself that he was still in charge of the situation. Amazingly, judges often let abusers get away with such antics, as though both parties deserved the judicial restraints that only one was seeking and only one had established a need for.

Rose was in no mood to contest the point, but she remembers thinking how absurd it was. "He had to be in control, kind of telling me, 'You can't come here, this is where I am,' " she remembers. "And I just said, 'Fine.' At that point, I didn't care. I just wanted him to leave me alone. And he smiled, and, you know, he didn't show any remorse throughout the whole thing."

Cartier was given a one-year sentence, with six months to be served at Deer Island and the other six suspended for a two-year probationary period. "Terms and conditions of probation," the court added, "are you're not to have any contact with Miss Ryan, either in person or by letter, and Miss Ryan, you won't have any contact with Mr. Cartier." All in one breath. It sounded as if Rose were being put on probation, too. She was certainly under court order to watch her step.

Cartier was transported back to Deer Island, a nasty, dangerous place that has since been closed down, to be replaced by a sewage treatment facility. By the time of his trial, he had been taken out of the general population. Murphy said he was under "medical observation" at the facility and, according to what Cartier told him, likely to be entered in a sixteen-week program at Bridgewater state hospital in light of his substance abuse problems and "mood disorders." State officials say there is no record of such a transfer.

Imprisonment at Deer Island reinforced Cartier's racist attitude. His Doc Martens boots, castleneck tattoo, and skinhead haircut made him an instant enemy of black inmates, according to Paul Zeizel, a psychologist who saw him frequently at the jail. "He was at risk at Deer Island," Zeizel said. He said he tried to get Cartier in the Bridgewater program but gave up when hospital officials told him the waiting list was so long that Cartier's term would be up before he could be admitted. According to Gene Cartier, his son was put in protective custody—isolated from the general prison population—after fighting with a black inmate who tried to rape him. Deer Island was "90 percent black," Gene Cartier asserted.[15] "Michael had an attitude. They tried pushing their weight around with him. He wouldn't take their shit. He was going to kill this dude because he wanted to fuck him up the ass. So they put him in PC [protective custody]."

Deer Island records reflect no such attack. They indicate he was put in PC for medical observation, as his lawyer stated. For Cartier, it was a way of staying out of trouble. His was a life full of fear. At one point, he was put on what amounted to red alert—a status called "MOA" (Medical Observation A). That meant he was put in a cell in his underwear—without any outerwear, without blanket, sheets, or pillow. "He probably threatened to kill himself," Zeizel said in a recent conversation. "Either my colleague, Dr. [Eric] Brown, or I put him on MOA," Zeizel said. But he said it may have been that Cartier simply wanted to get out of PC or whatever other predicament he was in. "I always got the feeling that he was saying to me, 'Hey, Zeizel, I'll do anything not to be in PC' or something like that. . . . And I would say, 'Okay, I'll make a deal with you: stay in control. I'll try to find some services for you.' "

Cartier told Zeizel and, later, another psychologist that he did get into some fights. But he preferred to avoid them, and not just at Deer Island. He used to "act crazy" so he wouldn't have to fight, Rose Ryan said. "He told me this. He said, 'I do it on purpose so people are scared of me.' He starts acting like he's nuts, and instead of fighting with him, people say, 'What's going on?' They just give it up. And that was kind of his defense, not to fight."

Even so, "he was scary to a lot of people, scary to me, too," Zeizel said. "I felt he was dangerous, to the community and to himself." But no one in Boston Municipal Court's probation office ever asked Zeizel for his opinion. He said probation officials rarely asked him about prisoners he treated. "I wish they had," he said.

In sentencing Cartier for the subway attack, the judge tried to remind him that his relationship with Rose Ryan was over. "The best thing for you to do is to realize that," the court said. "She doesn't want to have anything to do with you . . . move on with your life."

Cartier refused to let go. The harassment continued. He began making collect calls to the Ryan family home from jail, and he enlisted other inmates to write obscene letters. "He made calls from jail the whole time he was there or had other inmates call," Ryan said. The sisters called the district attorney's office in Boston, and a woman prosecutor they spoke with encouraged them to accept the collect charges so they could make a record on their phone bill and "prove that he was breaking probation already, while he was in jail." Rose still has a list of four that she recorded, along with a note from New England Telephone saying: "All 4 calls come from the east wing of the Deer Island Correctional Inst."

Rose was even more frightened about what Cartier might do when he got out. The prosecutor assured her she would be notified when he was released. Tina said the prosecutor told them, "The sad part is that he may be released [early] because he's been a very good prisoner and we're overcrowded." But "she never called us," Rose said.[16]

That is not an isolated problem. Battered women frequently aren't notified when their abusers are set free, even in states like Massachusetts, where the law entitles them to notification if they sign up for it. "It happens all the time," says Andrew Klein, chief probation officer in Quincy District Court. Victims can sign up with prosecutors or other designated agencies, but they aren't the ones who provide the notifications. "The prosecutors aren't supposed to do it," Klein said. "It's up to the sheriff. Anytime you deal with more than one agency, the chances increase geometrically that it's never going to get done."[17] In cases where notifications are made, according to other officials, the women often aren't told until the morning of the release, too late to put "a safety plan" together. In all too many corridors of the criminal justice system, "victims still live in the dark," as one prosecutor in the D.C. area puts it. "They are at the absolute bottom of the priority barrel." He recalled two separate homicides where the mother of the murder victim was not even told her son's killer had been arrested—and convicted. They found out only when a probation officer came calling in the course of a pre-sentence investigation. "There's a complete lack of human concern," he said. "We have laws to protect people, but we do everything except tell the people what's going on."[18]

Rose Ryan moved to a studio apartment in Salem near her sister's company. She lived alone and was afraid to go into Boston. She didn't tell anyone who knew Cartier where she'd gone. Still "I'd get nervous," she remembers. "I was just terrified that he was going to get out because I figured he was going to come after me. . . . I had a baseball bat in my car. I had Mace in my purse." She laid out a bunch of knives and other sharp objects next to her bed each night before going to sleep. "I always thought that he would come back and try to get me," she said. That isn't "domestic violence." That is terrorism. But the criminal justice system isn't accustomed to looking at it or dealing with it in that way.

Cartier was released early, on November 5, 1991, with time off for "good behavior." I was flabbergasted when I learned of that. I didn't know anything at that point about his conduct in prison, but I thought, surely this was a mistake, an aberration. Authorities were aware that Cartier had been harassing Rose from prison, or at least of allegations to that effect. This was "good behavior"?

The answer is that the jailers don't care. All they care about is whether the prisoners make a ruckus inside the jail, not outside. It is not at all uncommon for inmates to get "good time" while intimidating women over the telephone or through the mail. In Fairfax, Virginia, one prisoner serving time for violating probation by harassing an ex-girlfriend was convicted of making dozens of annoying calls to her and her father while incarcerated.[19] He still got good-time credits for all the time he spent in jail, including the days on which he made the phone calls. In one particular week, he made more than forty hangup calls.

In Oregon, another inmate serving time for manslaughter contrived to obtain the mail of the California woman he blamed for his problems by filing a change of address form with the local post office. When she found out about it and complained, a corrections official laughed in her face. "Inmates do that sort of thing all the time," he told her. The "prank" had no effect on his good-time credits. He served only four years of his fifteen-year sentence. The woman had moved by then, but he tracked her down from his prison cell by writing a letter to the

California Department of Motor Vehicles telling them she was a witness to an accident. The DMV sent him her new address in a letter mailed straight to the prison.[20] Later, serving a new prison term for molesting an eleven-year-old girl, the same felon managed to get copies of the woman's federal tax returns by using a forged power of attorney.

Why not cut off the incorrigible prisoner's mail? "We can't," the hounded woman, Linda Pride, was told. "It's in the California Prisoner's Bill of Rights. We can check his mail for contraband, and block certain pieces, but we can't completely stop his mail because that would be considered an invasion of his privacy."[21]

The postal service, which a former chairman of the House Government Information Subcommittee, Rep. Gary Condit, has called "the stalker's best friend," recently changed its mail-forwarding system in an effort to prevent such harassment. But in most jurisdictions, the "good time" just rolls on.[22]

Cartier had been given three months in jail on May 9, 1991, for violating probation and another six months on June 21, 1991, for attacking Rose Ryan with a dangerous weapon. He served about six total, counting time from the date of his arrest, probably longer than most good-time math formulas would prescribe. In most states, inmates are given generous early-release credits for taking part in prison rehabilitation programs or not being a disciplinary problem or simply to ease crowding.[23] They are frequently granted automatically under state law, without any requirement of good conduct. "Good time has become little more than a bribe to entice inmates' good behavior," says Edward Leddy, a professor of criminology at St. Leo College in Norfolk, Virginia.[24] "It's designed to make life easier for prison authorities—but often at the expense of public safety."

At Deer Island, Cartier had hardly been a model prisoner. On September 9, 1991, a "rec officer" told him to move out of a segregated psychiatric observation unit to the main prison, known as the Hill. He refused. A disciplinary board sent him to the West Wing to spend ten days in isolation, locked up for twenty-three hours a day.

The lockup was probably the only safe place for him. It was Cartier's first stint in the West Wing. "Most likely someone had it out for him, to put him there [in the West Wing]," Zeizel said. "It was basically a very difficult place for white inmates to be. Its nickname was 'the Wild Wild West.' If I had to see guys from the East Wing, I'd go up and see them. Guys from the West, I'd send for them."

A few days later, on September 16, he was cited for throwing food against a wall and sent back to "the Plant," a unit for troublemakers. He was found guilty by a disciplinary board and drew another ten days in the lockup there. He probably did that to get out of the West Wing, Zeizel said.

On October 29, still in protective custody, he earned another stint in lockup for throwing a burning piece of paper from his cell. When an officer asked him his first name, he said it was George. His guards wrote him up for "destruction of property, attempted arson, and lying to an officer."[25]

His release from Deer Island, with time off for good behavior, came a week later. Under a law that has since been repealed, he got fifteen days' good-time credit automatically, without doing anything to earn it.[26] He also got time off for taking part in a substance abuse program.

The isolation of different parts of the justice system from one another, their persistent, almost primitive failure to communicate with one another, became apparent with Cartier's release. We are inundated with talk these days about the information superhighway, but the justice system is still running on dirt roads. Cartier's probation officers were aware he'd been officially set loose, but they didn't know he'd been rearrested before he could leave the gates. One would think they should have known. Warrants to send him back to Lawrence for violating probation there had been delivered to Deer Island back in June. Cartier knew about them. He signed a slip of paper in August 1991 asking for a speedy trial on the charges. The authorities in Essex County (Lawrence) didn't want to see him on the streets even if officials in Boston didn't care. Probation officer Paul Dube in Lawrence knew Rose was still worried. He had talked to her after Cartier's commitment to Deer Island.

"She indicated she was in fear for her life," Dube said. So as soon as Cartier's time at Deer Island was up, he was taken into custody and transported back to Essex County to face charges of violating probation on both the Nader market burglary and the ketchup bottle incident in Andover. On November 6, 1991, he was brought into Lawrence District Court, adjudged guilty in the ketchup bottle caper, and sentenced to fifty-nine days in the Essex County jail.

Ostensibly, the reason for that curious sentence was the upside-down arithmetic of the penal system, where less can sometimes be more. "We wanted to keep him out of circulation for as long as we could," Dube told me. "The reason we had him committed for fifty-nine days was that for anything under sixty days, you're supposed to spend the entire period in jail. If you get anything sixty days or over, you are entitled to parole eligibility after half of the time served."

What that overlooks is the six-month suspended sentence Cartier had coming to him in Lawrence for the 1988 burglary at Nader's market. That was dismissed, wiped off the books. "That's amazing," said a probation officer who looked at the record at my request. "They dropped the more serious charges." Massachusetts Probation Commissioner Donald Cochran, who also looked at the record, agreed that Cartier got off lightly. "I'd guess that his defense attorney plea-bargained that arrangement," Cochran said. Had Cartier served that suspended sentence, Kristin might never have met him.

8

I was back in Boston again, poking around Kristin's flat, trying to pack up her artworks for temporary storage. I found them fascinating. Somber, elemental, angry, tormented. They had a power and intensity that kept me fixed on them. Some of that was doubtless due to the awful loss I was feeling, to the pride of a father ready to see talent at the slightest hint of it. But I was sure now, as I had never been before, that she would have been a success, artistically if not financially. Kristin was reaching deep down inside herself. Nothing seemed fake or copied. She'd struggled for two years at BU and learned important techniques at the art school there. But she found it too traditional, too confining. She wanted to switch to the School of the Museum of Fine Arts, which artist Robert Motherwell had called "an oasis of creativity." I encouraged her to apply. It was time to strike out on her own.

"This is really pretty scary but I'm sure it's the right thing for me to do," she wrote in April 1990 after submitting her application. "I'm glad I've gone to BU. I've definitely learned a lot, maybe things that I couldn't have gotten anywhere else. But I also feel that I would not benefit to stay here, that it would be best to take all the classic training I've gotten and take it to a school where I can be creatively inspired . . . somewhere that's more a part of the modern art scene."

BU, Kristin added parenthetically, "is known as an old fart school." But she said she still appreciated all the art history courses she'd taken there. I know she enjoyed most of them, but maybe she'd forgotten her comments on the first two she took. I can't find the letter, but I do remember her saying that one of the teachers was "a human sedative." In any case, she knew what her father wanted to hear. She would be taking her liberal arts courses at Tufts, "So you don't have to worry about me not getting a rounded education."

"Anyway, I just wanted you to know that I appreciate all that you're doing for me and I'm not an ingrate," Kristin wrote. "I really just want to learn all I can. I wish you could see some of my most recent work. I think you'd be impressed."

I was impressed. I wish I could have told her how much.

The Museum School notified Kristin in late May 1990 that she'd been accepted. Not all of her credits were transferable, and it would take at least three more years to get the degrees she wanted, a Museum School diploma and a bachelor of fine arts from Tufts, but Kristin was delighted by the opportunity. She stayed in Boston most of the summer to get ready. She had a summer job, and she wanted to move into a new apartment a few doors from the overpriced flat she'd been renting. She'd also started dating her friend Jason, who was studying art at BU, and whom she'd known since freshman year when they both lived on the tenth floor at Claflin Hall. But they spent the summer apart. Jason got a job as a crew member on a yacht plying the waters off the coast of Maine. He wrote her in late July to say that the fishing was terrible and that he missed her. Enclosed was a paycheck he asked her to keep until he got back; he said he was afraid his roommates would lose it.

Kristin took time out to come down to Jekyll Island for about ten days in August to play golf with her brothers, go crabbing with me, and sun herself on the beach with Helen and Rosemary. She brought a charcoal portrait of herself that she'd done at BU. She was quite proud of it, and she gave it to Helen for a birthday present. The Museum School scheduled registration before Labor Day, so Kristin hurried straight back to Boston while the rest of us dawdled. She got all the classes she wanted, including drawing, welded steel sculpture, jewelry making, and an art history course on film noir at Tufts.

At first, some of her new teachers and advisors told her, she was too reticent, too tentative. She felt that way herself. She had left art school at BU, as she told her first Museum School advisor, because "she felt it was all technique." She said she was "looking for more creative energy but feeling a little intimidated about finding it." Her Museum School teachers urged her to push on, to put aside her doubts, to trust herself and her ideas, to develop the artistic promise they saw. Kristin fell in love with the place.

"She was so happy at the school," her metalsmithing teacher, David E. Austin, remembered at a memorial service and show for Kristin's work that the school held after she was killed. "She felt she had come to a place where she could really experience and process her ideas. And she did."

A generous, gentle man, Austin worked very hard with her that first year because of the "remarkable things" he saw she could do. After that, he went on a year-long sabbatical, but he would see her on the subway almost every week, as she got out of her classes at Tufts just as he was coming home from dinner with friends. She told him about the courses she was taking, what she was making. He was struck by how enthusiastic and happy she was, how much she enjoyed the freedom of the school's open curriculum. At the Museum School, all studio courses are available to all students, regardless of their year level, subject only to class size limits and fulfillment of prerequisites. At the end of each semester, students present work from all their classes to a review board composed of faculty and students. The board makes suggestions for further study and awards a block of credits "appropriate to the term's accomplishments." The system is said to be unique among art schools.

"She was just so amazed at what was happening to her," Austin said. "And it was because this school was right for her. She could see that, with this freedom that she had here . . . it allowed her the latitude for her creative vision."

It isn't easy to be an artist of the inner self, but Kristin was plainly on her way. The less rigid atmosphere gave her a bit of "cultural shock," as she told her first review board in December 1990, but she soon adjusted, turning out what subsequent reviewers called "excellent" ceramics pieces, "a wonderful self-portrait," and a curved marble sculpture that was "more sensitive than most works at the school." The biggest reservation of her first-year teachers was that they felt she was still editing herself too much, showing them only what she considered "the good stuff," not taking enough chances.

First semester was hectic. Dating Jason apparently had its ups and downs, perhaps because he liked Kristin so much. A brown belt in karate as well as a sculpture major at BU, he was certainly capable of taking care of her. Rosemary and I could see how fond he was of Kristin whenever he came by the house in Washington to see her. His father was an assistant military attaché at the New Zealand Embassy, and they lived just a few miles away in Bethesda, Maryland. At first Jason had dated Kristin's roommate at Claflin Hall. For a long time they were just "best buddies." He would come calling frequently when they were home for school breaks or summer vacation. He even waited for her to get out of the shower. They shared a wry sense of humor, which relied heavily on snappy one-liners delivered deadpan.

In Boston, Kristin frequently went down to Bunratty's, just a block from her apartment, to see him and take in the music. Jason got a job there to help make ends meet, first as a bouncer, then as a bartender. He doesn't seem to have enjoyed it much. Not counting friends like Kristin, he wrote her from New Zealand in March 1991, a couple of months after returning there, "One thing Boston taught me was how repulsive humankind can be." Between bouncing and bartending and other things, he said, "I've seen some nasty traits come out in people and I've just been turned off. . . . Can't say I miss the States, but I've committed you and all my friends to memory so you'll never be forgotten. . . . P.S. Give all your useless flatmates and friends a smack in the head from me."

Jason had gone back to New Zealand in early 1991, with his father's tour of duty done. Kristin deemed his letter "snotty and obnoxious" in overall content and said she wasn't sure she'd answer it, but she did. Around the same time she got it, she doodled in one of her notepads: "Kristin's got no mates / No mates, No mates / Kristin's got no mates / No mates, No mates."

Lonesome or not, Kristin had more time for her art. She did the self-portrait, the marble piece, and other ceramic sculptures that won praise from her review board that May, but she told herself that she wasn't working hard enough. She found the atmosphere at the Museum School a bit "weird." All of her close friends were still at BU. "There's people here I speak to," she said in one letter, "but I haven't made any real friends."

The Museum School could seem unfriendly, even alienating for anyone not absorbed in art. You could stay there late into the night, but to work, not play. "Unlike BU," as one of Kristin's classmates, Kate Sutton, put it, "the Museum School has neither college campus nor student activities. The students tend to become self-absorbed in order to survive. Such is the nature of the art world."

Kristin embraced the school for what it was. She stayed late into the night. She could sense herself learning, progressing. And by the spring of 1992, she was overcoming her reticence, whether her teachers knew it or not. Most of her work was still in the flat as I rummaged around. All her roommates had moved out by now. The only sign of life was Circe, curled up in her terrarium. One of Kristin's old friends had promised to pick her up and take care of her, but he hadn't done that yet. I sat on Kristin's futon bed, poked through her books and papers, and made a little catalog of the art she'd left behind. A wide-banded brass ring had disappeared. Gone, too, was the curved marble sculpture. Kristin had promised it to Lauren, who had taken it with her, headed for New Orleans with Brian. They brought it back for the Museum School show that September.

David Austin, who hadn't seen her work for more than a year, was amazed at her progress when he came back for the show. It reminded him of something Robert Motherwell had said in a commencement speech about searching for something in a small studio he kept in SoHo and finding a painting he had done when he was very young. As soon as Motherwell saw it, he had a flash of recognition, a realization of how important that painting was in his development as an artist. He called it his gem.

"When we look at Kristin's work, we can feel that," Austin said. "That these pieces are her early works of transition."

At the Museum School that last year, there seems to have been concern for Kristin on another score. If so, it was at least partly my fault. She was going to have to spend most of her final year at Tufts. I felt the academic courses were important. I think she did, too. She enjoyed most of those she took at BU, but she thrived on the courses she took at Tufts, which she told me were light years better. But her art teachers seemed uncertain, perhaps a bit suspicious, of students who didn't hurl themselves completely into their artwork. The apprehension was understandable. They didn't want her to get rusty or become distracted.

"One more term here and the rest at Tufts," one of her reviewers wrote in December 1991. "Her artwork continues to grow, but will be curtailed by the academics. She knows in her heart that she wants to make art her life, but is anxious about leaving school . . . worried as to what's next. Will she experiment more with more challenging courses and keep developing her inner voice? Or will she go to a more craft/facility route, working more on jewelry and ceramics? Our strong suggestion is that she keep up the risk . . .

"Kris," the reviewer concluded, "you have a lot to say. It's simply a matter of expanding the dialect."

Kristin knew "the value of artistic adventure," as one of her advisors put it. But she didn't relish the penury that could go with it. She lived a very frugal existence in Boston. She dreamed of owning her own business, selling jewelry and ceramics and other handcrafted things. Rosemary had always wanted to open an art shop; maybe she could go into business with her mother. But all that was iffy. Kristin was worried about what to do after graduation. Her favorite pastime was, as she once wrote, "morbid self-reflection." She expected to graduate in the spring of 1993, but what then? She wanted to go on to graduate school. We would have helped but probably not enough to pay the whole bill. She knew she might have to go to work first to be able to afford it. A degree from Tufts would be useful in trying to nail down a regular paycheck.

And she was a Lardner. She liked to read, and she liked to write.

One of her favorite classes was "The Self in American Film," which she took in the fall of 1991. The idea of the course was to use movies to explore theories and ideas about "the self." The students watched *The Hustler,* with Paul Newman as a pool player, as an example of "the self at work" and *The Accused,* with Jodie Foster as a rape victim, as an example of "the role of women as property, masculinity and 'rapist ethics,'" among others. But the films were just a springboard for discussion and were followed by writing assignments designed to bring out the students' notions of identity. Kristin saw the self as a complex being, composed of an outer self and an inner self, with the inner self hiding some things consciously but also concealing a still deeper self that manifests itself in different ways, in attitude, in personality, but especially in art. "It is the inner self," she felt, "which gives power to art."

For her final paper, Kristin turned in an essay, a short story really, on what it was like to be an artist. She called herself Amy and wrote of the paradox of reaching down inside oneself and at the same time feeling that the raw material—the clay or the marble—has a life of its own, waiting to be released.

"Amy pulled her keys out of her pocket and unlocked the door. As she entered the studio she inhaled the smell of wood and stone, it smelled so good and comforting. She turned on the lights and went over to the shelves. Locating her piece, she carried it over to the bench. 'Okay,' she addressed the stone, 'what do you want to be?' She lifted the stone into her arms and closing her eyes, caressed it. Finding a spot, a feeling, she set the heavy piece slowly down again. Amy put on her hat, her goggles, her dust mask, and her gloves. Time to get serious.

"She positioned the chisel, raised the mallet and began chipping away. She knew there was something in there just screaming to get out, she could only hope to be the instrument through which it was released. Amy loved the stone carving studio when she could be alone. . . . Thoughts slowly wandered through her brain. In most of her work she took her memories and experiences and tried to translate them into a single entity. Trying to translate her feelings into her work was so frightening. It felt as though she was telling all her secrets to the world. Why would anyone want to know them anyway? But making things was all she wanted to do."

Kristin saw her art not only as an expression of what was hidden deep inside, but as something to be guarded closely.

"Art could be such a selfish thing. Everything she made she made for herself, and not one bit of it could she bear to be parted with. Whether she loved it, despised it, or was painfully ashamed of what she had made . . . she couldn't stand the thought of these little parts of her being taken away and put in someone else's possession."

Kristin said she knew there were many artists at her own school, "and thousands, millions more around the world," who were "a lot better than she was." So "what did she have to say that was so important? Why was she making art? Why does anyone create? . . . She still didn't know why she did what she did, but as long as she could continue to reach inside of herself and pull things out, she would have a reason to keep going on."

The thoughts and the story were heavily inspired by that marble sculpture, curving and sensual, that Kristin had made. It pleased her immensely even though "after the weeks of work she had devoted to it, she felt as though it had created itself. She couldn't possibly have had anything to do with it."

It must have been difficult to promise it away. But she did. She promised it to Lauren. Her friends were very important to her. When she told them she loved them, she really did. Kristin didn't use words lightly. She meant what she said, she spoke from the heart. "She had a heart of gold," said Amy Buettner, one of her first roommates on Glenville Avenue, now a metalsmith in Oregon who still has Kristin's photo on her coffee table. "She would totally bend over backwards for you."

Kristin's teacher for the film course, Ross Ellenhorn, was impressed with the paper and remembered it months later, after Kristin was killed. He remembered Kristin for other reasons, too. Ellenhorn happened to be a counselor at the Cambridge office of Emerge, the nation's first counseling service for male batterers.[1] He mentioned this to his students during one of his lectures. Kristin approached him after class. "A couple of her roommates had had trouble with boyfriends," he remembered. "She talked about them."

Could she have been talking about herself, too? This was before she ever met Michael Cartier. "Men are dogs," she sometimes told friends, because of the way they treated women she knew. I have no doubt she knew young women who had been hounded for sex, or subjected to abuse, or both. I'm sure she had her fill of grabby, grasping dates, too.

"She didn't go out with boys that much," Rosemary says. "She really resented guys coming on to her . . . pushing at her. She thought that was all they wanted. Years ago, mothers used to have chats with their daughters. Now they know more than you do."

Kristin and I talked about that, too, very briefly, in our last conversation the day before she was killed. Was there anything more that made her so outspoken? I don't know. It's too late to ask. But Kristin was quite dissatisfied with "the state of the gender thing," as Amber Lynch put it. Her writings showed that. Her artworks were even more outspoken in their anger. When I asked Andy Armstrong if he had ever hit her, he got very upset at the suggestion. He had shouted at her, even cursed at her, at a chance meeting after they had broken up and he had started drinking. But that was all, he said. I didn't even have to ask Jason. He knew Kristin wouldn't abide by such treatment. "I never hit her," he volunteered. "She was really strong about that sort of thing."

Kristin spent a busy summer in Boston, studying at Tufts, working part-time at a pastry shop, and looking around for a new apartment. Jason was in New Zealand, and she hadn't met Michael Cartier, who was simmering on Deer Island. With roommates moving to other places, the apartment at 20 Glenville was suddenly too big. After considerable searching, she, Lauren, and Matt found the flat in Brookline and arranged to move there in late August. Kristin took two courses at Tufts, one in Asian religions and the other in children's literature. She needed to build up credits, but she enjoyed both of them. Buddhism appealed to her, partly because of the respect it accorded women, who, she wrote, "were not seen as a lower form of being who had to be reborn as a man in order to achieve enlightenment." But she was puzzled by the concept that reality is fleeting and painful.

"Why is reality painful because it is fleeting?" she wondered. "If you accept that it is fleeting and live moment by moment, then reality is not painful, it just is. . . . Pain only comes when you try to hang on to what is impermanent. So all life need not be suffering. You can enjoy life if you do not expect anything from it."

The course in children's literature was just great fun. Kristin had read most of the books years earlier, and now she could get some credits by reading them again with a more critical eye. It gave her new insights into books like *Kidnapped,* the classic boy's story, and *Little Women,* the classic girl's story. She found *Little Women* too preachy and *Kidnapped* much more realistic, even though the so-called girl's book was based on the author's real-life experiences, while *Kidnapped* was an adventure story fashioned from the author's imagination. She had loved *Little Women* as a child but on reflection felt it was heavy-handed. "It actually made me get up, clean my room, do laundry and wash the dishes, just like a good little woman," she said. She decided that *Kidnapped* was a better example of the values of friendship and human bonds because it doesn't "put forth its values and morals in such a transparent manner . . ."

"I believe [*Kidnapped*] would influence a child to be trustworthy, honest and forthright," Kristin said in a paper contrasting the character influences in the two books. *"Little Women* also extolls these virtues, but they are eclipsed by a wife-and-mother sticky sweetness. . . . It is far too pious. It is a shame that the labels of 'boy's book' and 'girl's book' are attached to these works. I think boys would benefit from *Little Women* and girls would benefit from *Kidnapped."*

Her professor liked the paper, though he thought she should have expanded on the last point, at least to explain what benefit boys would get out of *Little Women.* Doing the dishes, perhaps. "What's here is great," he told her. "Observant, accurate, clear. You're a perceptive reader and a good writer—you have a way with words. . . . I have the impression, reading it, that you are a lot smarter than you realize." I always thought so, too.

Kristin's happiness spilled over in her notes home. For Father's Day, she sent me a lovely card, with an exquisite oil painting of a woman named Jutta on the cover and a note wishing me "the most wonderful of Dad Days" and adding: "I appreciate all that you & Mom have done to send me to school. Thank you—I try to make you proud of me."

She celebrated her twenty-first birthday the next month at a party with friends, a six-pack from a BU student she liked named Jorge (who unfortunately was going with another girl), and a massive water gun called a Super Soaker 100 that Lauren gave her. "When I got the Super Soaker," she wrote Amy Buettner a couple of days later, "I took the screen out of my window and sat on a ledge, legs hanging out of the window, and zapped everyone on Glenville." She had started dating another boy named Andy after Jason left, but that was over by now. He was always looking at other girls. "Andy's a complete loser and I never want to see him again," Kristin said.

"I knew lots of guys who liked her, who were really nice and who told me they liked her," Lauren Mace said. "One boy, Mitch, tried for a year to get her to go out with him. She liked him, but she wasn't attracted to him."

The months fluttered by, speeding past a two-week vacation in Jekyll that was highlighted for a few days by Kristin's presence. She found somebody to take care of Circe and managed to buy a round-trip ticket for $129. She didn't use the first half of the ticket because she wanted to drive down with Helen. Kristin hitched a ride to Washington and came down from there after she and Helen coaxed Mira into coming along. If she had any worries, they disappeared, as they did for the rest of us, as soon as we crossed the Jekyll bridge onto a divided highway dressed up with tropical flowers and shrubs. Rosemary always likened it to entering another world, where no cares could touch us. Kristin spotted deer and wild turkey on bumpy rides with Charlie down the island's dirt fireroads in his pickup truck. She caught a small shark from the bridge over the Jekyll River when Ed took her fishing. He took a great picture of her in her Metallica T-shirt, holding the shark on a line and smiling happily. She went beachcombing with Richard on the south end of the island and found "a perfect piece of driftwood" for Circe's terrarium. She went dolphin-watching on an evening boat cruise with Helen, and Mira saw a huge sea turtle jump out of the water. But she spent most of her time, as usual, on the beach, sunning herself and reading books in a beach chair next to Helen. She flew back to Boston loaded down with souvenirs, but almost missed the plane when an officious guard insisted on a prolonged search of her luggage. The driftwood had set off the metal detector, but the guard was convinced there was something more ominous to be found. We were quite emphatic in our protests. Kristin's ticket came with an explicit warning that "no changes are permitted once ticket is issued."

Michael Cartier was released from his last place of confinement, the Correctional Alternative Center in Lawrence, Massachusetts, on the day before Christmas, 1991. He'd been sent there on December 23 after serving most of his sentence at the new Essex County jail in Middleton. His fifty-nine-day term had been trimmed by ten, evidently for "good time" served. He should have been arrested again before he walked out the door, in part for harassing Rose Ryan by mail and over the phone while he was still at Deer Island. A warrant accusing him of violating his probation had been issued December 19 in Boston Municipal Court. Probation officials there didn't know he had been jailed again up in Lawrence.

"How would we have known?" the BMC's chief probation officer, John Tobin, protested when I pressed him on the point. All they had to do was read his rap sheet, I told him. The fifty-nine-day sentence he got in Essex County that started on November 6, the day after his release from Deer Island, was plainly listed. Tobin ignored the point. "Cartier was on probation in this [Boston Municipal] court," he declared. "He had a split sentence [jail, then probation]. We issued a warrant for failure to report [after his release from Deer Island]. We would still have issued a warrant even if he was incarcerated" somewhere else.[2]

Fine. But the warrant wasn't served. Tobin's office had been snoozing. It didn't know where Cartier was. He was in someone else's jail! I couldn't help thinking of that old stanza by John Collins Bossidy:

And this is good old Boston,
The home of the bean and the cod,
Where the Lowells talk to the Cabots
And the Cabots talk only to God.

In fact, Tobin's office didn't even put an officer on Cartier's case until a full month after he'd left Deer Island.[3] Only cursory supervision was prescribed. Cartier's file shows that he was assigned to "administrative" probation, which meant that all he had to do was meet certain minimal conditions.[4] He didn't even have to report to his probation officer on a regular basis. Massachusetts Probation Commissioner Donald Cochran told me that a "risk/need assessment" is routinely done for convicts about to be put on probation to determine how much attention they need: "maximum . . . moderate . . . [or] minimum." He said those convicted of violent crime are given "automatic maximum attention until they prove they've gotten better."[5]

Cartier didn't get maximum or even minimum attention because no risk/need assessment was made. Why? Apparently because too many probationers in Boston Municipal Court had already been given the relatively more expensive treatment that year.[6]

"This particular case, Michael Cartier, should have been a risk/need case," BMC probation chief Tobin acknowledged recently. The first assistant chief, Matthew Regan, now retired, was making the assignments and was trying to meet guidelines that said the office should hew to the statewide ratio of "70 percent risk need and 30 percent administrative." The BMC probation office wasn't meeting those guidelines when Cartier's case came up. "That's why I think this particular case ended up as 'administrative,' " Tobin said.[7]

The probation system is full of dangerous pitfalls and shortcuts, and not just in Massachusetts.[8] Only people like Tom Casey keep it from collapsing. He lost jurisdiction over Cartier in May of 1991. The supposedly hard-nosed professionals of BMC took over after that. Rose Ryan was absolutely right to be keeping knives near her pillow.

The assignment of a probation officer for Cartier should have been made in early November at the latest. It wasn't done until December 5 after a prosecutor in the Suffolk County DA's office, Susan Underwood, sounded the alarm, apparently in response to a call from the Ryan sisters. Underwood sent a memo concerning Cartier's alarming approaches to Rose Ryan to the probation office on December 4. The probation office called Underwood back and made contact the next day. According to a note made by Regan,[9] "Ms. Underwood disclosed that the principals [Cartier and Ryan] had been friends, that he knew of her address. [Underwood] also related that it is her understanding that there is a restraining order against the defendant in Lynn. He has made telephone calls and allegedly written letters. P.O. [probation office] acknowledged that P. O. D. Barrett [-Moeller] *would be assigned* to the case" (emphasis supplied).[10]

On December 5, the probation office "called Deer Island and learned the defendant was discharged on 11/5/91. He was picked up by the Andover Police, and he probably was arraigned in the Lawrence Court. His last known address was 43 Calumet St., Roxbury." The next call was to Lawrence District Court to ask if Cartier had been arraigned on November 5, but, of course, it "produced no information for that day."[11] Neither did a final call to the Andover police. The sleuths at BMC evidently didn't think to ask about November 6 when Cartier was brought into court.

At some point that same day, December 5, the case was turned over to Diane Barrett-Moeller, who made out a surrender notice for Cartier, to be delivered to him at his "last known address" in Roxbury. Obviously based on Underwood's report, it accused him of violating probation because of his "failure to stay away from Rose Ryan," his "failure to be evaluated for Alternatives to Violence Group," and his "failure to report to probation" since his release from Deer Island on November 5. The notice demanded Cartier's appearance in Boston Municipal Court on December 12 for a hearing on the aforesaid allegations.

Cartier, of course, couldn't show up. He didn't even know he was supposed to. He'd been in the Essex County House of Correction in Middleton since November 6. No matter. A warrant for his arrest was issued December 19 by Boston Municipal Court in light of his failure to appear there. But like the millions of warrants stacked up across the country, it was just another piece of paper, sounding ominous, signifying nothing. Cartier's new supervisors in Boston could have found out where he was by calling the probation office in Lawrence or just by looking at his CORI. It said that as of November 6, 1991, his probation status in Essex County had been "revised and revoked" and he had been given "59DA CMTD" (fifty-nine days committed). But with no "hold" placed on him, he walked out in time for Christmas.

Cartier had other things to cheer about. According to his father, his $17,000 insurance settlement had just become final. He got a part-time job as a bouncer at Bunratty's around the same time. He'd hung around there before. Jason remembered him, after Kristin was killed, as someone "from the hard-core scene."

"I didn't think of him as a decent guy," Jason said in his understated way. "He used to bounce at a few places, but not at Bunratty's. He had a bit of a temper on him. Whenever I was talking to him or around him, he was sort of withdrawn, but I had a friend that came up from D.C. for a while, and Mike got into a fight with my friend. Mike sort of beat the hell out of the guy. It was a boyfriend-girlfriend type thing." The fight, as Jason recalls it, was over Rose Ryan.[12]

Cartier kept bothering her even after he got out of jail. His possessiveness was plainly one-sided. As far as he was concerned, Rose "belonged" to him, but that didn't mean he belonged to Rose. He brought another girl home with him that Christmas eve, or shortly "after Christmas" at least. Gene Cartier thought, after the murder, that it had been Kristin. It wasn't. She was on the way home to Washington, D.C., on December 24 for Christmas vacation. "He had another girl with blonde hair. Susie, I think her name was," Gene Cartier said. "He was seeing girls before Kristin."

Abused women across the country know how Rose must have felt when she finally learned that Cartier was out. It happens again and again. "He kept calling my mother's house until I had a friend, a male friend, go into Boston and confront him," Ryan said.

That didn't happen until March. By then, Cartier was living in an apartment on Glenville Avenue in Allston, just a block away from

Kristin's old lodgings, and working at Bunratty's. The manager, J. D. Crump, felt sorry for him and decided to give him a break. "I knew he was in jail for assault," Crump told me. But he said he didn't know what the assault was all about until months later—when Kristin found out and told him.

A powerfully built man who was clearly quite capable of running a nightclub, Crump came close to tears as I talked to him in the dank, dark tavern. He had been fond of Kristin. Then thirty-six, he had been working at Bunratty's for about three years. He had once been a counselor at a place called Positive Life Styles, and he felt he knew how to handle people like Cartier. Crump knew Jason, too. Big cities are like that—a seemingly bewildering, basically simple collection of small slices of life where everyone seems to know everyone with similar tastes.

"Kristin used to hang around here all the time when she and Jason were dating," Crump said. "She was always the bright spot of the night. She was a ray of sunshine."

Cartier started working there not long after Christmas, but he was hardly a high-priced employee. Crump never could figure out how he could afford his lodgings on Glenville Avenue, which was often decried by BU students for its high rents and grasping landlords.

"A one-bedroom apartment in that neighborhood costs at least $550 a month," Crump said. "There was no way he could live there himself on what he was making here. I assume his dad helped him out. His average pay here was $130 a week at most. He only worked two shifts a week, except when he was cleaning up. When he was cleaning up, he did extra shifts."

Kristin arrived home for the 1991 holidays late on Christmas eve. She usually got home in time to decorate the Christmas tree, which she did better than anyone. This time she had special dispensation. She and Lauren had snagged "great seats" for a Metallica concert in Worcester, at the Spectrum, on December 23. Would we mind if she got home later than usual this time? Could she please go to the concert? They'd already paid for the seats. Et cetera, et cetera. Rosemary wasn't enthusiastic, but she said okay.

"It was a lot of heads banging together," Rosemary remembered. "I saw no need for it. But I thought Helen had bought the tickets [she hadn't; she'd paid for an earlier Metallica concert], so I said okay."

Kristin, I'm afraid, was an enthusiastic head-banger. Mira Suarez remembers going with her to another Metallica concert, the one Helen did finance, at the Capital Centre in Landover, Maryland. "It was absolutely crazy," Mira said. "I wasn't going to go, but Kristin said I had to come. The entire crowd was banging heads. The guards couldn't believe it. They were going around shining their flashlights on everybody." Mira had a fine time until she woke up the next morning with a very sore neck. She couldn't move it from one side to the other. Kristin massaged it for her, and she returned the favor.

Kristin slept late after the Boston spectacle and flew home in time for midnight mass with the rest of the family—her parents, sister Helen, her three brothers, and one sister-in-law, Richard's wife, Carol. We arrived late, as usual, and stood in the back of the church, as usual. Given a choice, Kristin would probably have preferred a Buddhist ceremony, but I don't think they celebrate Christmas. She and Helen slept upstairs that night in their old bedroom, the one with the star-studded ceiling. Kristin talked about how lonely she was, how most of the other girls she knew had boyfriends. "She just felt sad about that," Helen says.

Kristin got a ride back to Boston for the start of second semester at the Museum School January 13. Classes at Tufts began two days later. Kristin signed up for an anthropology course called "Myth, Ritual and Symbol."

Michael Cartier was getting closer. He had gotten his part-time job as a bouncer at Bunratty's by now, but there was still a warrant out for his arrest. He surrendered himself in Boston Municipal Court on January 17, accused of violating probation by failing to stay away from Rose Ryan, failing to report to the BMC probation office in early November following his release from Deer Island, and failing to respond to the December 12 surrender notice signed by Barrett-Moeller.

Two of the charges were obviously wide of the mark. Cartier couldn't have reported to the probation office in Boston until he had been released from jail in Essex County. He couldn't respond to the December 12 surrender notice—which was sent to an old address—for the same reason. But he had been harassing Rose Ryan. Evidence of that could easily have been adduced by asking her and her sister Tina. She was still living in fear, Mace in her purse, bat in her car, knives by the bed. He should have been ordered to complete the one-year sentence he got for attacking her. He was not only violating probation, he was violating Rose's restraining order, a separate crime in Massachusetts. The letter she got was obscene; the calls directed to her parents' house were chilling. Probation officials in Boston took a benign view. They had a limited report, and they seemed not to want to know any more.

Probation officials said they were aware of the letter to Rose, something written anonymously. "It was not determined whether he wrote it or whether he got someone in the institution to write it for him," Tobin told me. "Mrs. [Barrett-] Moeller concluded it was him anyway."

Case closed. Apparently, no one wanted any firsthand evidence. Officials in charge of Michael Cartier had already decided what was best for him. Rather than sending him back to jail for another six months as he deserved, they ordered him to attend a once-a-week class at the courthouse for six weeks called "Alternatives to Violence," apparently a pet project of municipal court officials. Barrett-Moeller was the principal instructor as well as the chief architect and promoter of the program.

"We thought we'd be in the vanguard of responding to the 209A's [domestic abuse complaints]," said Boston Municipal Court Chief Justice William J. Tierney, who authorized Barrett-Moeller to start the project around 1991. "We were expecting an increase. The question was how we would respond to it on a limited budget."[13]

In sentencing Cartier in June 1991, Judge Donovan prescribed

Barrett-Moeller's classes for Cartier as the main condition of probation. He was the judge who let him off the hook in January in the apartment-trashing case. Now the judge decided an anger-control course would be the best medicine for Cartier on getting out of Deer Island. Barrett-Moeller had told Donovan her Alternatives to Violence Group, as the class was called, was proving to be "very effective."[14] "It's been very effective," the judge asserted at the sentencing hearing.

That is simply nonsense when it comes to people like Cartier. A six-week program can do absolutely nothing to modify the behavior of such troubled individuals. It was designed for all sorts of ill-tempered defendants brought into court on various charges. They would explore their difficulties and their psyches each week with a probation officer (Barrett-Moeller) and a therapist, and then take a quiz.

"More and more attention is being paid to people who are violent," Tobin said in explaining the program to me several weeks after Kristin was killed.[15] "It's not a therapy program. It's more educational. It's for people who react to stress in different ways, not just batterers. We've had professors from MIT. We've had newspaper reporters. It is not designed just for abusers of women." (Tobin, I'm sure, did not mean to suggest that professors and reporters never abuse women, just that the ones he had in mind were ordered to the class for other reasons.)

Whatever the rationale, the course was too short, a placebo that pacifies the courts more than the convicts.[16] It simply gave officials an excuse for saying that the conditions of probation had been met. There is little reason to believe even longer or more intensive courses would be effective. We like to think that rehabilitation works, but there is no evidence, except in isolated instances, that it does. A landmark study in 1975 by the late Robert Martinson pointed that out. Many criminologists today think he was too pessimistic, but he reviewed the results of more than two hundred separate efforts to measure the effects of programs designed to rehabilitate convicted criminal offenders. His conclusion: "With few and isolated exceptions, the rehabilitative efforts that have been reported so far have had no appreciable effect on recidivism."[17]

The court's Alternatives to Violence program did not even meet state standards. Massachusetts was one of the few states to provide for state certification of batterer treatment programs. The standards, adopted in 1991 by a court-appointed commission, were aimed at ensuring that court-referred batterers were sent to "recognized" treatment programs formally certified by the state Department of Public Health. David Adams, a cofounder of Emerge and one of the commission members, said the rules were "full of loopholes" and amounted to a compromise with probation officers on the commission who wanted shorter programs than Adams and other members felt would be effective.[18]

The probation officers, Adams said, "felt the courts would rebel" if limited to programs like Emerge, which took forty-eight weeks of one-a-week sessions lasting two hours. The new rules required only forty hours, or twenty weeks of two-hour sessions.[19] The six-week Boston Municipal Court program was, of course, never certified.

"That was absurd," Adams said of the short duration. He said he opposed sending any batterers to the Alternatives to Violence program and urged state health officials to press the point with Probation Commissioner Cochran's office. "I felt they should be screening out batterers," Adams said. "They always assured me that was the case." The Alternatives to Violence–type programs were started by probation officers concerned about the lack of rehabilitation efforts, Adams said. "They meant well, but they were really naive about batterers and what it takes to change batterers."

In describing the program to me, Tobin said that Diane Barrett-Moeller was "a certified batterer's counselor. It's a relatively new position." He said she took "in-service courses" at a college in Dudley to qualify. Adams said there was no such position, at least not under the state standards. "Individuals are not certified," he said. "Programs can be certified. Their program was never certified."

New and more rigorous standards were adopted in Massachusetts in March 1995, requiring, among other things, a minimum of eighty hours, or forty weeks of two-hour sessions, and making plain that the programs that could be "recognized," the word used in state law, would have to be certified.

Greater effectiveness "is not the only—nor necessarily the most important—rationale for states to require longer treatment programs," Adams wrote recently. "Longer programs permit a lengthier period in which to monitor the abuser's behavior and to judge his commitment to nonviolence, something that is of great concern to the victims of abuse. Even for the untreated batterer, it is quite common for there to be a two- to four-month period between episodes of violence. Therefore, completion of a 12-week program does not necessarily demonstrate an offender's commitment to ending violence. It may reflect the abuser's successful manipulation of the program more than it indicates any changes in behavior or attitude."[20]

The new standards include many other revisions to enhance victim safety. For instance, they broaden the definition of "domestic violence" to include "stalking, harassment, on-going monitoring or pursuing of [the] victim," and they require that not only the victim (for example, Rose Ryan), but any "current partner" (for example, Kristin) be warned of any immediate or serious threats to their health or safety.

Only about twelve other states have promulgated any standards, Adams said. But compliance is another matter. Judges, like other people, don't always follow the law when it imposes obligations on them. "Massachusetts judges are still not referring to certified programs, even though the Judicial Standards and the law require them to do so," Adams said.

Donovan said he thought he was doing the right thing in giving Cartier a split sentence, first jail time and then treatment. In cases like this, he said, "I want them to know they have done wrong and have to pay a price, and I want them to get treatment." The judge said he also put Cartier on probation for two years so there would be "a club over his head" if he got out of line. "I thought I did a good disposition that would protect the victim [Rose Ryan]," Donovan said. Of course, he added, "this is going on the premise that everything works as it should, which often doesn't happen."[21]

In choosing Barrett-Moeller's course over alternatives such as Emerge, Donovan said, "I wanted [Cartier] to attend the most successful program and successfully complete it." He said he believed Barrett-Moeller had presented him with statistics indicating "that the program was working." But other probation officials found that she guarded it jealously and even discouraged supervisors from sitting in on the classes.[22] It was a case study in courthouse politics. She apparently had the judges on her side. Even after Kristin was killed, Barrett-Moeller was allowed to lengthen the program (to eight weeks) and was gradually relieved of all other duties so she could devote more time to it.

The Alternatives to Violence program was eventually terminated by Tierney in July 1993 amid a crossfire of recriminations. It turned out to have what Tobin described as "an inordinate recidivism rate" and a waiting list so long that one in four would be out of their probationary periods before they could enter it. Of the 117 probationers who had been accepted into the program, 52 percent had been rearrested. Four of ten on the waiting list had been rearrested or had subsequent restraining orders issued against them.[23]

"We cannot and must not perpetuate what does not work," Tobin said.[24]

Judge Donovan said he didn't know any of that at the time he sentenced Cartier and was still unaware of it when I called him. "I was aware the program was canceled, but I was never told why," he said. "There were rumors that it was money, that there were personality conflicts and such. All the reports we were getting at that time [1991] was that it was a very good program—and very effective."[25]

When Cartier finally turned himself in at Boston Municipal Court on January 17, 1992, the presiding judge held there was "probable cause" to revoke his probation, but it was just an artificial maneuver. The next week, on January 24, what officials deemed to be his "technical" violation of probation was set aside, and he was formally ordered to attend the Alternatives to Violence program starting in February.

With more than two weeks of school gone by, Kristin went over to Bunratty's on the evening of January 29 to meet Lauren and her new boyfriend, Brian Fazekas. Lauren had met him there the previous Friday. "It was the last place I thought I'd meet somebody I'd really like—in a bar," Lauren said. "Brian used to work there. He came up to me, and I asked him why he did that. He said the reason was I didn't look like I belonged there."

Cartier was working the door that evening. "That's where she actually noticed Mike," Brian said. "That's where she first saw him. . . . She didn't do anything or say anything. She just noticed him. And she said, 'You know, he's cute.' "

They met more formally and spoke together for the first time several days later. As a father, I think about it often. It was a meeting that depended on a long string of circumstances, an accident within an accident within an accident. If only he'd been in jail, I think . . . if only she'd stayed home . . . if . . . if . . . if . . .

Lauren and Kristin were thinking of going to Bunratty's again when Brian called and suggested they go to Axis instead. He had a good friend in one of the bands that was playing downstairs that night. It was a four-man group called Zen Under Fire, and it played what Brian called "a slightly alternative sort of guitar rock."

"I said, 'Well, Kristin and I had plans,' " Lauren remembers. "I invited her to come with me." Lauren offered to pay.

Kristin might still have stayed at home, but she remembered that she had a friend in another band playing upstairs at Axis that night. His name was Tim Blanchard, he was from Washington, D.C., and he was a student at the Berklee College of Music. He played guitar in an eight-piece band called The Even Up.

So she decided to go. Brian didn't have his car with him, so they walked over to the T. A slightly older woman named Christian—"she couldn't have been older than twenty-five," Lauren says—met them there. She worked with Lauren at Marty's, and she joined the group. "I didn't know her last name," Lauren said. "I just worked with her. We just went out that one night actually. She was very funny. She had a very good sense of humor. And she was making us laugh so hysterically I was embarrassed on the T."

The downstairs bands were still setting up when they got there, as Lauren recalls. They went upstairs to listen to Tim's group.

Kristin should have stayed there. But eventually they went back to listen to Brian's friends. Cartier was there. Kristin wanted to meet him. "She thought he was good-looking," Lauren said. "She kept saying, 'I want to meet him.' " But she wasn't about to walk up to him and say hi.

"Oh, I know him," Christian told her. "I'll introduce you to him."

Lauren said: "I think Christian was trying to be like the little matchmaker or something. She was, like, very bubbly and ditzy."

Lauren and Brian took a cab home. As Brian recalls it, Kristin and Cartier went to a late-night diner. Christian, it seems, disappeared.

Cartier must have thought he'd found the girl of his dreams. He liked noisy music with rebellious lyrics. So did she. He liked snakes. She liked snakes. He had a pet ball python named Mantis. She had a pet ball python named Circe. She even liked tattoos. Long before this, she had designed one for herself, a Celtic pattern to go around her ankle. Besides, he was big and strong. Kristin liked to go to places where a fellow like that could come in handy.

At the outset, Cartier did his best to make Kristin like him. He was sweet and generous. Sometimes he showed his better side by doting on his little half brother, Justin, now three, and taking the little boy with him to the Children's Museum and other spots in Boston.

"I tried very hard to get through to him," said Kimberly Cartier, Gene Cartier's third wife and Justin's mother. "He really was a good kid. He had a lot of anger in him. I don't know how old he was when they [Gene and Penny Cartier] separated, but I know that kid went through hell. For eight years, he was in state custody. When he got out, Gene thought he could take him, but it was really too late. He wouldn't let anybody close to him."

Kristin knew he could be considerate. She knew he could be a tough guy, too. She expected him to take care of her. What she didn't know were his secrets, his hatred of women who didn't do what he told them to do. Kristin had her secrets and turned them into art. He had his secrets and turned them into violence.

9

It took me months to discover how much slack the system had cut for Michael Cartier. I'm sure I still don't know how much he got away with. I'm sure no one else does either.

"He was obviously a very manipulative kind of guy, a guy who knew how to do what he had to do," Chief Probation Officer Tobin said after Kristin's murder. "But that wasn't as readily visible as it is now. Hindsight is great sight."

For instance, Tobin asserted, Cartier had done all that the BMC probation office expected of him, completing the Alternatives to Violence program as required. "Cartier went through it," Tobin told me in our first conversation in late June 1992. "He showed up each time. You don't send probationers away when they do what they're supposed to do."

What Tobin didn't tell me was that Cartier didn't do what he was supposed to do until he was given a second chance. He had actually dropped out of the course and, incredibly, was allowed to sign up for it again. I found that out a month after I spoke with Tobin, quite by accident, when I spoke with a helpful state official who agreed to give me a chronology compiled from official records. It showed that Cartier attended the first meeting of the Alternatives to Violence group on February 5, 1992, the starting date of a new six-week program, and then skipped the next class, February 12.[1]

Judge Donovan, who ordered Cartier into the program, said recently that he would have sent him straight to jail at that point to serve out the rest of his one-year term. "If I find someone in violation of probation, I send them off to jail immediately to complete their sentence," he said. As the sentencing judge, he remembered the case clearly.[2]

Unfortunately, there is no requirement to send such cases back to the judges who know something about them. It is a blind spot in the system that is especially troublesome in incidents of domestic violence where one judge's stern warnings mean little or nothing in the midst of the next judge's busy day. Cartier's case went before Linda Giles, a judge who had never dealt with him before. She revoked his probation at a hearing on February 14, 1992, but it was a paper edict. Evidently acting on Barrett-Moeller's recommendation, the judge "stayed" imposition of the six-month sentence until June, when the case could be reviewed. Instead of sending him back to jail, the court allowed Cartier to start the course over, beginning April 1. That gave him what amounted to a two-month holiday, more than enough time for some untutored mayhem.

Barrett-Moeller, who ran the program, declined to talk to me in the days following the murder, after consulting with Chief Justice Tierney.[3] She said there were "still legal limitations on what I can say," although she did not spell them out. She said she was sorry about what happened, but still could not talk.[4] Had Cartier conned her like most of the women he dealt with? Or was she being protective of the successes she'd been claiming for her Alternatives to Violence Group? Tobin said she was "a ferocious probation officer."

"We tend to be a punitive department," Tobin claimed. "We are not a bunch of social rehabilitators." In Michael Cartier's case, it was anything but punitive. Beyond that, the BMC probation office was a department that seemed to operate in a vacuum. Cartier's record of psychiatric problems, his admissions under Section 12 as a danger to himself or others, his reliance on a powerful drug to control manic depression should have disqualified him from the court-run rap sessions.

Tobin once again pleaded ignorance. "If we had information that he had a prior history of mental illness, or that he was treated in a clinic or that he had been hospitalized, then what we probably would have done is recommend that a full-scale psychological evaluation be done for him," Tobin told the *Boston Herald* in early June of 1992 after Kristin was killed. "We didn't know about it."[5]

There was, to put it plainly, no excuse for not knowing. Tom Casey, the probation officer in Brighton, knew. So, at least in part, did Rich DeAngelis in Malden. The psychologists at Deer Island knew. At one point, they'd even had his clothes taken away from him. All Tobin's office had to do was pick up the phone to find out what a menace Cartier was. Even more outrageous is Tobin's flaccid declaration of what would have happened if they had known: "a full-scale psychological evaluation."

Cartier told Kristin that he had been in trouble with the law before, but she was too pleased at having a new boyfriend to question his explanations. He was endearing. He was sincere. He wanted to be liked. "She told me about him the night she met him," Chris Dupre said. "She said, 'I met this good guy. He's really nice.' She seemed very enthusiastic about him."

She told big sister Helen about him, too. Helen was her confidante, the person she most admired. Helen paused when Kristin told her that Cartier was a bouncer at Bunratty's and had a very large tattoo.

"Well, ah, is he nice?" Helen asked.

"Well, he's nice to me," Kristin said.

On February 7, the day after Cartier's first violence class at the courthouse, there was a birthday party for Lauren at the house in Brookline. Kristin invited Cartier and introduced him to her friends. They were not impressed.

"I had a very bad feeling about him when I met him. Somebody told me he'd been in jail," said Lisa Esformes, a good friend of Kristin's who had gone to BU for a couple of years and then transferred to Colby-Sawyer College in New London, New Hampshire. "I asked Kristin about it," Lisa said of Cartier's jail time. "She said, 'I think he's learned his lesson.'"

Bekky Elstad met Cartier at the party, too. He wasn't much of a conversationalist. "Kristin said, 'Come over and meet my boyfriend,' " Elstad said. "I never really spoke with him. She said he was intimidated by her friends because they were all college educated."

Kristin knew Cartier was on probation, but all she had was his version of what happened. "She said he'd been in jail for beating up his old girlfriend," Chris Dupre remembers. "She knew that pretty early on."

"She did know that," Bekky Elstad said. "But when she talked to him about it, I think he minimized what he had done. I remember her being worried about that because she had a teacher and a friend [Ross Ellenhorn] who counseled her that when men say they slap women, they mean that they beat them. She wanted him to get counseling."

Above all, Kristin wanted to believe him and his excuses. She didn't know that he had a rap sheet three pages long, including an arrest for killing a kitten. "I think he told her that his mom had left him, that he'd always been raised in foster homes, that he was messed up," Amber Lynch said. He seems to have told her that all he did was slap Rose and that Rose hit him.

"She didn't know that Mike had attacked this woman with scissors," Lauren Mace said. "He told her it was a two-way thing, that he was the one who was sent away. He said that it was her fault, too, but she was a woman so she wasn't sent to jail. When she told me stuff like that, I thought of it as a basis for breaking up. Kristin had so many excuses for what he had done."

Lisa Esformes had the same experience. "I heard every excuse in the book from that guy, out of Kristin's mouth," Lisa said.

Kristin just couldn't believe that someone so "nice" to her could be that much at fault. Perhaps she didn't know that was a hallmark of many men who beat women. They hide their compulsions, at first. Like so many other women, Kristin was fooled. She felt sorry for him. Besides that, she was an artist. Perhaps she thought she had some interesting raw material, some promising stone that she could sculpt into shape.

Cartier did his best to give her that impression. He took her out to dinner and escorted her to nightclubs. He bought her little things, the kind she liked. For Valentine's Day, he gave her a rose, a heart, and a teddy bear. "For someone especially nice," he told her in a card. "I got the rose because I think you are very special. I got the teddy bear because you are huggable and warm. And the hart [*sic*] because I think you have a big one. Love, Mike."

Kristin couldn't afford much for herself. Rosemary and I didn't know it, but she was spending almost every bit of spare cash she had on the 14-karat gold sheets for the madonna she was painting for Rosemary. She often called on big brother Edmund, thirty-one, an assistant vice president at a brokerage firm in New York, or big sister Helen, thirty-two, a lawyer then in private practice in Washington, for help. Kristin sometimes referred to Ed as "the Bank of Edmund." In February, around the time Cartier started squiring her around, she called Ed for a quick loan to keep American Express from canceling her card. He sent her $350 in early March. She sent him a thank-you card with a note that said: "Dear Ed, Thanks for saving my ass. I'll pay you back as soon as I can."

It was the last time he heard from her in writing. He spoke with her once or twice by phone that semester, about plans for a summer vacation on Jekyll Island without Mom and Dad. Rosemary and I were planning to go west that fall to visit her brothers and other relatives. The Lardner children were arranging to get a place on Jekyll anyway. But Ed found it harder than ever to get Kristin on the phone.

I noticed the same thing, much more often than in years past. Kristin's roommates usually said she was down at the Museum School, working late. Sometimes I suppose she was, but I remember being a bit suspicious about that. I realize now that she was probably out with Cartier.

"I didn't like him, but he was really nice to her for a long time," Lauren said. "He'd buy her things . . . like the teddy bear with a rose. It didn't match him, but it was really sweet." Lauren didn't like him because of his looks and his manners. Too tough. Too angry. Too foulmouthed. And yet, she said, "He'd say hello, he'd get us into the bar he was working at for free. He was a little rude sometimes, but you'd just deal with that."

As the weeks wore on, Cartier started to argue with Kristin. One of the problems was his jealousy, another sign of trouble. Kristin didn't flirt with other men, but he would accuse her of it without a second thought. Lauren's ex-boyfriend Andy Meuse often came over to the house even after he broke up with Lauren. "We were still friends, and he'd come over and hang out," Lauren said. "Mike used to say to Kristin, 'Oh, are you going out with him, too?' He was really rude. She only went out with him for two months. She kept thinking nothing would happen to her. I said, 'Why? It's not like you knew him for a long, long time.' "

That's just the trouble. Finding a new boyfriend these days can be a dangerous game. American girls have always been freer to exercise their own judgment and see the world plainly, with all its vices and dangers on display. Even in the nineteenth century, as Tocqueville observed, "In no other country is a girl left so soon and so completely to look after herself. . . . Before she has completely left childhood behind, she already thinks for herself, speaks freely and acts on her own."[6] By the same token, marriage appears as much more of a constraint. The feminist movement of recent decades has, of course, emphasized the inequity of remaining barriers and the need for more freedom for women. But freedom has its risks, and not merely sexual ones. There is nothing new about violence against women, but the more equal and independent women become, the more danger they face from men like Cartier, men who can be engaging, attentive, and endearing until the women in their lives fail to do what they're told.[7]

Cartier told friends that Kristin broke up with him because she wanted to see other people. That wasn't true, but that's why he killed her. "If he couldn't have her, no one else was going to," Bekky Elstad said. "He was jealous. He was very, very insecure. That's what jealousy is."

Pathological jealousy that manifests itself in stalking and persistent surveillance when the woman leaves or attempts to leave is not evident in all men who batter. "Its presence should be seen as a significant indicator of potential homicidality," says David Adams of Emerge. "Closely related to this is extreme possessiveness, which is often manifested by the abuser's unwillingness to accept the end of the relationship. Women who leave this type of man are subjected to ongoing harassment and pressure tactics, including multiple phone calls, homicide or suicide threats, uninvited visits at home or work, and manipulation of the children."[8]

Cartier's antipathy toward blacks caused difficulties, too. Kristin had black friends, girls and boys. In high school she went to a prom with a black classmate. After they started dating, "Mike asked her if she ever went with a black guy," Lauren Mace remembers. "She said yes. Mike got mad. Kristin was never a prejudiced person. She should have seen this as a bad signal."

Rose Ryan was still worried that Cartier was going to come after her. She didn't know about Kristin, but she had learned from a friend in late February that Mike was out. He was still making obnoxious calls to her mother's house. But by now, Rose had a new boyfriend, Sean Casey, twenty-three. He was shorter but solidly built, and, as Rose puts it, "I think he intimidated Mike because he had more tattoos. Mike knew Sean from before." Sean decided it was time for a talk.

Around March 1, Cartier was working the front door at a nightclub called Man Ray when Sean Casey showed up. "He knew I was coming," Casey said. "He had a lot of friends there. I had a couple of people with me, too, but I just wanted it to be me and him. For six or seven months previous, I heard he was going around saying he was going to beat up anybody that goes with Rose. Then he found out she was going with me."

Cartier made sure Casey was searched at the door, and then both went inside. They eyed and avoided each other for a while. Finally Casey went up to him. Cartier was sitting down, with a bike seat in his hand.

"I heard you were going to start trouble with Rose or beat me up," Casey said to him.

"Oh no," Cartier assured him. "That's not true. I have no problems with you. No problems with Rose. It's other people trying to get me in trouble."

Casey nodded at the odd item in Cartier's hands.

"What are you going to do with the bike seat?" Casey asked him.

"Oh, nothing," Cartier said blandly. "I was just standing around with it."

Casey brought up Rose again. He told Cartier she should be able to go anywhere she wanted without worrying about what might happen.

"She can't come to Boston," Cartier responded. "I have a restraining order against her."

Casey couldn't believe what he'd just heard. "What? What restraining order? What are you talking about?" he asked Cartier.

"Well," Cartier amended, "she can't come to any shows where I might be. She has to stay away from me."

Casey wasn't buying that. "She can come to any shows she wants," he told Cartier. "She's going to go to shows and there's nothing you can do about it."

As they were talking, a young woman with chestnut hair walked by. It was Kristin. Cartier nodded at her as she passed. "I don't need Rose anymore," he told Casey. "I have my own girlfriend."

The encounter with Sean Casey made Cartier nastier, more belligerent. He was someone who had to take out his frustrations by lashing out at others. Kristin had no idea what happened at Man Ray. She had a good time that night. But shortly after that, Cartier hit her for the first time.

It happened after a party sometime in early March. Mike took Kristin, and once they were there, he got into a fight with Amber Lynch's boyfriend, Mitch. Some say Mitch provoked it, but Kristin was upset with Mike and went back to her flat. So did roommate Matt Newton, who was also at the party. Lisa Esformes, who was spending the weekend in Brookline, remembers the angry procession.

"All of a sudden, Matt stormed into the house," Lisa said. "Then Kristin stormed in. She said, 'Mike had to hit somebody.' Mike finally showed up. Matt didn't want to let him in the door, but he got in and went to Kristin's room."

"She told me he was really, really mean," Amber Lynch said later.

At first, Kristin told her that Cartier had called her dirty names. "But later, when I was over at her house, she said, 'Oh, he hit me. He punched me in the head.'"

Lisa, who was visiting at the time, remembered what it sounded like from the other side of Kristin's door. "I heard him screaming at her, calling her horrible names," Lisa said. "I could hear him punching the wall."

After that, Cartier seemed to quiet down. All of a sudden, he and Kristin walked out arm in arm. Later, Kristin called from Cartier's apartment, talking in a fast, low voice. "I'm at Mike's place," she told Lisa. "I have something to tell you, but I can't. Mike just walked in the door." Lisa offered to come over to talk. Cartier's apartment in Allston was just a few blocks away. "No, no, you can't," Kristin said in what struck Lisa as urgent, frightened tones. "Mike's here."

Kristin arrived back home in Brookline the next afternoon. She told Lisa that "we ended up in a huge fight." Kristin didn't say anything about Cartier's hitting her, but Lisa urged her to break off with him anyway.

"I said, 'Kristin, please get out of this relationship,'" Lisa said. "I didn't know he was abusing her physically."

"You don't understand," Kristin told her. "You don't have my background." What she seemed to be saying was that she understood people like Cartier, people with violent temperaments. What she seemed to be suggesting was that she could handle the situation.

"I think it had to do with people she knew when she went to school in Washington," Lisa said. "Punk rockers and the hard-core scene. . . . She was used to that. And I was over-reacting."

Lisa had known Kristin since their first week as freshmen at BU. They had different tastes in things like music, but they became very close. "She always wore black," Lisa said. "She said, 'I just can't wear colors.' We had a lot of fun. I loved her so much. I felt like she was my sister."

Lauren Mace didn't know about Mike's hitting Kristin, either. "She told me they were arguing in her room. She said he pushed her down," Lauren remembered. "But she wasn't like, hurt. I think she was scared to tell me some things about him because she knew I'd be mad, like a parent. He always used to take her out and buy her things, but they used to fight a lot. I could always hear them arguing, in her room."

But as far as Lauren knew, "he never laid a hand on her. Lisa and I were very, very apprehensive about that," Lauren said. "We were waiting for it to happen. Lisa would start fights with Kristin about it. If Mike was at our house, Lisa wouldn't come over. I told Lisa that was ridiculous, but we both had the same idea [that Kristin should not be going out with Cartier]. Lisa chose to aggravate her about it. I tried to be negative."

Kristin may have been too embarrassed to tell them more. She had always been outspoken in her disdain for men who abused women. Now she was making an exception for Cartier. She felt sorry for him. She knew what a tortured life he had even if she didn't know all the particulars. She couldn't bring herself to confide in Lauren or Lisa, but she told Bekky Elstad that he had hit her.

"She freaked out on that," Bekky said. "I think when it happened, she was saying, 'Get away from me. I don't want to talk to you.' That set him off. He told her he was sorry. He was all broken up. She wanted to believe him."

Amber Lynch said Kristin told her that she and Mike both cried after the fight. "After that, she said they weren't going to see each other for a while because he thought he was bad for her."

Kristin came home in mid-March for spring break, outwardly bright and cheerful. Kevin VanFlandern's mother remembers standing in line with Kevin at the neighborhood Safeway store on Connecticut Avenue when "a young, vibrant girl came up and gave Kevin a hug and said, 'I'm so glad to see you.' She seemed so full of life, so exuberant. I thought to myself, 'Gosh, why can't I feel that way?' "

That was Kristin, smiling that infectious smile of hers, even when she was gloomy on the inside. This, of course, is her father talking. Her friends noticed her moody spells more than I did. I rarely asked what was bothering her. Why should I when I got such a great hug and a

smile to boot? She sometimes moaned about her teachers and grades.
She sometimes worried about her chances of success without starvation.
I told her she was smart enough and talented enough to do anything
she wanted and make a go of it. If she seemed skeptical about such
cheerleading, I could bring back the laughter with a quip or a light
remark. Her friends used the same formula. It almost always worked.

On this trip, she showed how happy she was to be home by cook-
ing dinner for the entire family, something she'd never done before.
When I told her how much I liked it, she was really pleased. It was a
Greek recipe for chicken. Kristin told me what the name of it was, but
I'm afraid to say I remember only how wonderful it tasted. She learned
it from a boxful of fancy recipes Helen had sent her. They disappeared a
few weeks after she was killed when a crew renovating the apartment
for her landlords trashed most of her belongings a day before her brothers arrived in a pickup truck to retrieve them.

Kristin spent most of her time that week as she usually did on
spring break, going out with friends. One night she and Kevin went to
a bar in the Adams-Morgan section, a downstairs lounge called Hell
(the upstairs lounge is Heaven). She told him about her troubles with
Cartier.

"She told me a lot of the problems she was having," Kevin said.
"She basically said he was kind of a jerk and they weren't getting along.
She admitted he hit her a couple of times. She was trying to dump
him." But she didn't say she was afraid. "She had a pretty strong
pride," Kevin said. "She usually didn't show she was afraid of people."

Her mother and I can attest to that. We wanted all the children to
be independent minded, to think for themselves, even if we also wanted
them to do what we said. The result, I think, was a warm, noisy, argu-
mentative family. If the parents sometimes shouted to make a point,
about politics, sports, or teenage habits, so did the kids.

"Before I was sixteen, I'd get caught doing things I wasn't supposed to be doing," Lauren Mace said. "I was afraid to tell my parents
the truth. Kristin said she was the opposite. She'd yell and scream and
fight. But we handled problems the same way. I was really scared and
so, probably, was Kristin."

Sometimes I wonder about that. Is it better sometimes to admit weakness? To be afraid? To cry? After Kristin was killed, I asked a good friend who had lost a child in an auto accident how he handled it. "I cry a lot," he told me. So do I. It helps. Would things have turned out differently if Kristin had been afraid and said so, as loudly as she could? I don't know. I do know that she asserted her rights, as we taught her to. She relied on the law to keep her safe.

At the Lardner house, the spring break was memorable on another score. One morning—it had to be late morning if Kristin was up—Kristin was on the phone in the kitchen. She was in her bathrobe, fresh from the shower. Mira was there. She noticed a tattoo above Kristin's left ankle. Friends say she got it on a trip to New Hampshire from someone Cartier knew.

"Kristin, that's a cool Celtic cross," Mira told her.

Rosemary entered and noticed it, too. "What's that on your leg?" she asked Kristin.

Here accounts differ.

According to Mira, "Kristin said, 'It's a tattoo.'

"Mrs. Lardner said, 'No, it isn't.'

"Kristin said, 'Yes, it is.'

"Charlie came downstairs at that point. Mrs. Lardner said, 'Charlie, tell me that isn't a tattoo.' Charlie said, 'It isn't a tattoo.' Mrs. Lardner said, 'Good.' I guess she decided it was a stencil."

The other, shorter version is Rosemary's. "I knew it was a tattoo," she said. "I just decided not to recognize it as such. I said to Kristin, 'That's not a tattoo, is it?' And Kristin said, 'Okay, it isn't.' "

"You'd be so proud of me," Rosemary said after the murder when I asked her about the tattoo. With a smile she recalled all the curious stares and raised eyebrows she drew—in the back of the church, on the subway platform, and other places—because of Kristin's sweet rebelliousness. "You have no idea what I ignored."

Kristin was more enthusiastic than ever about her art that spring. She was "really getting it together," she told me. She talked with Rosemary at much greater length: about an encyclopedia on jewelry Rosemary had given her at Christmas, about a class Rosemary was taking at night at the Smithsonian on decorative matting and framing, about gilding and faux finishes and maybe starting a gallery together.

"She was talking about how neat she thought a place called the Artful Hand at Copley Square was when she first went up to Boston," Rosemary said. "I thought, 'Well, I can do these things. She has this modern approach. We could start a gallery.' It was the first time we talked seriously about it. Kristin was delighted. It solved her problem about what she was going to do."

They talked about how expensive art supplies were. But Kristin didn't mention how she'd been scrimping to buy the gold leaf for the madonna. Rosemary realized how expensive the madonna was as soon as she saw it, after the shooting. "It must have cost her every dime she had," Rosemary said. Her teacher in the Smithsonian class, Hugh Phipps, had made that plain. "He said he was going to teach us cheap gilding," Rosemary said. "He said nobody can really afford to do real gilding." The last scheduled class for Rosemary's course was on gilding. Rosemary didn't go. It was held June 4, 1992, the day we buried Kristin.

Spring break ended in the usual hurry. I drove Kristin to National Airport on the afternoon of March 22, 1992. She had yet to tell her parents that she had a boyfriend, much less a boyfriend who hit her. The Sunday traffic was thick, and she got out of the car for a long sprint from the terminal to catch her plane. She was dressed in black as usual, loaded down with a duffel bag and heavy luggage. She gave me a kiss and a hug and hurried off, skipping easily through a mass of cars. She seemed in wonderful spirits. I did not see her again until I went to the morgue.

When Kristin got back to Boston, Cartier tried to make up with her. He bought her a card with a printed message that said, "I've been thinking a lot about our misunderstanding. . . . I hope we can put this one behind us." And he gave her a kitten. "It was really cute—black with a little white triangle on its nose," Amber Lynch said. "It was teeny. It just wobbled around. He stole it from an Allston pet store."

It didn't live long. Cartier put it on top of a door jamb. Kristin told him not to do it. She said it was too little to keep its balance.

Cartier didn't listen. The kitten fell off, landing on its head. Kristin had to have it destroyed.

Devastated, she called home in tears and told Rosemary for the first time about her new boyfriend. Rosemary was home alone when the phone rang. Part of the conversation was picked up by a malfunctioning answering machine. Rosemary put in a new tape and set aside the old one. We remembered it after the funeral. Day after day, I stared at it, telling myself I would transcribe it that very afternoon. It took me a couple of months before I could bring myself to listen to it. Kristin's voice was wavering. It was clear she'd been crying.

Rosemary: What does Mike do?

Kristin: Well, he does the same thing Jason did, actually. He works at Bunratty's.

Rosemary: He does what?

Kristin: He works at Bunratty's.

Rosemary: Oh. Is he an artist also?

Kristin: No.

Rosemary: Well, that's what I was asking. What does he—? Is he a student?

Kristin: No. He just—he works. He's a bouncer.

"Oh," Rosemary said, asking a few moments later why she was going out with a boy who wasn't pursuing an education. Kristin told her she wanted to have a boyfriend, "just like everyone else does."

As soon as I got home from work that night, Rosemary said, "Call your daughter."

"Which one?" I asked. "Kristin," she said.

When I called, Kristin began crying again as she told me about the kitten. She was also upset because she'd given Cartier a piece of jewelry she wanted to show her review board at the Museum School in May. He told her he'd lost it.

I told her, as gently as I could, that I didn't think she should be wasting her time going out with a boy who did such stupid things. I said it was easy to see why she was so upset. We talked about school and classes for a few minutes more and said goodnight.

Charlie called her around the same time. He'd just entered Franklin & Marshall College in Lancaster, Pennsylvania, that winter at age twenty-five. A few years of blue-collar jobs, from pumping gas to filleting fish, had convinced him to try higher education. He made straight A's that semester but not without a lot of anxiety. He used to call Kristin and tell her his problems. She was a good listener. Now she told him her problems, bursting into tears again as she explained what happened to the kitten.

"Get rid of him," Charlie advised his sister. "He's a zero."

"She just said he made her sad," Charlie remembers. "She said he didn't mean to do it. I said it doesn't matter. It just shows how stupid he is."

The "accident" with the kitten was a heavy blow to Kristin. She grew up with cats, all belonging to one or another of the Lardner children. At one point, there were three in the house, not counting an occasional litter that had to be given away. The only resident feline in Washington at the time was T.C., born in 1986. He belonged to Charlie, but Kristin was the one who kept book on him. It's called *Cat Tales,* the kind of nicely bound journal that you buy to fill in the blanks. Carefully filled out in Kristin's hand, it comes complete with heavily inked pawprints, a snatch of fur, inoculation dates, photographs taken by Kristin, and notations that his favorite activities included "waking people up" and "chasing girls." Whenever she was home, he smelled of Poison, the perfume she wore. T.C. still likes to sleep at the foot of her bed.

March was coming to an end. Lisa went to a pet store in Somerville and bought Kristin a new kitten, a ten-week-old female with a crooked tail and orange tiger stripes. That was Stubby, and she was a fast learner. Kristin was hoping that Cartier could still learn something, too. His new Alternatives to Violence course was scheduled to begin on April 1. She encouraged him to go.

Cartier went, but he had much more than Kristin's urgings to impel him. He knew he was risking another six months on Deer Island if he played hooky again. He'd told J. D. Crump, perhaps others, that he would never go back to prison. Crump said he shrugged it off. "It was a typical thing, 'You're not going to take me back,' " he maintained after Cartier killed himself. "Any ex-convict is going to say that."

Kristin went out with Cartier for the last time on the night of April 15, 1992, after one of his Alternatives to Violence classes. They went to the Rathskeller, a nightspot on Kenmore Square, and got into another argument.

"There was some sort of huffy thing at the Rathskeller," Brian Fazekas said. "I don't know what it was. Maybe they didn't get in or they got in for a while and then one of them wanted to leave and the other didn't."9

On the way home, they kept arguing as they walked up Commonwealth Avenue. "Both of them were pretty hard-headed," Brian said. "Neither of them would ever back down. It didn't matter what it was about. It could have been, 'You dropped my pencil,' and it would have turned into something."

At Packard's Corner, just above the BU campus, Cartier shoved her down onto the sidewalk, cutting her hand. She got up and set out for home. Cartier followed, pelting her with small stones and pebbles he found in the street. She kept trying to walk away from him, but he kept grabbing at her then falling back and throwing things.

"I'm going home," she told him. "Get away from me."

Cartier couldn't handle that. They passed a small construction site outside a fast-food store called the Wing-It. He picked up a small piece of reinforcing rod and threw it low, hitting her in the calf.

Kristin stepped up her pace. He kept after her. Again and again, she told him to "go home and leave me alone." She began running. He kept following her until she turned up a side street in Allston. The sign said Griggs Street.

It was a bad turn. The street was deserted, lined on one side with shuttered auto repair shops.

"Get away from me. I never want to see you again," Kristin told him. He caught up with her, grabbed her, and threw her down, calling her all sorts of names.

"He was saying, 'Get up, you stupid this,' and 'Get up, you stupid that,' " Brian remembered from talking to Kristin shortly afterwards. "I don't want to get into all the stuff he said, but it was very graphic. I'm sure you can imagine what he said."

Kristin left out the epithets in the affidavit she filled out later, but she was quite explicit about the beating.

"He pulled me into the street, threw me down and kicked me repeatedly in the head and legs," she said. Cartier, she told police, kept shouting at her, "Get up or I'll kill you." The same words he had used with Rose Ryan.

Kristin struggled to her feet. It was around 2 A.M., April 16, but luckily, a car stopped and two men helped her home. She was crying hysterically when she stepped in the door. Lauren and Brian asked her what happened.

"They'd been down on Kenmore Square," Lauren said. "I didn't understand why she didn't get a cab instead of having him follow her. She said, 'I didn't know what to do. I'd been drinking.' They were probably in several arguments."

Kristin refused to see him again. Cartier refused to accept that, as he did with Rose Ryan. He wouldn't take no for an answer. He began haunting Kristin by telephone, calling ten or more times a day. He warned her bluntly not to go to the police. He knew a complaint from her could send him back to jail. He had six months hanging over him for beating up Rose Ryan, but he made clear to Kristin he would hold it against her if he had to do the time. He told her "he might have to do six months, but she better not be around when he gets out." He didn't explain why he stopped at six months. He seems to have assumed he wouldn't get so much as an extra day for kicking Kristin in the head, but I don't think she questioned him about his arithmetic.

The threat kept Kristin quiet at first. She had a bit more than a year to go before graduation. Cartier would be out in half that time. She didn't want to live through an entire semester in Boston in fear of another violent attack. What should she do? What could she do?

At one point around this time, Charlie remembers, she told him she would like to have a gun "to go shooting with." She didn't mention

Cartier when she said that. She'd been talking with Charlie over the phone about the time during spring break in 1991 when he'd taken her out to his favorite haunt in West Virginia, an abandoned quarry near the Shenandoah River. He let her try a semi-automatic rifle and a pistol he'd acquired.

The mountains enchanted Kristin. "It had recently rained," she wrote Amy Buettner a few days later, "so the sky was clear and the river was roaring. All the little mountain creeks were running clear and cold. I saw a huge turkey, found a cool turtle shell and shot a 10 mm. pistol."

"Kristin had a great time," Charlie says. "We did about sixty rounds on the rifle, shooting into the dirt. Then we heard sirens. We got all paranoid. We thought it was the police. But it was just fire trucks going to a town near the quarry. Then we went down to the railroad tracks by the river and fired off the pistol. It was a Colt 10-millimeter. We shot it at a tin can. She was good. She made it jump three or four times. I couldn't hit it."

Kristin always wanted her brother to take her to West Virginia again. They talked about it that final spring and about how Kristin wished she had a gun of her own. "She wanted a handgun," he remembers. "I told her Boston was probably one of the worst places in the world to be caught with one." It never occurred to Charlie that she might have been thinking of protecting herself. Now he wonders.

Her fears aside, Kristin wanted to encourage Cartier to keep his violent temper under control. She agreed to take a once-a-week phone call from him the day he went to his Alternatives to Violence class. I suspect that must have made her refusal to see him anymore a bit ambiguous. What he needed was a flat and final no. But Kristin, like too many other women in such circumstances, was too kind.

She also called her teacher Ross Ellenhorn in hopes of getting Cartier into Emerge. Kristin urged Cartier to try it. She already knew he wasn't the star pupil in the courthouse class. "One day she was laughing," Amber Lynch said. "She said, 'Oh, Mike went to his Alternatives to Violence class tonight. He got a lot of the answers wrong.' "

That may have been in early February, the one class Cartier took before dropping out. Kristin had just started dating him. But now, his failures in a classroom quiz were no longer a laughing matter. He was a menace in fact as well as on paper. She asked Ellenhorn what to do. It was either Friday, April 17, the day after the attack on Griggs Street, or the following Monday, April 20. The details were still fresh in her mind as she described what happened.

"I told her that with a guy that dangerous, there was no real way to avoid it happening again," Ellenhorn told me after Kristin's murder. "I wanted her to think about going into a shelter, to think about getting a restraining order. Although, I know, a restraining order is just a piece of paper. Mostly, I was trying to get her matched with reality."

Kristin may have told him Cartier had hit her before. She said nothing about his beating previous girlfriends. "She was concerned about herself, but mostly about getting him into Emerge," Ellenhorn remembered. "I made clear that Emerge isn't a panacea, that there was still a chance of him abusing her."

Ellenhorn gave her the phone number for Emerge; he called Kristin back that night around 10:30 P.M. to make sure she had given it to Cartier. She had. Cartier tried it, then called her back and yelled at her for giving him a number that just gave him a recording.

"He told her, 'This is just a stupid recording,' " Ellenhorn said. "That's typical. He wanted to make her responsible for him not going."

At that point, Ellenhorn and Kristin agreed on another approach. She would call Cartier again, give him a number that would work, and say nothing else to him.

"I tried to make clear to her that what he was doing was trying to keep control," Ellenhorn said. "I think he was also making her confused. I told her that he could kill her. A very large percentage of the guys in our program could kill. He was starting to fit the profile of a real killer. Because she was leaving him. That's when things get dangerous. I could sense she was getting more nervous." Ellenhorn had no more contact with Kristin after that, although he made it clear to her that she could call him anytime.

Like everyone else who knew Kristin—parents, relatives, friends, acquaintances who might have had a glimpse of trouble, even those who didn't—Ellenhorn scolded himself after she was killed for what he didn't do. For not searching for and contacting Cartier's probation offi-cer. For not contacting Kristin again. He tried several times, then gave up. He wishes he had done more. Rosemary and I wish we had done more. We are consumed by victimhood. We have produced a society that encourages us to blame ourselves or our loved ones for being raped, murdered, beaten, duped, or defrauded. We are told that we "asked for it" or at least provided the fertile ground. We have got to disabuse ourselves of the notion that "there are no bad boys, only bad societies." There are plenty of "bad boys" (and girls) out there, committing real crimes, and only a misguided society will keep making excuses for them.

Cartier showed up at Emerge's offices in Cambridge a week later, around April 28 by Ellenhorn's calculations. As one of the counselors, Ellenhorn happened to be on duty that Tuesday night. He'd never seen Cartier before, but he realized who he was when Cartier wrote down Kristin's name on the intake form under "Victim."

"Are you on probation?" Ellenhorn asked him. The question was a standard part of the process.

Cartier said that he was.

"I'm going to need the name of the probation officer," Ellenhorn told him.

"Fuck this," Cartier responded. "No way."

With that, he ripped up the intake form, ripped up the contract form, and carefully tucked the torn papers in his pocket. He wasn't about to leave them there.

"He knew," Ellenhorn said. "He knew what kind of connection would be made. The majority of the people we get want us to contact their probation officers—to show what good boys they've been. That was the last thing he wanted."

Cartier kept going to his classes at the Suffolk County courthouse until he "graduated." It was the only way to get rid of that suspended sentence. He was also hoping that Kristin would take him back. Abus-ers often say they're sorry and they may even mean it, until the next time they lose their temper or decide to lose it.[10]

He was rated as somewhat passive at the anti-violence classes, but he got through them without any more truancy on May 6. The next day he walked into Gay's Flowers and Gifts on Commonwealth Avenue, a few doors west of Marty's. It was a short walk from Cartier's apartment on Glenville, which parallels Commonwealth. He bought a dozen red roses for Kristin, and he gave the proprietors a brightly decorated card to be delivered with the flowers. The florist told me about the card, but I didn't know what it said until two years later, when I found it inside one of Kristin's notepads.

Dear Kristian [*sic*]

I hope you don't mind the roses. I bought them in thoughts of you because you are always on my mind. Because a lot of things have happened between us and I wish they didn't. So I'm going to do the things that we discussed because we both know that I need help. With your help and the people from Emerge we both know that I can become a better person inside for myself as well as for others. This is one reason I bought you roses because I appreciate what you are doing for me. And I love you for it. And one more reason is I hope you did well in school today. So what I'm trying to say is Kristian please don't give up on me. I know it's hard because I hurt you inside, but I'm trying to change because I love you and I don't want you to be afraid of me anymore. I know it will take some time because I know you're hurting inside because of me. So please just hang in there and don't give up on me.

> I love you very much
> Michael Cartier

The message may have been heartfelt, but Cartier didn't write it. The handwriting, except for the signature, belonged to Leslie North, a young woman who had known Cartier for years. They'd gone to Lawrence High School together before he dropped out. Her boyfriend was in the back seat of the car in the 1988 crash when Cartier suffered his injuries. She was his counselor, his advisor whenever lovelorn. Kristin couldn't stand her.

The first I heard about North was on a visit to Marty's Liquors.

She had worked there herself, just outside the main store in the redemption center, where customers returned empty bottles and cans. Later, in late spring, she moved to another Marty's store in Newton.

Some of the clerks at the Allston store mentioned North in connection with an incident that took place the afternoon Kristin was killed. They said a friend of North's had been harassing Kristin at the cash register, just a few hours before the shooting, and that North had been in the store around the same time.

Others at the store remembered North in connection with Cartier—and the gun he used to kill Kristin. "There's a girl who works at our Newton store," Martin Siegel, one of the store managers, told me. "She showed [Cartier] how to fire the gun. She knew how because she was in the army. She was there [at Cartier's apartment] the day he bought the gun."

Siegel said he'd heard this secondhand and then confronted North about it. She confirmed showing Cartier how to fire the gun, he said. "She said, 'I didn't want him to hurt himself,' " Siegel recalled. Siegel said he suspected that North knew where Cartier bought the weapon.

Louis Siegel, another store manager, said he spoke with North, too, and she said Cartier had told her he was going to kill Kristin. "She didn't believe him, I guess," Louis Siegel said.

I was amazed. I had the report of the homicide investigation. At least I thought I did. Unless it was incomplete, the police hadn't talked to Leslie North. It seemed to me it was time that someone did.

She was working the cash register at the redemption center in Newton when I walked in. Tall, dark-haired, and somewhat puffy-faced, she didn't seem surprised when I introduced myself. She said she'd known Cartier for years. They'd both been "in and out of foster homes." "He was hanging around with the wrong people," she explained. Then he moved in with North and a friend of hers named Hope. North said he stayed with them for "several years." He confided in her.

Sometimes North was his informer as well as his confidante. Rose Ryan remembers that there were times Cartier accused her of dating another boy when she and Mike weren't getting along. Leslie North saw Rose with that boy on the subway once, and, Rose says, "She reported it to Mike. She was like his good buddy. It was towards the end, when I was trying to get away from him. . . . The way she was with him, she would help with anything."

North said: "He always called me when he had a fight with his girlfriends. He did have a very bad temper. I've seen him really mad. He used to break windows, break into places all the time." She said Cartier told her that "his father used to beat him up a lot when he was younger."[11] But before Rose Ryan, she said, "I had never seen him touch another woman."

I was skeptical about that. I wondered, too, about North's claims that she and Kristin liked each other. Cartier had introduced them in February, but Kristin's friends said Kristin didn't like North at all, and I suspect the feeling was mutual. Kristin, I'm sure, would not have been happy if she'd known whose handwriting it was on the note that came with the roses.

North volunteered that the handwriting on the note was hers. "He told me what to write," she said. He said that he was trying to change, that he needed help, that he wanted to be a better person. He said, 'I'm trying to get back with her.' "

One of the proprietors at the flower shop, Alan Najarian, delivered the roses, and the card, to Kristin's flat. "One of her roommates took them," Najarian remembered. "He was kind of reluctant. I think he must have known who they were from."

A gentle, soft-spoken man, Najarian added that he had been reading a great deal "about how men go around brutalizing women. Domestic violence seems to have hit an all-time high. Something's got to be done about it."

Cartier had told Rose Ryan he had a gun. Perhaps he told Kristin, too. Boston police think he may have gotten the weapon the day of the murder, but Leslie North remembered his showing it to her "shortly after [he and Kristin] broke up," probably in early May.

Why did he get the gun? "He said, 'Ah, just to have one,' " North said. "I asked him, 'What do you need a gun for?' He said, 'You never know.' I didn't realize you're not supposed to get a gun if you've been in jail. I didn't tell anyone he had it."

North said Cartier told her he paid $750 for it. He had a box of bullets for the gun, too. Special bullets. It was sixty-one years old, a Colt .38 Super, serial number 13645, one of 65 to 70 million handguns loose in the United States. It was shipped brand-new on January 12, 1932, to a hardware store in Knoxville, Tennessee, where all traces of it disappeared.

"The sad but horrible truth is that with reasonable care, there's no reason it shouldn't last one hundred years or more," John C. Killorin, spokesman for the U.S. Bureau of Alcohol, Tobacco and Firearms, said of the old gun. Some authorities say $750 is far too high a price to pay for a gun like that, but as Killorin said, "The street price depends on how desperate you are to get a gun."

The .38 Super was designed in the thirties because some people thought the .45 wasn't powerful enough. Bullets for them are hard to find, and expensive. "It takes a very rare cartridge," Killorin said. "For some reason, the gun was never popular in the United States. The ammunition is available, but it's a tough gun to buy bullets for."

According to North, he got everything at once. "I was at his home the day he bought it," she said. "I was a little nervous. I asked him where he got it. He said, 'Oh, from some kid.' . . . I guess he bought the bullets with the gun. He had them in his hand, like six or eight of them. They were in a box. He took them out. I said, 'Geez, Mike.' "

There were rumors that North's stepfather had owned a gun and that North may have provided him with the weapon. She denied it. She said her stepfather didn't own a gun and had never had one as far as she knew. She also denied showing Cartier how to use the pistol.

"I was messing around with it," she said. "I showed him how to clean it. I was in the army a little while. I thought he was going to get a permit for it, get it legalized. . . . He knew how to load it. He knew how to aim it. I showed him just a little bit of safety, just how to hold it when you shoot. I told him, 'Just don't ever load it if you're not using it.' I just pretty much told him, 'Be careful.' "

North had been at Kristin's house in Brookline several times after Cartier introduced them. "Mike really loved her," North said.

Perhaps he thought he did. Michael Cartier never knew how to "really love" anyone. His sentiments were too self-centered, carrying sadness wherever they wandered. He wanted others to love him. When it became apparent that they did not, that they could not, he took revenge.

North remembered something else Cartier told her after he got the gun.

"If I kill Kristin, are you going to tell anyone?" he asked her.

" 'Of course I'm going to tell,' " she said she replied. "I didn't take him seriously. He just laughed. . . . He said that once or twice to me. This was like right after he got the gun. I should have said something and I didn't. I never took anything he said seriously anyhow."

I grimaced as I walked to my car. How many others, I wondered, had a glimmering of what Cartier might do? And what of the harassment Kristin was subjected to a few hours before she was killed? North professed to know nothing of it. "They all hate me over at Allston because I knew Mike," she protested. "I'm getting harassed at that store." But when I described the person who reportedly had been cursing at Kristin—thinning hair, bad teeth, in his thirties—North said, to my great surprise, "You just described my boyfriend to a T. But why should he be harassing somebody he doesn't know?"

I had no idea. Could someone have been playing surrogate stalker or substitute harasser on Cartier's behalf? If so, was this just a spontaneous effort, or part of a mean-spirited and deliberate plan? I got no help from the boyfriend, a surly fellow who testily denied bothering Kristin when I spoke with him on the phone that evening. He said he couldn't even remember being in Marty's that day.

After speaking with North and, more briefly, her boyfriend, it seemed to me that the police should have talked to her, too, so I called Billy Dwyer. He was working the night shift as usual. He said he'd tried to contact North, but she never responded to the messages he'd left. Now, he said, the case was closed. He had other homicides to deal with. The conversation was friendly, but the message was clear. He wasn't about to get back into the case unless I could get someone from the Suffolk County DA's office to tell him to do so.

I went down to the DA's office the next day. The district attorney, then Newman Flanagan, wasn't in, but his secretary helped arrange an appointment with Flanagan's first assistant, Paul Leary.

Leary had heard about my poking around. I found out that much on a rather contentious visit to the Brookline town attorney's office, a few hours after talking with North. The Brookline police sergeant who talked with Kristin said he couldn't talk to me without the town attorney's approval.

I think the town attorney would agree that we did not get along. His name was David Turner, and when I walked into his office, unannounced, he was on the phone with someone, talking about how the town could apply "pressure" if whatever they were talking about didn't go smoothly. I identified myself and told him I wanted to talk to the sergeant but understood I needed the approval of the town fathers, if not the Norfolk County DA's office, before talking to the police. He said that was standard policy throughout Massachusetts.

At that point I'm afraid I broke some of my own rules, but perhaps the exception proves them. I said to Turner that what he had just told me was incredible. He said it was at least true in Brookline. I disputed that on the basis of what I'd read in the Boston papers. Was he really insisting, after all the statements Brookline police had made to the local press, that they stonewall the victim's father? I suggested that might not look too good in print. The conversation deteriorated from there. He lectured me on the danger of jeopardizing criminal prosecutions. I said that I'd been covering criminal cases before he ever got out of law school and had yet to see a real-life example of what he was talking about. He took umbrage, drawing up to full height, and said that he was sixty-one and a former assistant attorney general for the Commonwealth. I think I said, So what? He asked me to leave his office. I asked him to repeat Brookline's so-called policy first, so I could take it down word for word. It seemed clear that he knew nothing about Kristin's case. I told him that it was closed, that no prosecution was planned, that the perpetrator had killed himself, and that this had all taken place in Suffolk, not Norfolk County. Fortunately, I had with me a letter from Flanagan, offering condolences and stating that the case was closed. I handed it to Turner, and he retired to another room to make a phone call. When he came out, he said he had spoken with Leary and there was no objection to my talking with police since the case was closed. But Turner also said Leary wanted me to get in touch with him if I had any "additional information."

I've often wondered what would have happened to some other father of some other young woman who had been murdered on the streets, somebody who didn't have a press card to wave around?

Leary saw me the next day around noon. He gave me a sympathetic hearing. I mentioned my conversation with North about the gun and the possibility that she might know more about it, especially in light of what others told me she'd said. Leary said he would have someone talk to her, called the homicide unit, and asked them to send over a detective named Billy Mahoney.

Billy Dwyer showed up instead. He said he, too, had picked up reports that North supplied Cartier with the gun and that she "did not like Kristin at all." But Dwyer said he still felt that Cartier hadn't gotten the .38 until shortly before the shooting. Cartier had been looking around for a crowbar that afternoon, presumably to break in someplace. "Because of the crowbar thing, we felt he had gone and stolen it [the gun]," Dwyer said.

There was, however, no evidence that Cartier ever found the crowbar he was looking for. And he was still searching for one until very shortly before the shooting. Perhaps if he'd found it he would have bludgeoned Kristin to death instead of shooting her.

In any case, Dwyer said he had tried three times to talk to North. Now that I'd talked to her, he didn't see any point to it. "The fence is up," he said. I felt that whatever she had to say should be a matter of official record. Dwyer agreed to try again, but as it turned out, she got a lawyer. The interview never took place.

Dwyer had a pained look on his face as we spoke in Leary's office. A compassionate man, he seemed teary-eyed at times. By the end, he had me on the verge of crying, too, though I'd swear he started it. "Let it go," he urged me. "Let it go."

I told him I couldn't do that.

IO

Kristin had spent too much time with Cartier that semester. Now she was trying to get ready for her review board. She plunged into her artwork after the breakup, regularly working past nightfall at the Museum School. "She spent a number of very long days there and overnight once," Brian Fazekas, who had moved into the flat in Brookline, remembers. Her sister Helen kept trying to get her on the phone, without much luck. When they did talk, Kristin said she was working overtime at the school studios, trying to catch up. Her review board was set for the last day she could take it, Friday, May 8.

Cartier called her on May 7, the same day he sent the flowers. By the time they'd finished talking, she was furious. His promise to become a better person had wilted long before the roses did. Cartier owed her $1,000 for letting him use her Discover card to order a NordicFlex machine. Despite his access to cash, he didn't have any credit cards of his own. His father said he didn't even have a picture ID. So Kristin let him use the card to finance the exercise machine. Now, she told him over the phone, she wanted him to return it to the manufacturer. Cartier laughed at her and said, "I guess you're out the $1,000."

"There's absolutely nothing you can do about it," he taunted. "I'll see you later. Bye." And he hung up.

Seething, Kristin promptly called Cartier's probation officer, Diane Barrett-Moeller, and gave her an earful: about the exercise machine and the beating.

Kristin's call was another of the probation office's secrets. Tobin said nothing about it to the Boston press in the days after Kristin's murder, when it was becoming obvious that there was something terribly wrong with the handling of Cartier's case. Tobin did discuss the call with me, but only in response to my asking him about it. I had found out about it from Kristin's friends. He said he didn't "volunteer that information to the newspapers because they didn't ask about it."

"Your daughter was concerned," Tobin said. "She put a lot of emphasis on the weight machine. Mrs. [Barrett-] Moeller said, 'Get your priorities straight. You should not be worrying about the weight machine. You should be worrying about your safety. . . . Get to Brookline court, seek an assault complaint, a larceny complaint, whatever it takes . . . and get a restraining order.' " With a restraining order in place, Cartier would be committing a crime if he followed her around or even bothered her on the telephone.

The probation office's administrative log for Cartier sums up the conversation in these words, jotted down by Barrett-Moeller: "Rec'd call from an unidentified woman who stated D[efendant] had beaten her up. She stated she did not want to see him in jail but would rather he get help. Advised her to obtain a restraining order at her local court. She indicated later in the conversation that she lived in Brookline. She was also distraught over the fact that the D[efendant] still had her new $1,000 exercise machine. We discussed her priorities and PO advised her for her safety she must seek a restraining order at Brookline Court. The woman would not agree to do this as she was adamant that he not be incarcerated."[1]

Kristin naively assumed that the system would treat him with stern efficiency, that applying for a restraining order would bring swift action by criminal authorities. Cartier himself expected "six months" if she blew the whistle on him. Why should she think any differently? She didn't know how blind justice can be, how courts, police, and probation officers inhabit their own circumscribed worlds and have difficulty communicating between those worlds, let alone to outsiders. She thought the system worked. She is dead because it didn't.

According to Tobin, Kristin wouldn't give her name, even

though Barrett-Moeller asked for it twice. "We can't revoke someone's probation on an anonymous phone call," he said.

That overlooks the fact that all Tobin's office had to do was call the Brookline courthouse or the police station the next week and ask if any complaints had been filed against Michael Cartier. They had a name attached to them. It was Kristin's.

Tobin also claimed that his office could have taken no action because Kristin was "not the woman in the case we were supervising." That was like saying that probationers in Boston Municipal Court should only take care not to rob the same bank twice. It certainly was no barrier to officials in Brighton and Lawrence, who protected Rose Ryan by having Cartier's probation revoked in cases that had nothing to do with her. He was being supervised in Brighton for malicious destruction of private property and in Lawrence for the ketchup bottle episode as well as a burglary. In both courts, he was given jail time for what he did to Rose while on probation, quite aside from the sentence he got downtown in municipal court for the attack itself.

For much of the next day, Friday, May 8, Kristin was busy at the Museum School with her review board. She couldn't lug down the self-portrait she'd done after the beating, but she brought in some clay sculptures she'd made to hang from ceilings, along with jewelry, glass sculpture, and a figure painting. The dangling clay sculptures—the man and woman bound in conflicting postures—were quite powerful. Her reviewers gave her a full fifteen credits, but they seem to have been on different wavelengths. One found the works Kristin presented "very elegant" but "not strong" enough. Another encouraged her to experiment more with bound figures and pieces, one of her favorite approaches. Another felt she was "missing a level of interpretation that is personal. Her approach is too cautious. . . . The dangling clay pieces are the most promising." When she got back to Brookline, Amber Lynch remembers, "She told me she had a bad review board, that they misunderstood her."

Cartier, meanwhile, was called downtown for a meeting with his probation officer. Instead of moving to revoke his probation, Barrett-Moeller, in effect, told him what was up. The probation log for May 8 says: "D[efendant] rep[orted]. He was told he must stay away from this (unidentified) woman and have no direct or indirect contact with her. D[efendant] advised me that he had contacted Emerge but wasn't sure if he would follow through—advised D[efendant] to contact them immediately and also set up appt. [with] Dr. Bill Hudgins, Ct. Clinic, for psych. eval. 5/14/92. D[efendant] reminded to have no contact."

If Barrett-Moeller asked Cartier whether he had beaten "this (unidentified) woman" and how badly, there is no sign of it in her brief summary. But the exercise machine did come up. Failure to do something about that could have led to a grand larceny charge. As Tobin recounted the conversation, Barrett-Moeller told Cartier "she had received a complaint about an exercise machine that he got from a woman. She told him to get the exercise machine back to her. She told him she didn't want to hear about it anymore. And she ordered a full-scale psychiatric evaluation of him.[2] She also ordered him to report to her every week until the evaluation was completed."

Cartier did most of what he was told, while planning Kristin's murder. He saw the court-designated psychologist, William Hudgins, on May 21, and was scheduled to see him again on June 4, five days after he killed her.

Cartier called Kristin again on May 8. By then, she must have been having second thoughts about a restraining order. She warned him that if he didn't return the exercise machine, she was going to take court action. Perhaps that was just before Cartier walked into Barrett-Moeller's office and talked to her. In any case, he wasted no time in calling Kristin back. Very shortly after she warned him, Brian Fazekas remembers, he called again, from a pay phone. "Okay, okay," he told her, "I'll return the stupid machine."

Kristin was skeptical about that. And she was worried about more violence. She was still having recurring headaches from the beating in April. The warnings of her friends, her brother Charlie, her teacher Ross Ellenhorn, and now Cartier's probation officer rang in her ears. Charlie said it best: "Get rid of him. He's a zero." Her art reflected her apprehensions.

Staying in Boston until graduation the next year worried her the most. Cartier kept popping up. There was a party in early May at the house of someone named Larrissa. Kristin went with Amber Lynch and her boyfriend, Mitch. Cartier was there, at the door. He took one look at Mitch, whom he'd already fought, and said, "I'll kill him." Kristin said she wanted to leave, and they did. Where could she go without running into him?

Her review board over, Kristin spent the next few days talking to friends and deciding what to do next. She was in a quandary, and it showed. Lisa Esformes graduated in New London on Saturday, May 9, and Kristin went up for the ceremony. She gave Lisa a pinky ring she'd made for her. Then they went back to Boston to spend the rest of the weekend with Lisa's family and Lauren and Brian. Lisa remembers that Kristin "didn't look too good."

Kristin wasn't just worried about Cartier. Everyone she loved was leaving her, too. Lisa and Bekky Elstad were going back to California. Lauren was going to New Orleans with Brian. Matt Newton was moving to Maine. Amber Lynch was headed for the New York area. Kristin didn't know who she was going to live with the next year or where. There would be virtually no one left in Boston but a violent ex-boyfriend who had threatened to kill her.

On Monday, May 11, Lisa went over to Kristin's place to pick up her cat, which she'd left there with Stubby, before flying back to California. "Kristin came out of the shower, crying hysterically," Lisa said. "She wanted me to stay with her. She was my best friend. I had a hard time leaving her."

Jennifer Jones, another old Glenville Avenue roommate, was visiting Boston and called around the same time. She and Kristin were a great example of the principle that opposites attract. They were both from Washington and in fact had first met at a high school party there. Kristin, from Wilson, was wearing all black, topped off with bright red lipstick. Jennifer, from the National Cathedral School, was wearing white shorts, a polo shirt, and docksiders. "We just looked at each other and backed off," Jennifer remembers. But as the party was breaking up, the two of them discovered that another girl, about sixteen, had been trying to kill herself.

"She'd been ingesting literally everything she could get her hands on," Jennifer said. "Drugs, alcohol, rat poison, film developer. Kristin and I were the only ones who were worried about her. We looked at her and said somebody has got to help this girl. We made the boys whose house it was promise to take care of her. It was a real mess. In the end, she was taken to the hospital. She was there a good number of weeks."

Kristin and Jennifer met again on Glenville Avenue, first as next-door neighbors and then as roommates, when both were at BU. It took them a few weeks before they remembered where they'd first met. It took them a bit longer to discover that they'd both dated Andy Armstrong, who obviously favored young teenagers. Jennifer went out with him first, when she was fourteen. "He was called Spike when I dated him, because of his hair," Jennifer said. "He was a street vendor in Georgetown when I met him, selling jewelry and bracelets and sterling silver pieces." But Jennifer gave him less of her time than Kristin did before deciding he wasn't quite the right match. "We went to three movies and dinner," Jennifer said.

When Jennifer called that weekend, Kristin was less distraught about being abandoned by friends, more concerned about Cartier. "She wanted to get a restraining order," Jennifer said, "but she was so concerned about making his life worse. She said he's had these problems, he's been screwed over so many times." Jennifer listened carefully. They were good friends partly because, as Jennifer put it, "we were the best listeners around. We could talk to each other for hours because we listened to each other."

Kristin told her about the beating on Griggs Street and the exercise machine. "She was afraid of him because he hit her," Jennifer said. "But when it came to the restraining order, it wasn't because she was afraid of what he would do to her. She was worrying about him, what would happen to him, what she was doing to him."

Kristin thought that authorities would crack down on him when she walked into court with her complaint. After all, he was on probation, wasn't he? She thought his criminal record, his suspended sentence, would catch up with him. Little did she know that the law didn't work that way. It was later changed in Massachusetts, in large part as a result of her murder, but it still doesn't work that way in most states.

Jennifer encouraged her to go to court. "I think she had a feeling he would be sent back to jail or go into heavy drug use," Jennifer said. "She had it all worked out in her head how even if she were just to pursue him for the exercise machine, he was going back to prison. That was the first half of the conversation. The second half, she told me about the beating. I said, 'Kristin, you didn't put him in this position.' I told her to stand up for herself. I told her that if she ever wanted to shake this creeping feeling of inadequacy she sometimes had, she had to stand up."

By Monday afternoon, May 11, Kristin had made up her mind. She was going to rely on the system. She was going to ask the courts for help. Late that afternoon, she went over to the Brookline police station with Lauren and Brian. The courts next door were closed. Kristin walked into the police station to find out what to do. "We waited in the lobby," Lauren said.

Brookline police sergeant Robert Simmons spent more than an hour with her. He had been out "on the street," covering the south side of town, when Kristin arrived at the station house, but the officer assigned to the north side, where Kristin lived, wasn't available. Simmons was called in to interview her.

Kristin was uncomfortable. "She came to me looking for a restraining order—period," Simmons said. "She wanted to get out the door." She told him about the beating and the NordicFlex. She wanted the machine returned, but that was no longer uppermost in her mind. She just wanted a court order protecting her from another attack like the one on April 16.

"I assume she lost consciousness [when Cartier kept kicking her]," Simmons said. "She said the last thing she remembered was him saying, 'Get up or I'll kill you.' The next thing she knew was two motorists picking her up."

As Kristin described the beating, Simmons realized, "We had a jurisdiction problem." Cartier lived in Allston, a part of Boston. The attack had taken place on Griggs Street, which is also in Allston. Brookline is a separate town in a different county. But Simmons was more worried that Kristin would "take a walk on me" and refuse to press any charges. He spoke to a lieutenant and decided to apply for a complaint against Cartier under his own signature. That would give Kristin a chance to reflect on what she wanted to do.

"I said to her, 'Do you want to press charges?' " Simmons recalled. "She said, 'I want to think about it.' "

While she was there, Simmons decided to check on Cartier's police record. Kristin knew he'd been in jail, and, according to Simmons, she'd also learned that his previous girlfriend had taken out a restraining order against him. Maybe Cartier had told her about it. In those days, such orders were not entered into the state's criminal history information system, but Massachusetts did have a computerized criminal record system that showed the details and disposition of each criminal charge.

The sergeant ran into some snags in calling up Cartier's history. Kristin had his first and last name right, but she wasn't sure about the middle initial. She remembered the name of Cartier's father but had Cartier's birthdate off by a year. Simmons found it after a bit of trial and error, and the three-page summary from the state's Criminal History Systems Board finally popped up on a printer in the Brookline police radio room.

Simmons looked at it and showed it to Kristin. "Hey, look at this arrest record," he told her. "You can see the violence escalating. You can't take care of him until you protect yourself."

Kristin was "nodding at all the right spots" as Simmons talked to her. "She was very intelligent, very articulate," he said. "She was trying to use the system." She also emphasized to Simmons that Cartier had warned her that he might have to go to jail for six months, "but she better not be around when he gets out." Considerate and reassuring, Simmons told her, "I'll take out the complaint."

"Taking out a complaint" means filling out a form declaring that certain crimes have been committed, naming the alleged perpetrator, and recommending that he or she be arrested or summoned to a hearing on the charges. This is called an "application for complaint" and it can be signed by the victim or by the police or other officers investigating the case. When Cartier killed his kitten, for instance, the application for a complaint charging Cartier with cruelty to animals was signed by the SPCA investigator. The application is then sent to the courthouse for review by a prosecutor or, more often in Massachusetts, a police liaison officer on duty at the courthouse and sometimes known as "the police prosecutor." If the application is approved, the criminal complaint itself is signed under oath by the complainant and issued by the court. This is a criminal procedure, completely separate from the civil law governing issuance of a restraining order.

Civil restraining or protective orders were developed in the 1970s in response to the ineffectiveness of criminal sanctions in dealing with domestic violence, especially in cases "of unclear or borderline criminality."[3] Their issuance does not preclude bringing criminal charges against the offender at the same time. In fact, according to a nationwide study for the Justice Department, "[s]ome judges recommend that victims of serious domestic violence consider pursuing their cases both civilly and criminally, at least in cases where there has been aggravated assault and battery or other felonious behavior." The orders can help prevent retaliation, intimidation, or other pressures, but immediate enforcement is crucial because, in contrast to stranger-to-stranger crimes, the defendant will often have a strong sense of having been wronged and easier ways to retaliate. The study found, however, that the "most serious limitation of civil protection orders . . . is widespread lack of enforcement."[4]

It was 5:30 P.M. at the Brookline police station. The sergeant typed up a one-page report recounting the April 16 attack on Kristin, Cartier's repeated phone calls, and his warning to her if she went to the police. Simmons wrote, "Criminal complaints will be sought for assault and battery with a dangerous weapon [Cartier's booted feet], violation of the abuse law, and intimidation of a witness." He said a complaint for larceny over $250 would be sought for the weight-lifting machine.

Before Kristin left, Simmons got a restraining order for her, too. He called a magistrate on after-hours duty that night, Superior Court Judge Patti B. Saris, and obtained her approval for an emergency order directing Cartier to stay away from her apartment, not to abuse or threaten her physically, and not to contact her "in person, by telephone, in writing or otherwise." Unlike the short-sighted laws of most other states, the statute in Massachusetts applies to "substantive" boyfriend-girlfriend relationships. But the order was good only until the courts closed the next day at 4 P.M. Kristin would have to come back before then to get a temporary restraining order, one that would last a week.

Kristin left the police station at 6 P.M. Brian and Lauren were still waiting. "You won't believe the size of this guy's police record," she told them. "It's three pages long. He's killed cats.[5] He beat up ex-girlfriends. Lots of breaking and entering. He [Sgt. Simmons] just flashed the length of it and said, 'Look what you're dealing with.'"

Simmons readied the paperwork for submission to district court the next morning. That included an application for a criminal complaint charging Cartier with the four offenses he'd mentioned in his report, three of them felonies. The application was signed in the morning by Lt. Finnegan, the police liaison officer on duty that day, and he turned it over to clerk magistrate John Connors for issuance of a summons.

The summons was never issued. Inexcusably, the application for it was still moldering on a desk in the clerk's office the day Kristin was killed, almost three weeks later. Other officials I spoke with, outside Brookline, were amazed by the lapse. Connors shrugged it off. "We don't have the help," he told me. "It was waiting to be typed."

The Museum School's second semester ended officially at 6 P.M., May 11. Kristin was free to return to court the next day without missing any classes. She appeared before Brookline District Judge Lawrence G. Shubow in midafternoon. A widely respected judge who had been on the bench for fourteen years, Shubow had a solid reputation for safeguarding defendants' rights and dealing with juvenile problems. As "a young, left-leaning lawyer in the 1950s," in the words of the *Boston Globe*,[6] he was outspoken against communist witchhunts. Before his appointment as a judge in 1978, he had represented "just about every disenfranchised group in the state," including a prostitutes' union and a group of Gypsies.[7] On the bench, he devoted himself to problems such as fair housing, juvenile delinquency, rent control, and family law. He had a fine sense of humor and of himself. He was known to refer to his judicial robe as his "little black dress." He also seems to have been rather lenient on perpetrators of domestic violence. According to the *Brookline Citizen,* of five men who had been found guilty of such charges around the time of Kristin's death, only one received jail time.[8]

One of the men who had avoided incarceration was Anthony Roberts, then thirty-two, a man with a long record of violating restraining orders and arrests for assault and battery. According to court records inspected by the *Citizen,* Roberts had been attacking the same woman on Brookline Housing Authority property for two to three years. In 1991 alone, he was apprehended four times at the property in question for trespassing or assault and battery. On one visit, he was allegedly drunk and abusive, wielding a machete and a kitchen knife. He was arrested on various charges, including one count of assaulting the woman and two counts of assaulting a police officer.

Three of the cases were tried before Shubow in January 1992. He gave the miscreant a suspended sentence of thirty days in jail, put him on probation for a year, and ordered him to undergo alcohol evaluation and to stay away from the woman. Roberts soon violated probation, got thirty days in jail from a different judge, and a few days after his release, was picked up again for trespassing and beating up the same woman.

Four days after Kristin's murder Roberts went before Shubow again, on June 3, 1992. The judge gave him consecutive sentences of six months for trespassing, eighteen months for assault, and another year for violating probation in one of the 1991 cases: three years in jail in all.[9]

The message was clear. Shubow should have been sterner to begin with, and he knew it. Ironically, Brookline is in Norfolk County, the same jurisdiction that produced a pioneering domestic violence program under now retired District Court Judge Albert Kramer in Quincy, Massachusetts. He held back-to-jail hearings within a week for anyone who violated probation. His court hadn't seen a homicide from domestic violence in five years. When he said no contact, he meant it. "If somebody sends a postcard just saying 'Happy Birthday,' " Kramer said, "he's facing jail time. That isn't a love message, it's a control message, and it's very alarming to the victim. You've got to take these guys seriously."[10]

When I spoke with Kramer, he had just sentenced a man for violating probation in a domestic violence case by beating up another woman—like Kristin after Rose Ryan. There was no need for a full-dress trial, or even the injured woman's testimony. "Anyone who is on probation is supposed to abide by our laws," Kramer said. With Cartier's record, Kristin's reluctance to see him put back in jail shouldn't have mattered. "If a judge sees the kind of record this guy had, that's when you take it out of the hands of the victim," Kramer said. "You have him picked up on a warrant."

After Kristin's death, Shubow and Gwen DeVasto, program director of the domestic violence unit in Norfolk County District Attorney William Delahunt's office, said changes were being instituted to give victims of domestic violence more help than Kristin received.

"We've had a model program in Quincy for the past 12 years that we're now expanding into the rest of the county courts," DeVasto told the *Brookline Citizen* a few days after Kristin was killed.[11]

In other words, Kramer's pioneering work got little replication outside of Kramer's court, even from the DA who had basked in the program's reflected glory.[12]

At the May 12 hearing Shubow was unaware of the criminal complaint facing Cartier, although the papers were sitting in the clerk's office down the hall. The judge didn't bother to ask about Cartier's criminal record, either. Restraining orders in Massachusetts, as in other states, have been treated for years by most judges as distasteful "civil matters," without much concern for the criminal behavior underlying the petitions. Until Kristin was killed, anyone with a rap sheet could walk into a Massachusetts courtroom and loudly deny allegations of brutal conduct under the domestic abuse law without worrying about his criminal record catching up with him, even if just to question his credibility.

An unflinchingly honest man, Shubow publicly expressed regret after Kristin's murder for not examining Cartier's record. "If there is one lesson I learned from this case," he told the *Boston Globe,*[13] "it was to ask myself whether this is a case where I should review his record. In a case that has an immediate level of danger, I could press for a warrant and immediate arrest."

According to John Englebretsen, assistant chief of probation in the Brookline court, his office "used to try to do record checks" in domestic abuse cases but dropped the effort because "some judges thought that was an invasion of privacy."

He was apparently referring to Shubow. Under the previous chief judge, Henry Crowley, petitioners like Kristin would be sent upstairs to the probation office after their initial appearance. "We would talk to the person individually, and then talk to the alleged perpetrator and get that person's version," Englebretsen said. If their accounts conflicted, "we would meet with them both." The procedure "went into abeyance" when Judge Crowley retired in December 1991, a few months too soon to be of any help to Kristin.

Englebretsen told the *Brookline Citizen* shortly after Kristin's death that his office still looked for "red flags" in domestic abuse cases,[14] but the flag, it was plain, had to be waved in their face.

"You said in the *Brookline Citizen* that 'probation regularly checks for red flags in domestic cases,'" I reminded Englebretsen. "You do check criminal records then?"

"Not regularly, no," he said.

"What is a 'red flag' then?"

"A red flag means a person known by the court or noted to us by the police [as someone with a record]," he said.

"But the police knew Cartier had a record," I said. "Sergeant Simmons had it printed out. He showed it to Kristin. He sent papers over for a complaint on assault and battery with a dangerous weapon and other charges. It was signed by Lieutenant Finnegan. He marked it down for a summons. The police knew he had a criminal record."

"They just didn't tell us," Englebretsen said. "Nobody noted it in the courtroom. We weren't alerted to it."

Instead, Shubow treated Docket No. 92-RO-060 as a routine matter. On May 12, Kristin was sworn in and, in response to brief questioning by the court, said she wanted an order that would last for a year. The judge explained that he would first have to give Cartier an opportunity to "come in and give his story." He then issued a temporary restraining order telling Cartier to stay away from Kristin's school, her apartment, and her place of work until May 19, when another hearing could be held by another judge on a "permanent" order, good for a year.

"The system failed her completely," Shubow told me after Kristin's death. "There is no such thing as a routine case. I don't live that, but I believe that. All bureaucrats should be reminded of that."

I showed him some of the papers concerning Kristin's case that I'd gotten from the Brookline court. The judge examined them, disapprovingly. He pointed to a missing signature here, a time of day left out there.

"This is just bureaucratic sloppiness," he said. "Decades, actually centuries of experience have taught people how to create the forms and processes necessary to carry out their mission. One shortcut and you have the potential for error. Some of my colleagues consider me a nit-picking idiot, but it is the only way to mark out a trail for ourselves. Any departure creates a potential for disaster."

Kristin's death weighed on the judge. Just that morning, before meeting with me, he had to deal with a young man who had repeatedly violated a stay-away order despite an explicit lecture from Shubow about not contacting the woman involved. Shubow ordered him held on $50,000 bond, which meant his parents would have had to put up $5,000 to get him out of jail.

"It was my way of saying, 'Kristin, really, we haven't forgotten you yet,'" the judge said.

After the shooting, "we were all second-guessing ourselves," Englebretsen said in a separate conversation. "It's something that shouldn't have happened."

That is what is so frightening. It shouldn't have happened, but it did, under the purview of well-meaning people going about business as usual, dealing with wrongdoers in a way that ignores their past crimes and puts their victims at risk. "If anything good comes out of this—

and I'd hate to think nothing would come out of it—I'd want the judges to look at a man's criminal record," Lauren Mace said. "To see if it was his first offense. In Mike's case, if only the judge knew . . . if only he'd asked."

11

Kristin said nothing about the court proceedings to Rosemary or to me. We thought the new boyfriend was now an ex-boyfriend, and we were happy for that. Kristin had, of course, confided in Helen but made her promise not to tell anyone. They could count on each other.

"The person I most admire is my sister Helen," she wrote in high school. "Besides being a successful lawyer, she is also very beautiful. Although our parents helped put her through college, she put herself through law school. She works hard at everything she does. . . . My sister has been there for me, helping me with my problems all my life. I love her very much."

Kristin called her big sister at some point on May 11 or 12 and told her, sparingly, about the beating and, angrily, about the exercise machine.

"She told me he threw her down on the sidewalk and kicked her," Helen said. "I said, 'He did *what?*' She backed off on the particulars. She was really incensed about the $1,000 on her credit card."

Helen's shocked reaction to the beating may have embarrassed Kristin from telling her more about it. But Kristin could still be indignant about the NordicFlex without being mortified. And perhaps she was angrier about that. We are taught to value our purse more than our person. That's one of the lessons of the law. Assault and battery is just a minor crime. Grand larceny can land you in state prison. Besides, Cartier's announcement that he was going to cheat her was fresher in her mind.

Kristin told Helen she had decided to get a restraining order. In fact, she may have gotten one already without telling Helen she'd done so. Helen told her to get down to the courthouse before it closed. Kristin said she had "until midnight." It seems likely that Sgt. Simmons had told her that at the police station while trying to reach Judge Saris on the telephone.

Helen kept the news to herself, as Kristin requested, along with other bits of information Kristin had compiled. She'd been doing some investigating of her own. "She said she found out what a loser he was. She said, 'He's even been taking drugs behind my back,' " Helen recalls.

He was snorting heroin, Leslie North affirmed. "He was doing a lot of heroin when he broke up with Kristin," she said. "He told me, 'It helps me stay calm.' " Cartier sometimes mainlined heroin, too. He had a black cross tattooed on his left arm to hide the needle marks.[1] He told his jailers at Deer Island that he was "sniffing 3 bags" of heroin regularly, snorting 1½ grams of cocaine on weekends, smoking a small amount of marijuana, and drinking a case of beer each weekend. He said he also took angel dust about twice a month and occasionally used mescaline.[2]

That should have been more than enough to disqualify Cartier from the Alternatives to Violence group in Boston Municipal Court. "Any defendant found to have an active substance abuse problem" was supposed to be excluded from the classes. But probation officials apparently made no effort to find out what his jailers knew. Probation Chief John Tobin also told me at one point, "If we had found out about the restraining order, we would have moved immediately" to revoke his probation. But Tobin's office made no effort to find that out, either. Cartier's probation officer, Diane Barrett-Moeller, did nothing to get him off the streets.

Kristin, by contrast, took the criminal charges Sgt. Simmons listed quite seriously. She mentioned them in a phone call to Jennifer Jones on May 12, the day she got her temporary order from Judge Shubow. "Talked to Kristin today," Jennifer wrote in her journal. "Finally got a restraining order against this creep. Filed charges to boot. Lots of them."

When versions of my *Washington Post* article about what happened to Kristin appeared in the Boston newspapers in November of 1992, Tobin continued to insist, as the *Boston Herald* put it, that "his department did the best it could at the time, given what it knew."

"We can argue all day, but none of us have 20–20 hindsight," he told the *Herald*. "If you're looking for accountability, the accountability was exemplary as far as this department is concerned. If you look at what happened on the dates when Cartier was in contact with BMC's probation department, we did not allow any grass to grow under this guy's feet."

I don't think Kristin would have seen it that way. Cartier was still harassing her day and night. He knew about the restraining order, but he pretended not to know. "He was calling constantly," Brian Fazekas said. "I talked to him. I said, 'Look, man, there's a restraining order, you're not supposed to call.' He says he never got served the order. [Sometimes] the phone would ring at 3 A.M. I'd pick it up, say 'hello,' and there would be no one at the other end. A few times I would say, 'Mike, it's three in the morning.' I think this was mostly before the first [restraining] order, but it happened after as well."

Usually Kristin refused to talk to him, but sometimes she happened to pick up the phone and find Cartier on the line. "Some of it was about the machine," Brian said. "She wanted to know what was up, when he was going to return it. Sometimes she'd be really quiet. Sometimes he called pretty much to insult her."

Helen talked to Kristin again on Thursday, May 14, to make sure she had gotten the restraining order. She had, but she told Helen he was still calling. "She didn't let the calls bother her," Helen said, "but she was annoyed by them. One day she just sat there and let the answering machine pick them up. She said the machine was going on and off all night. He kept hanging up without leaving a message. But she knew it was him."

Helen tried to alert us without breaking any promises. Sometime that week, she came over in the evening and told Rosemary that things weren't going too well for Kristin and that she should come home. Helen had already urged Kristin to do that, but Kristin said she had just gotten a new job and she couldn't afford to leave. Rosemary didn't ask for particulars. She wanted to see Kristin again anyway.

"Kristin wants to come home," Rosemary told me as soon as I walked into the room, "but she thinks we can't afford it." A bit puzzled, I walked to the kitchen phone, got Kristin on the line, and told her what I'd just been told. "You can come home anytime you want," I assured her. "We'd love to see you."

It was Kristin's turn to be puzzled. She said she didn't want to come home. She couldn't walk out on her job so soon after getting it. "Everything's fine," she said.

I was glad to hear it. I told her we would still like to see her for a few days if she got a chance to take a break before summer school started. I told myself whatever problems there were seemed to have disappeared.

Kristin was planning to stay in Boston that summer and take a course or two at Tufts so that she could graduate the next year without having an impossible schedule in her final semesters. She had begun working at Marty's on April 27, shortly after breaking off with Cartier. Now with classes out, she was hoping to get as many hours as she could. On one shift, she looked up and saw Cartier inside the store, staring at her.

"She didn't see him come in. He walked up in front and was staring at her," Brian Fazekas recounted. "She didn't see him at first. She saw him at the last moment. Someone told her he'd been staring at her. She came home and mentioned it. I think it was definitely after the temporary restraining order, but before the permanent. . . . He had told her he was going to go into Marty's and check up on her, make sure she wasn't flirting with the customers."

At another point, it isn't clear when, Cartier angrily knocked on the front door of the Brookline flat. He had come round to pick up a piece of driftwood for his snake's glass cage and spotted someone else looking into a side window. It was probably one of Matt Newton's friends, trying to see if anybody was home. Whoever it was, he took off when Cartier came by.

"I told him Kristin didn't want to see him right now," Brian remembers. "He was really mad because he thought he'd seen someone looking in Kristin's window. He went storming off, saying he was going to find the guy and kill him. It's possible this happened before even the first restraining order because I don't remember telling him he wasn't supposed to be there."

Cartier seems to have been skulking about the Brookline flat afterwards as well. Lauren Mace said Kristin told her "she saw Mike poking around" the house the night Shubow issued his order or the next day. "She was probably more upset inside than she let on," Lauren said. "Kristin didn't like to come off as a scared person. She said something like, 'Well, that really scares me. What if he's sneaking around all the time when I'm there.' "

Kristin was obviously distracted that week. She left her wallet with her credit cards on a counter at the Bay Bank on May 13. Someone snatched them up quickly. By nightfall, a total of $2,167.82 had been charged to her American Express card, most of it at a computer store in Cambridge. Investigators for American Express contacted the merchants but were unable to track down the culprit. She took the incident calmly. I found out about it that night when American Express, unable to reach Kristin in Boston, called me at home in Washington to report the suspicious purchases. When I reached her later that night, she told me about losing the wallet earlier in the day, but she didn't seem as concerned about the fraudulent charges as I thought she would be. Obviously, she had other things on her mind.

On Thursday, May 14, Kristin called Brookline police and asked why the court order hadn't been served yet. "They said, 'Well, he wasn't home.' She said, 'Well, like, what's the point?' " Brian said.

Massachusetts law had recently been amended to eliminate a requirement that restraining orders be delivered by hand, usually by police officers, and to permit them to be sent by mail. But personal service was still the general rule. Part of the problem was that the order had been issued in Brookline, but Cartier lived in Allston, part of Boston.

At the Brookline police station, dispatcher Diane Mahon took Kristin's call and went out of her way to respond. "She was upset," Mahon remembered. "She wasn't sure what to do. She said, 'I want to make sure he gets notice of this because if he doesn't, he can keep going, thinking it's okay.' She wanted to make sure he knew he was supposed to appear in court. She wanted to make him aware he could get in trouble if he didn't appear."

First Mahon called Boston police. "They said if I faxed them a copy of the order, they would issue it when they could," Mahon remembered. "I said that wasn't good enough." So she talked to one of the brass on duty, Lt. Daniel O'Leary. When he found out that Cartier lived just across the line in Allston, he sent a squad car to deliver the order. Officer Jim Grogan went to the address but got no answer on the downstairs buzzer. "He gained entrance to the building," as Lt. Finnegan later summarized it, "and slipped a copy of the 209A [the restraining order] under the door to Cartier's apartment."

Perhaps Cartier was downtown at the time, meeting with a probation officer. Barrett-Moeller had told him to report every week until his evaluation was completed, but she wasn't there when he showed up on May 14. According to the probation file, she was on a "personal day" off. The file also says that Cartier "kept [his] ct. clinic appt." that day, but it seems he was simply told to come back the following week. The report of the clinic interview says it took place May 21. The clock was ticking, but no one at Boston Municipal Court was listening. Cartier could reassure himself on that point. After all, the exercise machine was being returned to the manufacturer. What else did he have to worry about? There were no witnesses to his attack on Kristin. Hanging on to the $1,000 NordicFlex while Kristin was being billed for it could lead to a grand larceny charge, a felony. That could lock him up for a longer time than the six months he had coming to him, but no one would prosecute him for it if she got a refund.

Kristin called Brookline police again shortly after midnight on May 19. Her request for a permanent restraining order was scheduled to come up for a hearing that morning. Now, in plain violation of the May 12 order, Cartier had called around midnight, got Kristin on the line, and urged her not to go back to court. This time Kristin didn't hesitate. She called the cops.

Sgt. Simmons, on duty that night as shift commander, took the call. He advised Kristin to file a complaint and sent officer Kevin Mealy to talk to her. Mealy, who was patrolling the neighborhood in a squad car, arrived at her apartment at 1:10 A.M.

Kristin met him at the door. "She informed me that her ex-boyfriend had contacted her by telephone on 5-19-92 at 12:00 A.M.," Mealy said in his report. "This conduct is in violation of a restraining order issued against the ex-boyfriend. . . . Ms. Lardner said that Mr. Cartier attempted to persuade her not to file for an extension of the order. She said that he did not threaten her but wanted her to drop all criminal action against him, saying that he would not hurt her again. A criminal complaint application has been made out against Mr. Cartier for violating the existing restraining order."

Cartier was evidently aware that he faced criminal charges for what he had done to Kristin. He wanted her to drop "all criminal action," not just the civil restraining order. And in calling her, he had committed another crime. The order slipped under his door clearly stated at the top, in capital letters, "VIOLATION OF THIS ORDER IS A CRIMINAL OFFENSE punishable by imprisonment or fine or both." According to the abuse prevention law, "Any violation of such order shall be punishable by a fine of not more than five thousand dollars, or by imprisonment for not more than two and one-half years in a house of correction, or by both such fine and imprisonment."[3]

Sgt. Simmons had Mealy do his paperwork as soon as he got back to the station house. "I told Kevin, 'They've got a hearing in the morning.' The documents went over there, but who reads them?"

Kristin arrived at the Brookline courthouse around 11:30 A.M. with Lauren Mace and Amber Lynch.

"He [Cartier] was in front of the courthouse when we got there," Lynch said. "I didn't look at him. We all just walked in quickly. We waited a long time. He kept walking in and out of the courtroom. I think he was staring at her. . . . [Kristin] said, 'Oh yeah, he called me last night asking me not to do this.' "

The week before, Judge Shubow had interrupted the case he was hearing to deal with Kristin's temporary order. He told me that abuse orders "are supposed to take priority." Someone else was presiding on May 19, District Judge Paul McGill, a visiting magistrate from Roxbury.

"We had to be quiet," Lynch says. "We couldn't read anything. Some poor lady was being evicted. Kristin [who had evidently made some inquiries] said the judge was going to go to lunch if we didn't get there by a certain time."

There was no one in the courtroom from the Norfolk County DA's office to advise Kristin. District Attorney William Delahunt had set up a domestic violence unit in 1979 after a Cohasset man, James Quirk, murdered his wife and three children before killing himself. But the unit had still not expanded much beyond Quincy, where Judge Kramer held sway. The DA had an office downstairs in the Brookline courthouse, but the woman described to me as "the victim-witness advocate" there, Gail Wood, said she was really "the DA's administrative assistant" in Brookline. "I don't counsel victims," she protested when I told her how her duties had been described to me. "That's not in my job description." She said her job was "to take [victims] up to the court and go into the courtroom and stand by them with the judge and explain to them what to expect. That's not counseling."

And on May 19? "I was out sick," she said.

Brookline probation officials didn't talk to Kristin either. They had no idea that Cartier was on probation in Boston Municipal Court for beating up another woman. Neither did Judge McGill. He knew nothing about Cartier that wasn't in an affidavit Kristin filled out, even though the conduct she described was clearly criminal. Like Shubow, he didn't check Cartier's criminal record. Unlike Shubow, it didn't trouble him. To him, it was a routine hearing. Kristin was looking for protection. She was processed like a slice of cheese.

"She thought he [Cartier] was going to be arrested," Brian Fazekas said. "It was her understanding that as soon as she got the permanent restraining order, he was going to be surrendered" for violating probation, or charged with violating Shubow's order, or both.

Kristin had every right to think he was going to be hauled off. Under the abuse law, police "shall" arrest any person whom a law officer "has probable cause to believe has violated a temporary or permanent vacate, restraining or no-contact order. . . ." Cartier had done just that twelve hours earlier. Kristin reported it promptly. The report of the officer she spoke with leaves no doubt that a violation had occurred. Officer Mealy may have had no jurisdiction to march over the line into Allston and arrest Cartier at his apartment, but Brookline police had every right, and duty, to apprehend him at the courthouse.

"What he [Cartier] did on the nineteenth was a crime," David Lowy, legal advisor to Governor Weld and a former prosecutor, said of the midnight call. "He should have been placed under arrest right then and there."

The hearing was short. "My confluence with your daughter lasted five minutes," Judge McGill said later. Actually it was closer to ten. It would have been shorter except for a typical bit of arrogance from Cartier, trying to stay in control in the face of his third series of restraining orders in eighteen months. He spent several minutes arguing for the right to go into Marty's Liquors, Kristin's place of work. In the process, he came close to admitting that he had been going there in violation of the temporary restraining order. The judge didn't catch it, or question him about it. Instead, he let Cartier walk away with the impression that Kristin was also being ordered to stay away from him.

McGill started the session by having Kristin sign and date an affidavit she had written out about the April 16 beating on Griggs Street, when Cartier "threw me down into the street and kicked me repeatedly in the head and legs." She said, "There was also another previous incident where he became unreasonable and punched me in the head."

"I just need you to sign down there," he told Kristin. "And put today's date in the appropriate place. Today is the nineteenth. It just says that all the statements contained therein are true." Not once during the hearing did McGill ask Cartier about the beating, admonish him against any future violence, or warn him that any violation of the restraining order would be a crime.

Preliminaries completed, McGill began by noting that both parties were present, standing at separate microphones. Cartier spoke into his clearly and distinctly, dominating the proceeding, sometimes interrupting the judge. Kristin stood back from hers. Her words were hard to make out on the tape that constitutes the official transcript. She was asked to speak only once.

"All right," McGill said. "I have before me Kristin Lardner and [pause] Mr.—"

"Cartier," said Cartier, giving it the proper pronunciation.

"Michael Cartier," the judge intoned. "Ms. Lardner has requested the court to order Mr. Cartier not to abuse her. Do you have any problem with that?"

"No, your honor," Cartier responded in earnest tones, as though it were a silly question.

"No," the judge repeated. "Good for you."

McGill may have meant the "good for you" sarcastically. It is just as likely that Cartier took it as a pat on the back.

"And number two," the judge said, "not to contact her. Do you have any problem with that?"

"No sir," Cartier assured him.

"All right," McGill said. "And she's also requesting that you stay away from 236 Winchester Street in Brookline. Any problem there?"

"No sir," Cartier replied.

"Okay," the judge continued. "And to stay away from Marty's Liquors. Any problem with that?"

"Yes, I do," Cartier told the court.

"All right," McGill responded. "I'll hear you on that. Tell me about that, sir, if you would."

"Well, sir," Cartier told him. "I happen to live right around the corner from there. And that's her place of employment. It's also a liquor store. I've been going in there for years, and she's only recently been employed there. If I go in there, I don't look at her, and I don't even go into the aisle she's working at, that register. I totally avoid her. I say nothing to her. Not even make eye contact with her."

The judge let the admission fly right past him. So Cartier had been going into Marty's? When? And why? Hadn't Judge Shubow's order been slipped under his door? How did he find out about today's hearing? How much nonsense did he expect the court to put up with?

In fact, the courts put up with an overdose, every day of the week. This isn't a problem confined to Massachusetts. It happens again and again before judges assigned to domestic restraining order cases. Women are usually treated sympathetically if the abuser isn't present. But if he shows up, the microphone is his. In many, perhaps most, American courtrooms, it's still a man's world. Numerous gender-bias studies commissioned by the courts themselves attest to that.

In fairness to McGill, it should be pointed out that he didn't interrupt Kristin. He simply didn't talk to her very much at all, although there was much he could have asked. When had she started working at Marty's? Had Cartier come into Marty's after the May 11 emergency restraining order Judge Saris issued? How often had Kristin seen him there? What did she think he was doing? Checking up on her to make sure she wasn't flirting with the customers?

"I usually don't force the victims to say anything," McGill said later. "They've filled out an affidavit. . . . I don't put them on the spot. I just talk to the defendant. I say, 'and you are to stay away from the home,' and so forth. 'You don't have a problem with that, do you?' "[4]

It sounds fine, on paper. In practice, I suspect, it makes the complainant, usually a woman, feel as though she doesn't count. It is an ordeal for a battered person to come into a courtroom and put her safety, if not her life, in jeopardy. I suspect that having done that, she would rather be asked to speak up than be expected, once again, to say nothing.

McGill reminded Cartier that there were a series of other liquor stores not far from the intersection of Harvard and Commonwealth, where Marty's was located.

Cartier said that would mean a longer walk for him. He said that "sometimes it's just easier" to go to Marty's.

Patiently, too patiently, the judge explained that he had ordered Cartier to stay at least two hundred yards away from Kristin under the no-contact provision. "That's the length of two football fields," McGill said. There was no way he could stay that far from her if he went into the store. "So if she even sees you, you'd be in violation," McGill told him.

Cartier saw an opening. "I live right up the street. That's less than two hundred yards," he told the court. "I mean it's less than two football fields . . . and I work at Bunratty's. That's right across the street."

"Well, listen," McGill said. "There are two different issues here. The first one is whether or not you have to go into Marty's Liquors."

Cartier: "I don't have to, but sometimes it's easier."

The court: "It may be easier, sir, but if you do, you're in violation of the order."

Cartier: "What if she's not working—she's not working that day?"

The court: "How do you know if she is or isn't?"

Cartier: "I don't—"

The court: "Then you're—"

Cartier: "I can see in the window."

The court: "—violating my order. My order as it stands. Right? You can't go in there."

"Okay," Cartier finally agreed, even though he would continue looking in the window.

McGill then ordered Cartier to stay away from "230 The Fenway" after Kristin, speaking up distinctly for the first time, explained that this was the address of the Museum School.

Cartier said he would have "no problem" staying away from the school, but he kept pushing to stay in charge of the situation, pressing the fact that he worked at Bunratty's. "I'm a doorman," he told McGill. "And that's right across the street. And I'd like for the record to have an order that she stays away from there, too."

McGill ignored him for a moment. The judge was concentrating instead on amending the order so that it told Cartier to stay at least two hundred yards away from Kristin "except when the defendant leaves his home or is at work."

"If this becomes problematic, then come back in here," McGill told them, as though both sides were on an equal footing. McGill said the order would stand for a year, but "of course, either or both parties can come in here to request that it be modified before then."

Cartier was emboldened. Once again, he asked the court to tell Kristin that "she should stay away from my work, don't enter my work. Because I work in a nightclub."

McGill fed the noisy ego. "Is there any need for you to go into Bunratty's?" he asked Kristin.

No, she told the judge. She used to go there with her friends all the time, but she didn't have to do that anymore. Her friends were graduating. She was facing another year in Boston, with Michael Cartier nipping at her heels. Everyone was moving out of 236 Winchester Street. She didn't even know where she was going to wind up for the summer.

"All right," Cartier said triumphantly. "So that's no problem."

"All right," the judge repeated, without realizing his complicity. "If you'll wait, you'll be able to get a copy of this momentarily, both of you."

The paper record does not reflect issuance of a "mutual restraining order," but that, in effect, was what McGill had just handed down orally. The National Council of Juvenile and Family Court Judges had formally frowned on such edicts since 1990.

"Judges should not issue mutual protective or restraining orders," the council said in a set of formal recommendations aimed at improving court practice. "This practice has emerged as a major problem in some areas, and has been cited in several states' gender bias reports as evidence of continued bias in the court's response to family violence.

"Frequently, mutual orders of protection are issued even when the respondent has filed no cross petition nor alleged any violence by the petitioner. Thus, both parties are labeled as abusers and are treated as equally blameworthy. The message to the batterer is that such behavior is excusable, was perhaps provoked, and he or she will not be held accountable for the violence. Victims who have not engaged in violent behavior are confused, humiliated, and stigmatized when such orders are issued against them . . .

"Mutual restraining orders create significant problems of enforcement which render them ineffective in preventing further abuse. They are confusing to law enforcement and unenforceable. When an order is violated, police have no way of determining who needs to be arrested. Often, they will arrest both parties, further victimizing the victim.

"If both parties are alleged offenders, there should be two separate applications, hearings, findings of good cause, and separate orders issued."[5]

With the hearing over, Cartier walked out of the courthouse scot-free. The Massachusetts mandatory arrest law for restraining order violations, enacted in 1990, went by the boards. In addition, a new state law making "stalking" a crime, especially in violation of a restraining order, had been signed by Governor William Weld the day before, on May 18, 1992. Cartier seemed well on his way to breaking that one, too, although it requires repeated acts of harassment and threatening conduct. The stalking law went into effect at 11:33 A.M., the minute Weld signed it on May 18, half a day before Cartier's phone call.

Cartier would have been sent to jail if the hearing had been held in Quincy before Judge Kramer. He routinely reviewed the criminal records of defendants in restraining order cases. Lawyers familiar with the way Kramer did business say he would have issued a warrant for Cartier's immediate arrest, notified probation officials in Boston, and set him down for a fast-track trial in Quincy, probably within a month, on the charge of violating a restraining order. "He would have been held on bail and faced jail time in both courts [Quincy and Boston]," said a knowledgeable attorney. "He had done time for similar acts. Now this. Around here [Quincy], you just do not walk the streets with a record like that."

McGill later said that if he'd known Cartier had violated his restraining order by calling Kristin that morning, he would have turned the hearing into a criminal session. "He would have been taken into custody if she had said, 'Judge, he called me,'" McGill said. "But I could only act on the information I had available that day."

Kristin assumed the court knew. She'd reported it to the police, hadn't she? This was her first encounter with the criminal justice system. She was trusting enough to think it worked.

"Kristin could have said something [in court], I suppose," Lauren said. "But she just figured that after that, he would be out of her life. She said, 'Let's go home.' She felt very relieved that she had this restraining order."

The Brookline police, to put it plainly, weren't hard-nosed enough. Perhaps they had been trying to accommodate Kristin. That was understandable when she came in to complain about Cartier's having beaten her up weeks earlier. Without her testimony about that, they had nothing. But when he violated the restraining order by asking her not to go back to court, she blew the whistle on him right away. She was a willing witness. She thought he was going to be arrested. Nothing happened.

The application for a complaint charging Cartier with violating Shubow's order was moldering in clerk John Connors's offices. The form has boxes at the top, one of them to be filled in with an X, labeled "Arrest," "Hearing," "Summons," and "Complaint." It was unsigned, but someone had marked "Summons" rather than "Arrest." Like the earlier complaint accusing Cartier of assault with a deadly weapon, it was still sitting in the clerk's office the day Kristin was killed.

12

The hearing concluded, Kristin went back to Winchester Street and began doing her best to forget about Michael Cartier. She talked enthusiastically about going to Europe after graduation, only a year away. The trip was a graduation present that Rosemary and I had promised her in memory of her grandmother, who had left some money for Kristin and the other children. She was going to go with Lauren, even though the two would be living apart in the meantime. After that, Kristin was thinking of graduate school. She had lost interest in boys. She wanted to concentrate on her art.

"She was really staying away from boys," Amber Lynch said. "She told me one day, 'I saw a really cute boy at work,' but then she said, 'The boys I like aren't so good so I'm just going to stay away from them.'"

Kristin didn't want to get married. She told Amber that would be "boring." "I don't think she wanted to have a normal suburban life," Amber said. "She also knew the state-of-the-gender thing was wrong."

Her essays for school, lucid and well written, reflected that. They showed a great deal of thought about art, religion, and the status of women. She wondered about death, too, and at least philosophically, had no fear of it. "Is death why we have religion?" she wrote in a note I found in her bedroom. "Religion is the only method humans use to explain the only question they can't possibly answer." She believed in the Buddhist view of existence as a continuing cycle of death and re-birth. She was convinced that she would be back again in some form, seeking enlightenment. For Kristin, the way to strive for that was through her art. She dreamed of being a great artist. She wanted to make a difference.

For now, she busied herself with the bulletin for summer school. She was still trying to pick out the courses she wanted. With a lonely year ahead of her, she also thought wistfully of Jason. "I think she missed Jason," Amber said. "After she realized how bad [Cartier] was, she started talking about Jason." Perhaps, deep down, she was hoping he would come back and protect her, but she never said that, to Jason or anyone else. Kristin wrote him not long before she was killed, but without any sense of urgency. She told him about her art and her tattoo and how she never expected to meet anyone like him again.

He sent her a fond response from Christchurch a few weeks later. He'd acquired a cat named Splinter and was still deep into his karate. He said he was now aiming for a diplomatic career and might be re-turning to the United States one day. "I really hope to see you again someday," Jason told her. "Anyway, I hope you never find a replace-ment for me either." He wrote the letter in June 1992. He didn't know Kristin was already dead.

At Marty's, Kristin quickly made friends with other college stu-dents who worked there. Cartier was still hanging around from his perch at Bunratty's, but Kristin didn't let it bother her for long. With her pink "plaintiff's copy" of the restraining order, she was beginning to feel comfortable for the first time in weeks. Chris Dupre spoke to her on the phone the night before she was killed. "She was in a great mood," he said. "She was like the most optimistic and happiest she'd been in months. She knew what she wanted to do with herself and her art. She was at a point where she didn't want a relationship. She felt good about what she was doing. She felt good about herself."

On Wednesday night, May 27, three days before the shooting, Tim Blanchard saw Kristin and Bekky Elstad walk into a nightspot near Fenway Park where he and his band were playing. Both were tot-ing cameras.

"She was probably in the best state of mind that I'd seen her in a long time," said Blanchard, an old friend from high school days who had moved to Boston to study music. "Her eyes were a little brighter. She seemed up."

Kristin and Bekky, a photojournalism major at BU, both scurried about, taking pictures of Tim and his band. Kristin had the Pentax K-1000 that she liked to use. Years before she had learned to be quite a good photographer at the Corcoran. She had even thought of switching to a photography major at BU before the Museum School accepted her.

"I went over to Kristin's place on Friday [May 29], to get the pictures pretty much," Blanchard said. "They came out great."

Kristin was still only a part-timer at Marty's. She was spending most of her time between semesters at the apartment in Brookline, painting and hanging out with what seems to have been a steady stream of visitors. It was a popular place, busy with preparations for a going-away party for Lauren that was set for Sunday, May 31. She was planning to move to New Orleans with Brian the following week. Kristin was looking forward to it with mixed feelings, excited about the party, sad to say goodbye. Lisa had already left. Now Lauren. Matt Newton, their other roommate, was moving to Maine. Kristin still wasn't sure where she was going to be living or who her new roommates might be. Friends say she had talked about getting a place with Andy Meuse, a frequent visitor who was once Lauren's boyfriend, but Kristin wasn't speaking with him anymore. It seems Andy had gone to Bunratty's even after the beating and spoken in a friendly way with Cartier, who let him in for free.

"Kristin was real hurt for a friend to be buddy-buddy [with Cartier] like that," Lauren said. "After the beating she wouldn't even talk to him. I wouldn't talk to him. Andy never called the house to say he was sorry. When Kristin was killed, Andy felt really bad because he felt all this guilt. She probably would have forgiven him. But she was really mad."

Wiley Hyde stopped by on the afternoon of May 28 and took Kristin for the bike ride during which she spotted that "weirdo" Cartier peeking into Marty's window. Wiley doesn't think he noticed them. I think he did. Why else would he have played the tough guy at Bunratty's later that night, pressing to find out where Wiley lived? I think it's what pushed him over the edge. Kristin had dared go out with another man.

"He couldn't handle bad news, he couldn't handle pressure," a long-time friend, Timothy McKernan, told the *Lawrence Eagle-Tribune*. "He'd get under pressure, he'd start breathing heavily and start talking all wild."[1] Andy Meuse told the *Boston Globe* that Cartier had been in several scuffles with friends in recent months. In one of those incidents, he allegedly pulled a knife on a friend outside the nightclub.[2] Sometimes he would be playing pool at Bunratty's and fly into a rage for no apparent reason, acting as though he were going to kill someone with a pool cue. "You'd back away from him because you didn't know what he was going to do," a friend said.[3] At the Middle East nightclub that spring, about a month before he shot Kristin, he took umbrage at one of the members of an all-girl band from New York, grabbed a beer pitcher, and banged it down on her head.[4]

This was the man BMC's "ferocious" probation officers wanted to "evaluate." Cartier submitted, dutiful as ever to official authority. He reported to Room 512, the court clinic at the "new courthouse" in downtown Boston, on May 21, 1992, for an interview with psychologist William Hudgins. In his two-page report, Hudgins observed that Cartier had completed Diane Barrett-Moeller's six-week program "and several weeks thereafter was in court for the same problem that had gotten him in the program in the first place. He had gotten into a fight with a new girlfriend and she took out a restraining order on him."[5]

"Gotten into a fight with a new girlfriend"? He'd kicked her with his boots while she was lying on the ground. "Get up or I'll kill you," he told her. That wasn't a fight. That was assault with a deadly weapon. And it had happened while he was taking Barrett-Moeller's course, not afterwards. Those details, and more, were on file at Brookline District Court as well as the Brookline police station. The "new girlfriend" had not only obtained a restraining order by now, she'd accused Cartier of violating it.

Hudgins said he explained "the non-confidential and voluntary nature of the evaluation and Mr. Cartier agreed to speak with me." By way of background, Cartier gave "the sad history of being in group homes and foster care situations" since the age of five. "His mother lives in the area, but I believe she has a drug problem," the report continued. "Since reaching his 18th birthday, he has done about 10 months worth of time at both Deer Island and the Essex House of Correction for assaults."

Cartier acknowledged a disturbing pattern to his behavior, telling Hudgins that "his problems with different women friends seem to occur after they have been dating 1–2 months. At that point Mr. Cartier claims that he 'becomes more demanding' and starts to act meaner and pick fights with them. He could not articulate what he meant by becoming more demanding but he seemed genuinely frustrated and worried about what he felt was a pattern of getting into fights with the women he dated."

Alluding to his attack on Rose Ryan, Cartier admitted hitting her and claimed he was "going to cut off her hair" but "stopped himself." He said he had "gotten into some fights in prison," too, "but mostly he was left alone." He had a reputation since adolescence "as someone who was difficult to manage and had a temper." He told Hudgins he realized that "he had a problem with women and he wanted to gain control of it so that he was not always driving away the women he was involved with."

There is, of course, nothing wrong with trying to help Cartier and others like him. But the dice were loaded in Cartier's favor before he showed up for the evaluation. It had already been decided not to revoke his probation. "What I was doing was seeing what could be done for the guy," Hudgins told me. He said Cartier's probation officers had decided in advance not to send him back to jail. Hudgins said it wasn't his function to recommend incarceration, in any event. Had Cartier displayed any nasty tendencies during the interview, the psychologist said, "I could say to probation, 'This person has an attitude problem,' " but that would have been all.[6]

"I often feel I am operating as a piece of software that will help the court access the mental health services," Hudgins said. "With an adult,

I cannot say this person should be in jail. That is up to the judge. I can say this person is mentally ill, or not."

What is unsettling about the "treatment ideology" underlying such efforts is the supposition that it works when there is little evidence that it does.[7] What is even more disturbing is the clinical lack of concern it inevitably displays for the victims of crime. The criminal is transformed from a prisoner into a patient.[8] The public at large becomes an object, a testing ground for whatever "medicine" is prescribed. Did Michael Cartier beat up another woman? Kick her senseless? Well, that's too bad. Let's talk to him again and see what happens.

Hudgins described Cartier as "a good looking, tall man with several professional tattoos, the most arresting being a dragon that went from the right side of his neck down his right arm.[9] He was quite articulate in the presentation of his past and present problems." He admitted taking "different drugs" but did not feel he was an addict. He told Hudgins he was interested in music, "particularly 'underground' music, which is 'political.' " "What that means is not so clear," said Hudgins, obviously not a punk rocker or heavy metal fan.

Cartier seems to have had no trouble with the interview. He knew how to comport himself. He had, as Hudgins observed, "spent a lifetime protecting himself and operating in the human services system." He admitted that he had "a violent streak" and did not trust many people. Hudgins noticed that "he had a 'springy' paranoid quality about him." Having said all that, the psychologist concluded: "He has been in treatment and appears motivated to gain more self control."

Hudgins had not seen Cartier's Deer Island records and so was unaware of the extent of his drug taking. The psychologist had not seen his criminal history, or rap sheet, either, and so was unaware that he had been arrested for "cruelty to animals," a charge that had obviously been dropped as part of a plea bargain.

"If anyone mistreats an animal, you are dealing with a very, very disturbed person," Hudgins said. "I don't mean kicking the dog, though I don't approve of that, but a sadistic act. That's a sure sign you are dealing with a very disturbed person."[10]

Hudgins probably would have ended up by recommending one-on-one counseling in a community mental health program. He apparently regarded batterer treatment programs such as Emerge as too confrontational. "The people conducting those programs take a very assaultive role," he said. "They say, 'You're a batterer, you've got a lot of problems.' That works, or it doesn't work. . . . With community mental health, that's one on one. It's a judgment of what's going to be palatable. You can set a person up so they will fail and go back to jail."[11] You can also set a person up so he finds it easy to do what he wants, even to commit more crimes. That's usually the way "back to jail." Experts in battering cases say a common problem with "traditional mental health centers" is their overriding concern with patient confidentiality.

"They have alcohol programs; they don't have any real experience with battering," says David Adams, cofounder of Emerge. "They say there's no need to contact the victim, that it violates confidentiality. We argue that a victim's right to safety far outweighs a client's right to confidentiality."[12]

Adams spoke not long after waging a stiff battle to upgrade standards for batterer treatment programs in Massachusetts, including a requirement for at least eighty hours of treatment. "The traditional mental health communities mobilized against them," Adams said. "They said [the proposed standards] weren't sympathetic enough to the batterers."

In most states, where there are no standards at all, anyone can hang out a shingle. "Anything goes," he said. "There are some incredible horror stories. It's like where the bad drives out the good." Even in Massachusetts, where programs need to be certified by the state Department of Public Health, some experts say monitoring has been so inadequate that many second-rate programs have gone unnoticed.[13]

Toward the end of the interview, Hudgins offered to meet with Cartier several more times, "to see if we can better understand his problems with women and to try to work out a course of treatment." The next session was set for June 4, two weeks away.

Kristin had nine days to live.

Cartier's probation officers never saw him again. He was supposed to report on May 28, but he didn't show up. That was the day he was stalking Kristin, peeking into Marty's. He'd already missed his appointment with Barrett-Moeller by then. Perhaps he had been snooping around the flat on Winchester Street, too. Kristin and Wiley had been there, playing chess and Scrabble before they went out to eat.

If Kristin was bothered by Cartier's spying, she seemed to have put it out of her mind by the next morning. The usual stream of friends moved through the house all day. Friday, May 29, was Lauren's last day at Marty's. When she got home, there was sort of a party in advance of the party set for Sunday. Friends from work came over. One of them, David Bowden, had taken introductory classes at the Museum School when he was twelve. He and Kristin talked about what the school had been like then and what it was like now. Bowden thought Kristin was "cool."[14] She introduced him to Circe and put the four-foot snake around his neck. He left with a friend.

"Does she have a boyfriend?" Bowden asked.

"No," his friend replied. "Not anymore. She's been going out with a real jerk."

Bowden had met Cartier before and agreed with the assessment. He had been at Leslie North's place one day, sitting around and drinking beer, when Cartier walked in. North handled the introductions.

"This is my friend, David," she told Cartier. Tall, handsome, and black, Bowden extended his hand. Cartier slapped it in a very hostile manner.

"He was a jerk—and an asshole," Bowden said. "It makes sense that Kristin broke up with him."

Wiley Hyde came by that night, too, but he didn't tell Kristin anything about his odd conversation with Cartier. "Why should I bring up an old boyfriend she doesn't like?" he said later. "She wouldn't have thought anything of it anyway. She would have just laughed."

At the BMC probation office downtown, Cartier's failure to report the day before was duly noted. He was in violation of his probation once again, but no one got excited about it. A "non-compliance" letter was sent out, instructing him to report to the probation office the following Friday, June 5. "FAILURE TO REPORT, *AS REQUESTED,*" the letter said in capital letters that belied the mild wording, *"MAY* RESULT IN ADDITIONAL COURT ACTION" (emphasis supplied).

Kristin called me at the *Washington Post* that afternoon in a cheerful, upbeat mood. I was busy collecting details on the Bush administration's prewar courtship of Saddam Hussein, which was prematurely coming to be known as Iraq-gate, and the call was a welcome interruption. If it had lasted just a minute, it would have been unforgettable, but it was much longer and more enjoyable than a brief exchange of last words. I never had a better conversation with her. She was happy, confident, enthusiastic. We talked about summer school. She hadn't registered yet and was still mulling over what courses to take. I told her, as I had a few days earlier, that she was welcome to fly home at parental expense, but she said she would rather stay in Boston and try to earn a few dollars before summer school started. Leaving a part-time job abruptly might mean no job when she got back. We talked about her Museum School evaluation—intense but fair, she said—and half a dozen other things. She had a big smile in her voice. All I knew about Cartier was that she had gotten rid of him, a fact that she obliquely confirmed. She said she wasn't going with anyone just then. That prompted me to make some grumpy reference to boyfriends in general. I think I told her to tell them to get lost if they got too pushy. She laughed a deep, rich laugh and said, "That's because you're my dad."

Cartier called his father that day, too. Leslie North said that Michael told her "his father beat him up a lot when he was younger, [but] as time progressed they got closer." Especially, she said, after the birth of his half brother, Justin.

Gene Cartier had a persistent drinking problem, but he denied ever hitting his son. He said he was convinced, while conceding he had no evidence, that the state-funded schools were at fault for his son's malfunctions. Although officials say there is no record of it, he suspects his son was sexually abused. Perhaps he was. But what then? Would that excuse his violence against women? Or anyone? "His attitude was 'Don't fuck with me and I won't fuck with you,'" Gene Cartier told me. "Temperamentally he was very quick, very defensive. I guess he could only show his feelings out through anger. That was the only way he could express himself. . . . While he was in the schools, I imagine he was abused. He wasn't abused by me or Penny."

Cartier's father no doubt tried to help his son once he left the Harbor School. But the effort may have been bogged down by the example. Rose Ryan remembered that when she went with Michael to the homestead in Lawrence for Justin's birthday party, "Mike said his father had just gotten out of [alcohol] rehab for the seventh time, [and] they were sitting there drinking! His father had a shot and a beer in front of him."

Gene Cartier knew about Kristin and about the restraining order, but he said he didn't know it involved any violence. "I asked him about what happened," the older Cartier said. "He said, 'Well, me and my girlfriend had a fight.' I figured they argued. I've had plenty of fights, but I never physically abused any woman I was married to or living with."

Gene Cartier said he didn't know about his son's attack on Rose Ryan either. "I didn't know about that until after—after he died," the father said. "I know he was on Deer Island. He called me from there. What he told me was that it was for violation of probation."

There was an excuse for everything. Even the violation of probation, the elder Cartier contended, was based on a bum rap. "He wasn't the one who put the blood in the bottle," Gene Cartier insisted. "He took a rap for his friend. The friend was on probation so he took the rap for him. That was the kind of guy Michael was. He didn't think it was such a big deal.[15]

"I don't know if it was hereditary or it was some emotional problem he had," Gene Cartier said. "But he wasn't a bad kid. . . . He loved animals. He loved children. He wouldn't hurt a fly."

What about the kitten Cartier had hurled to its death?

"He threw a cat out a window?" Gene Cartier said. "I didn't know that. I never saw that side of him."

Gene Cartier's third wife, Kimberly, remembered how her stepson liked to take three-year-old Justin on train rides to Boston for the day and had promised to take him to the Aquarium on their next trip.

"He liked to show him off to his friends." She said that Michael was "very sensitive," that he cried on hearing that she and Gene were having marital difficulties. "He was concerned about Justin," she told the *Lawrence Eagle-Tribune.* "He didn't want what happened to him to happen to Justin. We assured him that his father was much older and wiser now." Like her husband, she said, "I didn't think he was capable of hurting a fly."

At times, Gene Cartier seemed to confuse Kristin with other girlfriends his son had, but his son's last phone call stuck firmly in his mind. "He said, 'She's busting my balls again.' I think she was seeing another guy—in front of Michael—to get him jealous. . . . He did love her. He was obsessed with her."

Kristin went to bed that night with a smile. It had been one of the best days she could remember. "We were having a really, really good time," Lauren Mace said. "I remember I said, 'Good night, Kristin.' I gave her a hug. The next morning, I saw her taking her bike down the street, on the way to work. I did not see her again."

Saturday, May 30, was a breathtaking spring day in Boston, a light breeze rustling the trees on Winchester Street below the flat. The sun poked through Kristin's window early that morning, brightening the brown and ocher sheets on her futon bed. The moon had already risen. Circe was balled up comfortably in a glass cage against the wall. Near the foot of her bed was a packing crate neatly stacked with LP's. Kristin had been listening to Stravinsky's "Rite of Spring." It was a present from Jason.

On the wall was a richly colored calendar with each month dedicated to a religious goddess. May was for Lakshmi, the Hindu Goddess of Good Fortune and Prosperity. Atop a bedside bookshelf was a Tufts summer school bulletin with a half-filled-out registration form. She still had plenty of time to decide what courses to take.

Kristin got up early enough for her usual long shower. She'd gotten in only a few hours at Marty's that week, and she was looking forward to a full day's work, starting at nine. Lauren was supposed to meet her at the store at six when she was done. They were going to buy a keg of beer for the party on Sunday. Kristin opened the hallway closet where she kept most of her clothes and picked out her favorite combination: black on black. Slacks, sweatshirt, shirt, shoes, and belt. She grabbed a black leather knapsack and hopped on her bike, a spray-painted hand-me-down a friend had given her months earlier. She'd asked me to buy her a bike so she could ride to the Museum School, but I'd procrastinated. I didn't like the idea of her pedaling that far every day in Boston's pell-mell traffic and thought she was still taking the T.

One of the managers at the liquor store, David Bergman, was having lunch across the street at the Inbound Pizza that afternoon when Kristin walked in. It is a frugally furnished place with bench tables and a walk-up counter with delicious selections. He waved her over to his table. She was in high spirits, but she'd skipped breakfast as usual, and, Bergman remembers, "she was really hungry." She had a slice of Sicilian pizza and then two more. "We talked for half an hour, about her hopes and aspirations," he said. "She was going to travel in Europe with her friend, Lauren. She had all these plans laid on."

After lunch, the day turned sour. Leslie North walked into the liquor store with another girl. One or both of them had reportedly consoled Cartier after he beat up Kristin. Kristin thought that was ridiculous. North says she said hi to Kristin.

Another customer walked in the door around the same time—a man with bad teeth and thinning hair—North's boyfriend. He got in Kristin's checkout line and started cursing at her. Kristin was shocked—and nervous. She ran up to two other clerks on duty at the time, Brooke Mezo and Julie Blankstein.

"Did you hear what he just said to me?" Kristin asked them. "He was swearing at me, saying 'fuck you' and things like that. We've got to get him kicked out of here. We can't have that guy in the store anymore."

"Why don't you tell Louis [Siegel, the manager]?" Julie asked her.

Kristin hesitated. Neither of the other clerks had heard the foul-mouthed outburst. She probably suspected Cartier's friends were harassing her on his behalf. She didn't want to make a big deal with the boss over her personal predicament. "I don't want to get in trouble," she told Blankstein.

Not long after North and her friends left the store, J. D. Crump, the manager at Bunratty's, walked in to get a sandwich at the Gourmet Deli a few steps from the checkout counters. He asked Kristin how she was doing. "She said she was having a tough day," Crump told the *Boston Globe.* "The customers were being mean. I told her it would get better."

It was around 4:30 P.M. when Crump spoke with Kristin that day. Cartier was at a noisy gathering at the Rathskeller on Kenmore Square around the same time, making what later seemed to be an ostentatious farewell to friends. Friends told the *Lawrence Eagle-Tribune* that he was acting strangely, greeting people with long hugs instead of the usual punch in the arm or a handshake. "He wasn't the hugging type," said Timothy McKernan. "I think he knew what he was going to do."

At some point after her visit to Marty's, Leslie North walked into the club. Could she have mentioned that she saw Kristin at Marty's, working that day? She said that Cartier "seemed fine" when she saw him, but "he left early. The show wasn't over."

To Anthony DeBaggis, another friend, who first met Cartier after his car accident, he seemed distracted. His eyes were darting around the Rathskeller, and he wasn't following conversations. Suddenly, he announced that he had to leave and ran out the door.

He was hurrying back to Allston, a quick ride on the T. Around 5:40 P.M., he rushed into the Reading Room, a smoke shop on Glenville Avenue just a few steps away from Harvard Avenue. "He was looking for a crowbar," the young proprietor, Jim Farris, said. "I asked him why he wanted a crowbar. He said he had to go hurt somebody. . . . The guy was a psycho. . . . I knew another girl he'd been dating. He hit her head against a brick wall."

Farris said Cartier had come into his shop weeks earlier, asking where he could get some bullets. "I said, nah, I didn't have a clue. This was at least a month before, maybe six weeks." And the proprietor said what so many others have echoed: "This could have been prevented if somebody had opened their mouths. Nobody talked."

Cartier rushed out of the store, reportedly still looking for a crowbar. He had about twenty minutes before Kristin was scheduled to get off work. In fact, she had already left. She was supposed to work the day shift, from nine to six, but at five, she was told, to her dismay, to leave early, losing an hour's pay. "We had other cashiers coming in at five," Bergman explained.

Kristin expressed her disappointment to David Bowden, who was working in the back room, packing boxes. "David, do you know they changed my schedule?" she asked him.

"No," he told her. "Why don't you work with us, packing boxes in the back? Punch back in. You can work with us."

"No," Kristin told him. "I don't want too many punches on my time card." She could come back later. She walked up Commonwealth to make an express deposit at the Bay Bank at 5:17 P.M., continued to the end of the block, and turned right onto Spofford Road, where Bekky Elstad lived. Instead of going home or hanging around to wait for Lauren, she decided to go to Bekky's apartment and return to Marty's at six. It was a decision that seems to have cost her her life.

Lauren had come by Marty's at 5:40 P.M., around the time that Cartier was rushing into the smoke shop a block away. She left when she was told that Kristin had already punched out and returned to the flat on Winchester Street, thinking she would find Kristin there. "I thought she'd gone home," Lauren said. "I keep thinking if I'd been with her, he wouldn't have done it. Or maybe he would have shot me, too. It was like something pushed me out of the way."

Kristin was still at Bekky's, keeping her eye on the clock, her good spirits bubbling back up. She had been upset, but now she was smiling, briskly recounting how this "disgusting . . . slimy person" had been cursing at her at the cash register.

"She was laughing about how gross he was and then his being with these two girls—friends of Michael's—who were so gross," Bekky Elstad said. "She was putting in a new cash register tape. The guy came up to her, and she said, 'If you want to go to another register, go ahead, I'll be a while.' He said, 'No, I'll wait,' and then he got annoyed. She

said he left and came back in with Michael's friends, these two girls."
But that couldn't keep Kristin down for long. "She seemed in a pretty
good mood," Bekky said. "They were having a going-away party for
Lauren Sunday. She was pretty excited about that."

It was getting close to six. After leaving the Reading Room, Cartier went over to Bunratty's, still looking for a crowbar and still coming
up empty. Police think he was looking for the tool to break in someplace and get a gun. They think he stole the weapon shortly before the
shooting. It's more likely that he had the gun all along. Maybe he had
been thinking of using a crowbar to bludgeon Kristin. As it turned out,
all he had was a gun. No crowbar was ever found. Whatever the
weapon, it's clear he was determined to kill her when she got off work
that day.

At one minute to six, Kristin was hurrying back down Commonwealth Avenue toward Marty's. Cartier, approaching from the other direction, had a shorter distance to travel. He had just stopped at a Store
24 convenience store on the other side of Harvard Avenue. J. D. Crump
was in there, buying a pack of cigarettes. According to the police report: "[Crump] stated that recently [Cartier] had been asking people if
they could get a gun. Crump stated that he had a conversation with
Cartier about that and [Cartier] tried to make light of it but then stated
that he was going to shoot someone.

"[Cartier] had been in Bunratty's earlier in the day looking for a
crowbar and stated that he was going to get someone. Crump stated
that while in Store 24 a short time before the shooting he saw Mike and
asked him [if] he was going to work that night. Mike said that he was
but had [to] shoot someone first. Crump stated that he did not take
him seriously and walked away from him."

The shots rang out seconds later. Cartier must have seen Kristin
first. He strode past a tall, lanky man with thinning red hair and confronted her outside the Philadelphia Steak and Hoagie restaurant. The
red-haired man, Daniel Graham, noticed them just a couple of steps
ahead of him as he was walking west on Commonwealth. At first, he
thought Cartier was simply another unhappy boyfriend.

"The two crossed paths just in front of me," Graham said. "He said something to her. He asked her if he could see her that night or something like that. She said no, no. She made it clear that she wasn't interested. Basically, she brushed him off. It didn't seem that out of the ordinary."16

Cartier kept walking west, Kristin kept going in the opposite direction, toward Marty's. "Oh yeah, a jilted boyfriend," Graham said to himself. "She didn't seem worried. She just kept walking down the street."

They kept walking away from each other. The next thing Graham knew, Cartier wheeled around, moved toward Kristin, and aimed a gun at the back of her head. Graham saw the weapon glint in the sun.

It was more than Kristin saw. Cartier fired once. "He stretched his arm out," Graham remembered. "It was almost point-blank at her head."

Mike Dillon, the clerk at Marty's who clocked out at six, had just stepped onto the sidewalk at that point. He looked up instantly and saw Kristin fall outside the Soap-A-Rama, just next door to the restaurant.

Graham froze. "Maybe this is a prank," he thought. "Maybe there's a camera recording this."

Cartier retreated, never saying a word. He ducked into an alley between Arbuckle's Restaurant and the Heads Up hair salon, the last stores in the commercial row. Just as abruptly, he came back out of the alley, rushed over to Kristin, and leaned forward.

"He shot her twice more in the head," Graham said. "I ducked into a doorway, not knowing what he was going to do."

Scott Morales, another clerk at Marty's, had been loading a case of beer into a customer's car when he heard the three shots. "A black man shouted out, 'There's a girl down,' " Morales said. "I ran up. Mike turned around. He said, 'It's Kristin.' I said, 'No way.' Then I turned around. I saw this guy [Cartier]. I'm in shock for like fifteen seconds. I thought to myself, 'Can I do anything?' I saw Gay in the flower shop. I said, 'Did you call the cops?' She said yes."17

Some youngsters were playing games at the Soap-A-Rama. One of them, Paul Pitts, fourteen, a special student at a South End school, heard the first shot and saw Kristin on the sidewalk. He thought she was playing a game, too. Then, in the words of the police report, "He observed this man stand over the woman and fire two more shots into the front of her forehead."[18]

Chris Toher, the proprietor at Soap-A-Rama, heard the first shot from the back of his store and hurried up to the doorway to find out what happened. Some kids were trailing behind him. He was afraid that Cartier would come in shooting. He pushed them back.

"I saw him fire the final shots," Toher said. "It happened so fast she never had a chance. She was completely unconscious at the point he ran up to her. Her eyes were shut."[19]

A brave young woman was dead.

The killer fled down the alley to a parking area behind the stores and then to Glenville Avenue, where he lived in a red brick apartment building with a combination lock on the main door. Back on Commonwealth Avenue, police and an ambulance arrived within minutes. The ambulance crew had been eating at the Boston Chicken store on Commonwealth and Harvard when bystanders began pounding on the hood of their vehicle, telling them it was needed. The crew hurried to the scene. Police arrived moments later.

"A whole group of people ran down to get it [the ambulance]," Gay Sheldon said at the flower shop. "It made some people think that was the direction the shooter took."

The police were soon set straight. J. D. Crump told them where Cartier lived. Crump had been on his way back to Bunratty's when he heard the shots and hurried back over to Commonwealth. Scott Morales accosted him near the corner.

"Do you know where Mike is?" Morales demanded. "Does he have an alibi?"

"No, why?" Crump responded.

"Kristin!" Morales told him.

"My God, I just saw him at Store 24 a few seconds ago."

Crump hurried into the Soap-A-Rama. His girlfriend was there. He was afraid something might have happened to her. He had been at Store 24 getting cigarettes for her. After seeing Cartier, he said, "I walked back to Bunratty's. I heard it. It was the worst seventy-five seconds of my life."

Police conducted their questioning at the Soap-A-Rama. It was Detective Dwyer, a solid veteran, who made out the report about the encounter at Store 24, quoting Crump as saying, "Mike said that he . . . had to shoot someone first."

Brooke Mezo, the clerk from Marty's, witnessed the interrogation. She said she heard Crump quoting Cartier as saying at Store 24 that "he had to take care of something." However, she added, Crump "did say that Michael had spoken to him in the past couple of weeks and said he couldn't live without her, that he was going to kill her. And he talked about getting a gun."

Distraught and shaken, Crump scolded himself repeatedly when I talked to him. Kristin had told him not long before the shooting how worried she was, how badly Cartier had beaten her, and that he had been in jail for beating another woman. Crump said Cartier had said to him on occasion, "I want to kill her," and then would add, "But you can't do that." The Bunratty's manager told me he confronted Cartier "two days before" and threatened to call his probation officer if he hit her again.

"I gave him the tough-guy routine," Crump said, his eyes moist with tears. "I told him, 'You touch her one more time and you'll be gone.' "

"I'll be cool," he said Cartier had told him. "I'll take care of it."

"Mike asked me to butt out, and I did," Crump told the *Boston Globe* immediately after the shooting. "That's a regret."

The ambulance took Kristin to Brigham & Women's Hospital, where she was pronounced dead at 6:25 P.M. I remember clinging to the hope that they could still save her when Helen told me over the phone that that was where she'd been taken. "That's a good hospital," I said. Helen had already talked to Dr. Souther. She didn't want to fan false hopes. "No, Dad," she said, "she's dead."

* * *

Police sealed off a four-block area around Cartier's apartment building, anticipating a shootout.

"Cartier was believed to still be in possession of a firearm and believed to be extremely dangerous," Dwyer said later that night in his formal report. "He had apparently made statements to several people that he hated policemen and had no reservations about shooting a cop. He stated that he would never go back to prison again."

A police forced-entry team entered Cartier's apartment around 8:30 P.M. with a key from the building's owners. They found him dead, lying on his bed with the .38 he used to kill Kristin in his right hand. He had put it to his head and fired once. Police recovered the spent shell from the bedroom wall. They found three other shell casings in the area where he murdered Kristin.

According to his father, the autopsy showed he had not been high on anything. "They said drugs and alcohol were not involved," Gene Cartier said. "There were no drugs in his system: heroin, speed, cocaine, nothing.[20] He did love her. He wanted to marry her, believe it or not."

Later that night, Leslie North walked into Bunratty's, looking for Cartier. "I said, 'He shot Kristin,' " J. D. Crump said. "She didn't look surprised. I said, 'Then he went and shot himself.' At that point, she lost it. She started screaming, 'What a waste! What a waste! He's dead!' "

Crump later said, "I've had to live the past couple of weeks feeling I could have stopped him. I should have called his probation officer."

It's doubtful that would have done any good. The system is so witless that when the dead Cartier failed to show up in Boston Municipal Court as scheduled on June 19, a warrant was issued for his arrest. It was still outstanding when the *Post* article I wrote was published the following November. John Tobin told the *Boston Herald* at that point that he would have the warrant withdrawn. He said it was mistakenly written up by a clerk who didn't recognize Cartier's name.

"We have thousands of people coming in here," Tobin said. "The name probably didn't leap off the page."

That's just the trouble. Despite all the warning signals he sent out, Cartier's name didn't leap off the page when it should have. There are thousands of people like him. When the criminal justice system picks them up, it lets them go again and again. The killers on our streets are becoming younger and younger.[21] And the younger they are, the more they can get away with. "To wink at a fault causes trouble," the Book of Proverbs says. The next line is: "But a bold reproof makes peace."

13

The gong kept banging dolefully in the great hall of the Boston State House. Hundreds of T-shirts waved from jury-rigged clothes-lines, each shirt with a searing message about a particular woman's experience. The gong was struck as a signal that a woman is battered somewhere in the United States every fifteen seconds. The T-shirts fluttered in all sizes, grim reminders of how old the women were when they were raped, assaulted, or killed. Some belonged to little girls. One was infant-sized, commemorating a baby born dead after her mother was kicked in the belly by her partner.[1]

It was April 26, 1994, precisely one year, ten months, and twenty-seven days after Kristin's murder. I was back in Boston because of what had happened to her. This was Victim's Rights Week, and I'd been invited to take part in a day-long conference devoted to victims, the kind of people who make the criminal justice system uncomfortable. When a defendant's life or liberty is at risk, it's easy, too easy, to forget the innocent people who have already lost theirs. Massachusetts was one of the first states to enact a victim's bill of rights. Most states have them now. But in Massachusetts, as in most states, they aren't real rights. Rather, as a staff study for the Massachusetts Office for Victim Assistance pointed out, "They are services and courtesies that the District Attorney and the courts may provide." Throughout the country, assailants are still released on bond without regard for their victim's safety. Plea bargains are struck without notice to the victims. Some victims, like Rose Ryan, are shocked to learn of a convicted attacker's release from custody without a word of warning.

When my turn at the lectern came, all too soon for someone who would rather write than talk, I tried to stress what struck me as the inattention paid to the real costs of crime in contrast to the expense of fighting it. It had occurred to me that one of the biggest failings of the justice system is the underlying assumption that it would cost too much to keep it from failing. Cartier should have been in jail the day he killed Kristin, whatever the price tag. It costs less to nip crime in the bud than to deal, repeatedly, with its consequences.[2] It's often said that domestic violence, in particular, needs to be addressed by all facets of society, but that doesn't excuse the justice system from doing its job. Some judges contend it is wrong and even dangerous to look for weak links in the system after each new tragedy because it "sends the false message that people will no longer be in danger when we get the system in order."[3] A search for weak links sends no such message and poses no dangers, except perhaps to the weak links. What is dangerous is a justice system that pretends to be just an emergency room, entitled to sit back and wait for the dead and dying to show up. What is dangerous is a system full of "juris doctors" who fail to see how mightily they contributed to those emergencies or, if they see it, simply shrug their shoulders and go on to the next emergency. What is needed is a justice system that works in the most mundane of ways, a system that pays attention to the "little things" before they become emergencies, a system that enforces the laws instead of complaining that it can't.

According to the most recent Justice Department study of the system's resources, only 3.3 cents of every government dollar spent in a single year—that's federal, state, and local—goes to justice activities, criminal and civil.[4] That's little more than three pennies for everything: police, courts, prosecutors, public defenders, prisons, probation, parole, the works. Little more than a penny (1.1 cents) went for "corrections," including probation and parole. Americans spend less per person on their justice system than the residents of England and Wales spend on theirs.[5] As a special committee of the American Bar Association observed several years ago, "The entire criminal justice system is starved for resources."[6] The omnibus crime bill enacted by Congress in 1994 may help on the margins, but it is not going to change the arithmetic by much.[7] Under that crime bill, the federal dollars will disappear before long, creating consternation at state and local levels, which already shoulder much more of that 3.3 percent of the costs than Washington does. We just don't like to spend much money on law enforcement. As James Q. Wilson puts it, "For most of us, the criminal justice system is intended for the other fellow, and since the other fellow is thought to be wicked, we can easily justify to ourselves a pinch-penny attitude toward the system. It is, after all, designed not to help us, but to hurt him."[8]

Is there a more fundamental government function than the public safety? Yet we—again the "we" is federal, state, and local—spend six times more on social insurance payments, almost five times as much on national defense and international relations, four times as much on education and libraries, more than three times as much on interest on debt, twice as much on housing and the environment, and almost twice as much on public welfare.[9] The federal government alone spends nearly $25 billion a year on job-training and job-related programs, including training loans for jobs that don't exist.[10] But when new prisons are proposed, what we often hear is editorial thunder about how this is going to bankrupt us. That is plain nonsense. It also ignores the persistent overcrowding that the same pundits so frequently deplore. The columns of leading newspapers, including my own, are often peppered with talk about how too many minor, first-time offenders are clogging our prison cells. In fact, 94 percent of those in state prisons across the country—which is where most of the inmates are—are violent or repeat offenders.[11]

The first thing prison opponents tell us is that it costs $25,000 to house a single prisoner for a single year, a figure that, they like to add, is comparable to what it costs to send a child to Harvard. You won't hear them presenting prison costs in per capita terms, which is the commonly accepted practice. Why not? Because the per capita cost is so low. The annual cost to every citizen to keep all one million inmates in all 1,600 prisons (state and federal) in the United States for an entire year is roughly $100 (assuming the $25,000 cost per prisoner is correct).[12] Actually, the cost is probably closer to $21,900 a year—or $78 a person, less than many of us spend on cable TV.

But no matter how the costs are measured, it can cost even more to set them loose. According to an expert panel of the National Academy of Sciences, the near tripling of the prison population between 1975 and 1989 reduced the potential level of violent crime by 10 to 15 percent during that period through incapacitation alone—"the isolation that prevents prisoners from committing crimes in the community."[13] As columnist Ben Wattenberg has put it, "A thug in prison can't shoot your sister."[14] Or, I might add, your daughter.

According to Patrick Langan, senior statistician at the Bureau of Justice Statistics, had the prison population not grown over this period, and the 10 to 15 percent reduction therefore not occurred, there would have been at least 390,000 more murders, rapes, robberies, and aggravated assaults in 1989 than were actually reported.[15]

Three years later, the trend was the same. Imprisonments were still going up, and the crime rates were still below what they were in the seventies. Looking back, Langan points out that if the crime rates in 1973 had still been afflicting us in 1992, there would have been almost half a million more rapes, robberies, and aggravated assaults. If prisons averted only 50 or even 25 percent of that amount, it would still leave them responsible for sizable reductions in crime.[16]

"If you put people in prison who commit violent crimes, you'll get fewer violent crimes than you would if they weren't in prison," Langan said. "It doesn't take a degree in physics to figure this out."[17]

Those crimes cause turmoil for their victims. And they have costs that can be expressed in terms of dollars. The National Council on Crime and Delinquency, which doesn't like prisons, has estimated the cost of an average rape—for the person raped—at just $357.[18] It was part of an effort by NCCD to demonstrate the virtues of an Illinois program for early release from prison. The Justice Department's Bureau of Justice Statistics takes a similar approach. It put the costs of rape to a victim in 1992 at $234, but it counts only out-of-pocket expenses and only for six months after the crime was committed.[19]

I didn't know about Dina Badia when I spoke at the conference. I read about her later. But her ordeal illustrates the point. A twenty-five-year-old waitress in Dade County, Florida, she was accosted from behind as she approached her apartment in the early morning of April 17, 1993. Her attacker led her to a nearby lake after telling her he would kill her if she screamed. She had no purse. "I thought he was going to rape me," she told the *Miami Herald*.[20] What else could he have wanted? "If he was going to rob me, why did he walk me down to the lake?"

She got away by spraying Mace in his face. Her attacker, Lazarus Banks, was caught a week later while breaking into a Kendall apartment and linked to more than sixty burglaries. Badia wanted him sent to prison. Charged with strong-arm robbery for his attack on her, along with five counts of armed burglary, he got probation, thanks to a plea bargain. The judge kept the burglary cases off his record by withholding adjudication. Dade County prosecutors notified Badia by mail. She couldn't believe it. She couldn't leave her apartment for five days after the attack. Months later, she was still angry and upset. When she goes around a corner and hears a frog croaking, she jumps. When she gets home, she runs from her car to the door. "I'm going to be affected for life," she says.[21]

All that, by the Justice Department's calculus, was worth only $555. And that's assuming it was classified as a robbery. If it had been treated as an "attempted rape," officialdom would have put the cost at $234. Yet even this shortsighted math says that crime victims in 1992 lost $17.6 billion in "direct costs" for rape, robbery, assault, personal and household theft, burglary, and motor vehicle theft.[22]

How much more such crimes really cost their victims was spelled out in a study published in *Health Affairs* in 1993. Using jury awards and other data, it took pain, suffering, risk of death, lost income, and other long-term medical and mental health expenses into account. It estimated the cost of each murder at $2.8 million (updated to 1993 dollars). Each attempted or completed rape posed a lifetime cost to the victim of $56,000; robbery, $23,000; and assault, $17,000. Put another way, for the victims alone, the total lifetime costs of the violent crimes committed each year is $208 billion.[23] That's more than twice what all levels of government spend on the American justice system, civil and criminal.[24]

Other studies indicate that the costs of crimes committed by a serious offender on the street each year are about twice as high as the costs of putting him in prison. The typical state prison inmate, studies by Princeton's John DeIulio showed, committed a dozen property or violent crimes in the year before he was put in his cell—with each crime costing up to $6,000 a year.[25]

Given that level of damages, the New Jersey Sentencing Policy Commission concluded: "Prison often pays." The social costs of the crimes that would have been committed by the typical New Jersey inmate in a single year were estimated at more than $70,000, compared to an annual cost of $31,466 for incarceration. Unfortunately, as the commission noted, discussions about the costs of imprisonment do not usually "take into account the financial benefits of locking up criminals."[26]

That doesn't mean that everyone convicted of a crime deserves prison or that it would "pay" to lock up every convicted felon. Imprisoning drug offenders, who are occupying more and more cells, may save less.[27] But a strong case can be made for the proposition that it would be best to lock up many offenders, particularly violent offenders, earlier rather than later in their careers, instead of introducing them to the revolving-door system of which they are so scornful. The peak age for a criminal is between sixteen and eighteen. The average prison inmate is ten years older. Those older offenders draw the stiffest sentences not simply because they are adults, but because they have been given so many breaks.[28] The idea that we are spending "an exorbitant amount of money each year to warehouse petty criminals," a complaint that an unquestioning Tom Wicker once echoed in the *New York Times,* is simply false.[29]

The prisons, for their part, should offer humane conditions of confinement, and those must include treatment, education, recreation, and work programs. Good prison management requires them. Idleness is dangerous. As one study of prisons in Michigan, California, and Texas found, "It appears that little of a desirable nature can happen in prisons unless prison authorities maintain order. Commenting on his experiences in prison classrooms, a Michigan inmate said, 'It's hard to look at the blackboard when you're worried about getting stabbed.' "[30] But if our criminal laws are to have any meaning, the main purpose of prisons must be punishment and the protection of society. They should not be judged on whether they reform or rehabilitate their inmates. Too many critics of prisons judge them solely by whether they reduce the crime rate or transform their inmates. It is a utilitarian standard that ignores the crimes already committed and insults their victims. It tells them that they don't count, that only the criminals do.[31]

"It is the duty of prisons to govern fairly and well within their own walls," criminologists Charles H. Logan and Gerald G. Gaes wrote recently in *Justice Quarterly.* "It is not their duty to reform, rehabilitate, or reintegrate offenders into society. Though they *may* attempt these things, it is not their *duty* even to attempt these goals, let alone their obligation to achieve them."[32]

Efforts to prevent crime and to rehabilitate offenders—or even, in many cases, to habilitate them—especially when they are young, are vital, too. But we should recognize that many of those efforts are a case of too little too late, as they were with Michael Cartier.

He was headed for a life of crime at age seven, when his mother had him installed at the New England Home. He had an awful childhood, starting with a serious illness shortly after he was born. He tortured his pet rabbit, tried to beat up his first-grade teacher, and was constantly attempting to run away from home. He was convinced he had been abandoned when he was put in the New England Home, and no parental disclaimers could change that fact. Thinking he was abandoned made it so. His mother's repeated failures to meet him at appointed times made him worse.

Against all that, the New England Home had impressive facilities. A residential treatment program, it had one staffer for every two children during the daytime and two staffers for every four or five during the evening. The social workers usually had master's degrees, and the teachers were all certified for special education. Cartier was one of about twenty-four youngsters, aged five to twelve, in the home's Child

Care Center. It had a psychologist who tested and consulted for the program, and it provided regular psychiatric consultations.

"The amount of energy and effort that went into each of those kids was tremendous," Cartier's child-care worker, Tom Walsh, said. "On Friday afternoons, they would have case conferences and they would have a good ten to fifteen people there to discuss just one kid at a time. The teachers would be there, the child-care workers who were handling the kids on the halls, the school nurse if there were medications involved, maybe the Department of Social Services people if they were around. And they would make decisions on which way to proceed. . . . Sometimes you miss things. Sometimes you just can't do enough. And sometimes, it wouldn't have mattered what you did. . . . The window of opportunity for dealing with a lot of these kids was probably anywhere between six and eight years old."

The program no doubt helped some of the children it treated. But Cartier was too damaged. He stayed five years. When he left, former director Octavia Ossola remembers, "All of us were very sad, very concerned that here was a youngster who was going to have fairly serious trouble . . ."[33]

Sociologist Robert Martinson studied programs aimed at older ages and concluded that hardly anything worked. "Most criminologists think Martinson's original conclusion was too gloomy," James Q. Wilson says, while adding that he remains "somewhat agnostic" on the point.[34] A relatively new, and controversial, way of looking at old programs, called meta-analysis, has found some merit in juvenile programs that was not apparent before by pooling them into one sweeping "mega-evaluation."[35] But one by one, the programs have minimal effect, if any, and "collectively," as Wilson has observed, "the best estimate of the crime-reduction value of these programs is quite modest, on the order of 5 or 10 percent."[36] Even that slender result may not be applicable to adult offenders.[37]

Fear of crime, violent crime, has come to dominate public concern, even though crime rates are lower than they were some twenty years ago.[38] The rates, as measured by the National Crime Victimization Survey, have actually gone down since 1973, when the survey was first conducted. The volume has gone up, from 5.3 million violent crimes in 1973 to 6.6 million in 1992, but so has the population. In terms of the number of crimes per 1,000 people, rapes declined by 28 percent, robberies by 11.9 percent, and assaults by 11 percent.[39] Similarly, there were 4,120 more homicides in 1992 than there were in 1973, but the rate remained about the same, 9.3 killings per thousand in 1992 compared to 9.4 in 1973.[40] The peak year for all violent crime was 1981, but it drew little attention. The press was preoccupied with Ronald Reagan, Iran, the economy, and the cold war. So, perhaps, was the public. One reason the crime rates went down was the increasing tendency of judges to send offenders to jail. Other factors, experts say, included the aging of the postwar baby boomers and a growing wariness on the part of potential victims.[41] Young and old, they're protecting themselves, by staying home at night, by not going to parties, by being careful.

But it isn't the crime rates alone that matter. It isn't the rates that make people wary. It's the realization that the law isn't protecting them properly, that it doesn't have enough teeth.[42] It's the fact that almost three out of every four people serving a criminal sentence on any given day in this country are walking the streets. It's the fact that only one serious crime in twelve results in a felony arrest, and fewer than half of those arrests result in felony convictions.[43] It's the fact that fewer than half of those convicted are sent to prison, and those who are imprisoned serve little more than a third of their sentences.[44] It's the fact that the typical state prison inmate spends only thirteen months behind bars now, compared to thirty months at the end of World War II and twenty-one months when John F. Kennedy was elected.[45] It's the fact that almost two-thirds of those released from prison are rearrested for a serious crime in less than three years, and almost two out of every three felony probationers are rearrested for another felony or charged with violating the terms of their probation within three years.[46] It's the sense that there are more and more thugs and killers growing up in our midst, about to enter the same revolving door.

Our most frightening criminals are the youngest. In Chicago, an eleven-year-old boy slashes his eighty-four-year-old neighbor's throat.

In Maryland, a D.C. teenager who shot six people at a municipal swimming pool escapes from a minimum security youth center; with him is another boy accused of a double murder. Back in Chicago, a five-year-old is killed when two other boys, one ten and the other eleven, push him out a fourteenth-floor window because he refused to steal candy for them. Both boys have juvenile records. The ten-year-old was on probation for unlawful use of a weapon. Youthful killers, to be sure, commit only a small fraction of all homicides, but that is not at all reassuring when one considers the unpredictability of their violence. Crime has become more horrific. We can blame television, news and entertainment, for bringing it home so starkly, but the violence is too real to be turned off with a remote control button. Americans are quite right, as Wilson says, in believing that something fundamental has changed in our patterns of crime. "We are terrified by the prospect of innocent people being gunned down at random, without warning and almost without motive, by youngsters who afterward show us the blank, unremorseful faces of seemingly feral, presocial beings."[47]

Some seem to think the schools can make a big difference, in helping to cut down on violence, in teaching young boys that girls are not "objects of play." They should certainly try, but the expectation is somewhat ironic when many teachers fear for their own safety. Every day, according to estimates of the National School Safety Center, about 135,000 students nationwide carry guns into schools.[48] In troubled inner-city high schools, more than one in five male students own a gun, nearly one in ten brings it to school at least "now and then," and more than one in three have access to a gun and occasionally take one when they go outdoors. The custom may be spreading to elementary school. In Washington, D.C., recently, a five-year-old kindergarten student was apprehended taking a fully loaded .380-caliber handgun from his bookbag and showing it to two other boys in the back of their classroom.[49]

Most say they do it mainly to protect themselves.[50] What used to wind up in a fistfight all too often ends with a shooting. But ever stricter gun control laws aren't going to settle that. There are already plenty of laws on the books. They need to be enforced. Handgun crimes soared to record levels in 1992, reaching a level of more than 930,000, but experts believe that only about 2 percent of the 200 million guns in private hands are used to commit those crimes.[51] Almost all of the illegal weapons are handguns, and they are usually borrowed, stolen, or acquired in private transactions, not from a gunstore or pawnshop. Yet as James Wilson points out, "The average police officer will make *no* weapons arrests and confiscate *no* guns during any given year." In 1992, police across the country arrested only about 240,000 people for illegally possessing or carrying a weapon. Four times as many people were arrested for public drunkenness.[52]

In the view of some experts, there is nothing new about the youthful violence of today except in the "tools" that are used. But I think it goes beyond that. There is a very real "culture of violence" in American society that encourages aggression at every high-tech turn we take. As sociologist Elijah Anderson points out, affirming one's manhood today for many teenagers means much more than refusing to run from a fight. It means throwing the first punch or firing the first shot. It means not caring whether you live or die.[53]

Juvenile judges recognize the problem. They see those faces. In fact, according to a recent poll by the *National Law Journal,* most juvenile judges think today's youth are more "depraved" than those of fifteen years ago.[54] And they don't know what to do with them. Almost half of the judges, 48 percent, say flatly that the juvenile justice system is failing, and another 17 percent are inclined to believe that it is. A vast majority of the judges favor tougher measures, such as fingerprinting juveniles (93 percent), opening up their records to adult law enforcement authorities (91 percent), and conducting open court hearings for juveniles accused of felonies (68 percent). Four out of ten of the judges say juveniles as young as fourteen should be tried for murder as adults and even subject under certain circumstances to the death penalty. Yet they cling to the belief that most of the offenders who come before them could be rehabilitated if only first-rate, well-financed programs were available. Perhaps that should not be surprising for a group dedicated to the proposition that they can make a difference, that they can somehow turn their troubled charges into law-abiding citizens. As one expert told the *National Law Journal:* "Juvenile court judges see themselves as the last hope between salvageable kids and adult crime."[55]

The key word is "salvageable." No doubt many of them are. Others will mature on their own, without judicial intervention. As Hunter Hurst, director of the Pittsburgh-based National Center for Juvenile Justice, says, "Most of the kids who enter the system don't grow up to be criminals." But it is the most intractable ones who keep coming back to plague the system, especially in the larger cities, where they get one free pass after another. "We have a long history of throwing the big money at the poor risk," Hurst said. "We do that in health, we do that in crime. We do that in many areas of life. And when you back off and look at it, it doesn't make a whole lot of sense."[56]

The persistent lawbreakers are just a small fraction of any particular age group, but for them even the best-financed programs fail to make a difference. One of the most discouraging efforts was an ambitious program launched in the mid-1980s at the Paint Creek Youth Center in southern Ohio. A combination of the latest concepts considered "critical to success," it was specially "tailored to the individual requirements" of thirty to thirty-five youths convicted of serious felonies, in contrast to the traditional state training schools that house several hundred. The Paint Creek youths spent at least a year at the center and were not locked in. They received home furloughs, family visits, meticulous guidance and counseling, and toward the end of the program, part-time jobs for pay.[57]

The results? One year after release, according to a glum 1993 evaluation by the Rand Corporation, there were "no significant differences in arrests or self-reported delinquency" between those who went to Paint Creek and those who did not. In fact, more of the Paint Creek youths owned up to a misdemeanor assault during the first year they were home than those from the training schools. "It may be," the Rand report said, "that the somewhat chaotic and calloused environment of [the traditional training school] does just as good a job of preparing youths for the outside world as the Positive Peer Culture of PCYC . . ."[58]

There is something else that must be understood. The teenagers may have been too old to reform. Both groups consisted of serious felons over sixteen. Only in America do we pretend that our children need so long to grow up, that they aren't really responsible for their actions until, or after, they're old enough to be sent to war. What we forget is how quickly most of us reach the age of reason and acquire a sense of right and wrong, how young we were when we were doing good or bad and knew that we were doing it. How we are brought up, of course, has a lot to do with our moral sense, but it has a lot to do with it at a very early age. And it has a lot to do with what the children themselves bring to the table.

As Wilson says, "What is striking about the newer findings of child psychologists is that the emergence of a moral sense occurs before the child has acquired much in the way of a language. . . . Beginning at an early age, children can tell the difference between moral and nonmoral issues. That is to say, when asked if it is all right to do something even if there is no rule against it, children draw distinctions between actions that are always wrong (for example, lying, stealing, and unprovoked hitting) and things that are wrong only when there are rules against it (for example, boys entering the girls' bathroom, not going to school every day, or staring at someone while they undress). Moreover, there are some things that children regard as wrong whether they are middle-class residents of Hyde Park [in Chicago], Illinois, or Hindus living in the Indian village of Bhubaneswar. These include breaking a promise, stealing flowers, kicking a harmless animal, and destroying another's property."[59] Children are neither blank tablets nor pint-sized adults. Parents do make a difference in how they turn out, but probably more in terms of their morality than their personality. That moral difference, in turn, may depend on how the individual child is treated, compared to, say, his brother or sister. It is impossible for parents to treat two children alike, unless, perhaps, they are identical twins. "And though we may wish to give equal attention to both a cuddly, obedient child and a restless, obstinate one, we know that we cannot."[60] Life is unfair, and it can be unfair at a very early age. Children know that, even if they forget it as parents.

What all this means in terms of how a child will turn out, Wilson says, is not well understood, but "social scientists have made some headway. The single most important discovery has been the importance to the child of having a strong and affectionate bond to the parents, especially to the mother."[61] As a three-year study for the Carnegie Corporation of New York recently documented, those bonds are becoming more and more strained. The report, prepared by a prominent thirty-member panel, said that millions of infants and toddlers are so deprived of medical attention, loving care, and intellectual stimulation that their chances of becoming healthy, responsible adults are threatened. There is a huge pool of potential Michael Cartiers out there. Nearly three million American children, a fourth of all infants and toddlers under the age of three, live in poverty, the panel said. Divorce rates, births to unmarried women, and single-parent households had grown alarmingly over the previous thirty years. Twenty-eight percent of the children born in 1990 were born to unmarried mothers, compared to 5 percent in 1960, and 27 percent of the children under three were living with one parent, compared to 7 percent in 1960.[62]

Reports of child abuse were also rising, with almost one in every three abused children being a baby less than a year old. More than half of the women with children that age were working. Many of the children were spending most of their time in child care of such substandard quality that it adversely affected their development. At the same time, new medical studies indicate that the earliest years, from birth to age three, are critical to the development of the human brain. Other research indicates that early stress releases hormones that can hamper learning and memory, supporting the belief that such tensions in children can lead to intellectual and behavioral problems.[63]

Child welfare agencies are often unreliable sources of help. In the District of Columbia, the city's social workers have for years had too few cars to pick up children in imminent danger, no paper on which to take notes, limited access to telephones, and no diapers or formula for at-risk babies.[64] In New York City, according to a recent report by the city comptroller, the city's Child Welfare Administration is so fixated on returning children to their natural parents that it often violates state law as well as its own policies. "There is a compulsion to keep going to parents who are no longer interested or caring," City Comptroller Alan G. Hevesi said. He found one girl who was returned to her mother at age six, after five years in uninterrupted foster care.[65]

What is surprising is not how many children turn out badly under such circumstances, and by "badly" I mean serious, protracted criminal behavior, but how few do. Children who have been abused and neglected are more likely to be arrested as juveniles (by 53 percent), more likely to be arrested as adults (38 percent), and more likely to commit violent crimes (by 38 percent).[66] But the majority of abused and neglected children do not become delinquents, adult criminals, or violent offenders. They may, of course, have other problems in their lives. And there is much that we don't know. The findings are based on official arrest records, which say nothing about other violent behavior, "especially unrecorded or unreported family violence."[67]

But it is not my purpose to stray much beyond the justice system. Its failings are our failings. Its priorities are our priorities, but later rather than sooner. It takes the courts a long time to catch on and follow "th' illiction returns."[68] But too often the demands are for harsher and harsher penalties, instead of swift and certain punishment. Harsher sentences are often deserved, but quicker ones are more effective. What is forgotten is that the most ominous penalties are the least likely to be carried out. What is ignored is the snail-like pace of the justice system that takes far too long to impose any penalty at all. The crime issue was shamelessly exploited in the last campaign by candidates promising to "hang 'em high" and distorted by others claiming there really was no problem.[69] Former New York Governor Mario Cuomo put his finger on one of the biggest problems during his unsuccessful re-election campaign when he expressed his exasperation at the kind of criminal the justice system increasingly faces today:

"You can't stop them with a gun. A lot of them don't even care about your gun. You know what it is. You lock them up. You look at them. You say, 'You just killed somebody,' and they look right through you, some of these kids. Like they don't know what you are talking about. Like, 'What's the big deal?' "[70]

Nit-pickers might quarrel with Cuomo on one point. Guns would "stop them," just as "these kids" could have told him from long nights with Clint Eastwood and Arnold Schwarzenegger, not to mention their own excursions into real life. For these kids, violence is truly as American as apple pie. For them, it isn't so much a matter of might making right. For them, might is right. It's a message they can receive day and night by turning on the TV, playing a videogame, listening to heavy-metal or rap music, or even picking up a comic book. The good guys are the ones who win by killing everybody else, aren't they? As Myriam Miedzian has written in her study of links between masculinity and violence: "Whether it be on the TV or in films, at wrestling matches, heavy metal or rap concerts, hockey and football games, or in toys—the message far too often is that violence is acceptable, violence is fun."[71]

Common sense tells us that those who grow up in a violence-ridden society will produce more of it. Ninety percent of the juvenile judges polled by the *National Law Journal* said the media make youths more prone to violence. No one who has listened to heavy-metal or rap lyrics could doubt that, especially when it comes to violence against women. "Sick of chicks—they're all bitches," says one tune by Suicidal Tendencies. "Sick of living—gonna die." Or how about this from an album called *Girls, Girls, Girls* by Motley Crue: "Those last few nights it [the blade of my knife] turned and sliced you apart / Laid out cold, now we're both alone . . . / But killing you helped keep me home."[72] Rap music degrades women, too. "Faggots, bitches / look how their ass switches," sings a group called Just-Ice. Another of their songs goes: "Don't try to get too close / And try to kiss me and hug me . . . / It's only rhythm that I ride / The only love I got is psychopathic homicide."[73]

Despite all that and more, many scholars are dubious about how much violence is *caused* by the media.[74] There are more obvious footprints: unfit parents, chaotic neighborhoods, childhood temperaments. Rehabilitation isn't going to come about simply by invoking the word or even spending money on it. Amid all the debate last year about what became the Violent Crime Control and Law Enforcement Act of 1994, there was much talk about the need for programs to prevent crime and not just punish it. Billions of dollars were earmarked for sports, recreation, and job-training programs, primarily for teenagers. There may be much to be said for these efforts, but as Wilson observes, "Crime prevention is not one of them." We must recognize what we are up against. "The typical high-rate offender is well-launched on his career before he becomes a teenager or has ever encountered the labor market."[75]

What's surprising is how concentrated the criminality is. One study after another has come up with the same ratio: about 6 percent of the boys born in a given year will commit more than half of all the serious crimes committed by boys of that age and almost three-quarters of all the violent crimes.[76] Many of them come from quarrelsome, unloving families, and their parents may have criminal records. They may have a quick temper and a cold heart, do poorly in school, and start getting in trouble by the time they're in the third grade. As Wilson points out, "Prevention, if it can be made to work at all, must start early in life, perhaps as early as the first two or three years, and given the odds it faces—childhood impulsivity, low verbal facility, incompetent parenting, disorderly neighborhoods—it must be massive in scope."[77]

The trouble is, it's easy to describe the unruly crowd, but not to pick out the individuals who are going to commit the most crimes. It's one thing to lump a lot of rehabilitation programs together and point to an aggregate of modestly positive results, but quite another to design a particular program that is going to work. Even more unlikely is the prospect of an efficient bureaucracy rescuing small, at-risk children from the dangers that surround them before the damage is done. Michael Cartier, remember, began his new life when he was seven. It was probably too late. Yet the law paid little more than passing attention to him until he became a murderer at age twenty-two. Then he went home and killed himself, all on a day when he should have been in jail for having violated the terms of his probation weeks earlier.

The highlight of the Boston conference was the announcement that legislative leaders had just reached agreement on a new victim's rights law that would, among other things, give victims the right to confer with prosecutors before any plea bargain is made final and to consult with probation officers before the filing of any pre-sentence recommendation. But the "rights" were circumscribed by the willingness of courts and prosecutors to bestow them "to the greatest extent possible and subject to available resources." I hadn't quite realized until I scanned the bill and the eleven-year-old law it was to replace[78] that I was, as the parent of "a homicide victim," legally a victim myself.

One of the speakers, Massachusetts Probation Commissioner Donald Cochran, spoke of the frustrations that lack of communication within the justice system can cause, a point that drew an emphatic nod from me. "The basic flaw of bureaucracy," Cochran said, "is that it consists of isolated islands" inundated by "paperwork within paperwork" that no one shares with the other islands. He called it "insane" and said it was one of the main reasons domestic violence was such an overwhelming problem.

Another speaker, Mary Ann Hinkle, head of the sexual assault unit for the Norfolk County district attorney's office, emphasized the need for domestic violence advocates in all the state's district and probate courts. A survey conducted in 1993 by the Massachusetts Office of Victim Assistance showed that 70 percent of those courts lacked full-time, trained advocates.

Such experts can be quite helpful, but they can also be a mixed blessing. In some courts, they are treated as second-class staffers assigned to second-class cases that judges and prosecutors can then ignore. But their presence is still an important improvement over past practice. As Laila Yasin, legal coordinator for the Casa Myrna Vasquez shelter, told the *Boston Globe* when the survey was made public: "You really need someone on your side to make the system work for you and help you go from being a victim to being a survivor."[79]

Hinkle said the Norfolk DA's office now had advocates in all five of its district courts. I was glad to hear that. Brookline is one of those courts. There was nobody there to help Kristin when she walked in.

14

The night the conference ended, I got a phone call in my hotel room from a member of the board of Emerge, the place where Cartier had ripped up his application papers. His name was Magueye Seck, and he used to be a counselor there. He was struck by how difficult it was to change an abusive man's behavior toward his wife or girlfriend. He was often frightened himself.

"I used to be terrified," he said. "I would come home and tell my wife, 'I cannot sleep.' Once I had a client going to shelter after shelter, to find out where his 'woman' was. And he found it. He just sat in front of the shelter, waiting for her to come out. I had to call the police."

The skies were overcast the next morning. I decided to go back to Allston. I wanted to talk to the florist again. I wanted to see if Bunratty's was still there. I wondered if the paint on the sidewalk had faded. It was a depressing, disturbing trip. The T rumbled up Commonwealth Avenue, past Kristin's old dormitory and the Paradise nightclub, one of the places where where she and Cartier had gone on dates. Minutes later, it stopped at Harvard Avenue.

Bunratty's had changed but not that much. It was now Local 186, with Live Reggae Every Thursday Evening and Jamaica Good Beer. But it still looked dank and dark, with its painted black wood storefront. It wasn't even noon. The door was locked. I crossed the street to Marty's and turned up Commonwealth.

The gray paint marking Kristin's body was still there, wearing thin, but I was startled when I came up to it. It seemed to have moved. It wasn't outside the Soap-A-Rama anymore. I'm not sure why that bothered me, but it did. I guess it was like finding her grave in a different place. Alan Najarian in the flower shop set me straight. It was an illusion. The sidewalk hadn't moved. The Soap-A-Rama had shrunk, giving up half its space to a new fast-food store.

"The neighborhood's gotten a little better, a little quieter," he said. Local 186 was still about as noisy as Bunratty's had been, but the new owners had "cleaned it up a bit."

"It's not as seedy," he said. "They even have women working there now."

A short distance away was the alley Cartier ran into after the shooting, its metal gate open as usual. I'd never walked down it before. I felt I should. Some things, I quickly discovered, never change. The alley was littered with hand-out ads on yellow and pink paper, apparently tossed away by someone tired of handing them out to passersby. On the frame wall forming one side of the alley were graffiti in bold black paint, commemorating Michael Cartier.

"Castleneck [swastika] Lives [swastika]," said one.

"Viva La Castleneck," said another.

Violence against women is still malignantly alive and well. It is properly deplored in all the right forums, but there is a resentful audience out there that doesn't want to hear about it. Unfortunately, that audience includes not a few members of the criminal justice system, including judges and prosecutors who pretend to have more important business to attend to. They forget, or ignore, the old saw that says if you take care of the little things, the big things will take care of themselves. They don't care, if they ever knew, that there is no such thing as a routine case.

One example of the newfound attention running up against the old indifference lies in what I have taken to calling "Kristin's law," a new statute passed in large measure as a result of what happened to her. Her murder created shock waves in Boston, in part because of the growing pattern of violence it illustrated, in part because of the sustained and thorough coverage by the *Globe* and the *Herald* and the rest of the Boston media. As a result, it is no longer permissible for Massachusetts judges to treat cases of domestic violence as routine civil matters. In September 1992, less than four months after the shooting, the Massachusetts legislature passed a bill creating a computerized, statewide domestic violence registry and requiring judges to check it whenever a request for a restraining order is submitted to them. Kristin's death had prompted State Senator Michael Barrett (D., Cambridge) to introduce the common-sense measure in June; he called it "a memorial" to her and other women killed by batterers.

A nationwide first, the new system includes a registry of all civil restraining and other protective orders, violations of those orders, and all data from the state's criminal record information system about those named in the orders, including a defendant's probation status and the existence of any outstanding warrants. Massachusetts courts no longer have an excuse for being in the dark about people like Michael Cartier.

Judges in other states rarely make such checks, but a little-noticed provision added on the House floor to last year's crime bill enables and encourages them to do so. Accepted by the Senate and now federal law,[1] it opens up FBI records for the first time to civil as well as criminal courts for use in domestic violence and stalking cases and authorizes creation of a nationwide registry patterned after the one in Massachusetts. State and local governments that intend to compile and enter their domestic violence records into the system will be eligible for a total of $6 million in federal grants over the next three years. The measure also calls for the development of plans to increase "intrastate communication between civil and criminal courts" and for training programs to ensure that "a judge issuing an order in a stalking or domestic violence case has all available criminal history and other information, whether from state or federal sources."

Once again, the law, introduced by Representative Joseph Kennedy (D., Mass.), was a result of what had been happening in Massachusetts, where domestic violence in 1992 claimed a murder victim every eight days. Even before Kristin's death, Governor Weld had declared "the epidemic of domestic violence" in the state a public safety emergency. There had been another brutal murder the same week Kristin was shot. Suzanne Hoeg, twenty-seven, was brutally beaten and stabbed to death by her husband in their Brockton home, as two of their three children looked on. The homicide was another tragic reflection of the inaction and inattention of the justice system. Hoeg had taken out two restraining orders against her husband, Roger, and let them lapse. But there was a month-old warrant out for his arrest, charging him with assault and threat-to-murder for trying to strangle his wife and threatening to kill her. Eight days before the murder, police responding to a call for help confronted a drunken Roger Hoeg at the family's home, and instead of checking for warrants, gave him a ride to his mother's house. The warrant wasn't served until the day after Suzanne Hoeg's murder.

What is now dubbed the National Stalker and Domestic Violence Reduction Act—the federal version of Kristin's law—was a combination of a bill drafted by then Senate Judiciary Committee Chairman Joseph Biden (D., Del.) along the lines of the registry law enacted in Massachusetts and elements of a bill Joseph Kennedy had introduced in the House to improve reporting of stalking violations. It is sometimes said that 200,000 women are stalked each year in this country, but in fact no one knows how much takes place against either men or women. No one even keeps count of the relatively few arrests and prosecutions there have been. "Generally, they're very badly written statutes," asserts one veteran prosecutor, Robert Horan, the commonwealth's attorney for Fairfax County, Virginia. "Almost every state in the Union that's gotten into this game has gone back after a year or two to amend it."[2] The best strategy, proposed in October 1993 by a federally funded task force, would be to tighten the definition of stalking, limiting it to instances that cause fear of bodily injury or death, and make it a felony. But more than a year later, only three states, Virginia, Iowa, and Utah, had adopted the task force model.[3]

The federal stalker act would in any case give the courts a grip on the extent of the problem as well as the dangers posed by individual defendants such as Cartier. It was stitched into the omnibus crime bill with bipartisan support. Biden never had a chance to introduce his version in the Senate because of an unacceptable rider a colleague wanted to add to it, but once Kennedy got his proposal to the House floor, it was assured of passage.[4] Biden was chairman of the Senate conferees on the overall crime bill, and he was committed to keeping the amendment in it. Both Kennedy and Representative Connie Morella (R., Md.), chairman of the Women's Issues Task Force on Violence, mentioned Kristin's death in floor statements urging passage of the measure. Kennedy, I was glad to see, also cited Helen's testimony before Biden's committee a year earlier. "The courage of Kristin's family has turned their loss into hope for others," Kennedy said generously. "Her sister, Helen Lardner, testified before the Congress that, 'My sister might be alive today if the judge at the hearing had checked her eventual killer's record.' "[5]

I didn't lobby for the bill myself. In a way, I'm ashamed to say that, but as a reporter for the *Post,* I was, and am, prohibited from lobbying for legislation or even testifying for it. That's a bit of hypocrisy, I think. A fig leaf. Journalists are effectively "lobbying" for changes in law or prevailing assumptions all the time, by writing about this or that unaddressed outrage. Shouting from the rooftops is what they're supposed to do. But from that exposed position, I suppose a fig leaf is better than nothing.

In Massachusetts, the new law went into effect promptly in September 1992, enacted despite grumbling from some judges who didn't want the practice imposed on them by statute. It may be one of those little things, but it was aimed at one of the biggest weaknesses of the judicial system, or of any large institution: the failure of its parts to communicate with one another. Governor Weld predicted at the signing ceremony that it would increase the effectiveness of restraining orders, which he described as the "number one weapon" women have against their abusers.

"For a long time, this crime was virtually ignored, and women who came forward seeking help were told to go home and be a good wife. That's an attitude that has to change," Weld said. "Men who batter or stalk or otherwise terrorize their wives or girlfriends must know that their violence is a crime just like any other crime [and] will be treated as such."[6]

The old indifference remains a formidable obstacle. In many Massachusetts courts, as a recent study in the *Boston Globe* showed, judges and prosecutors still aren't taking the crime seriously enough. Although disobeying a restraining order is a criminal misdemeanor, district courts in several parts of the state were regularly dismissing most violations—"sometimes even those involving assaults with bats, knives and other dangerous weapons."[7] The relatively few violations that resulted in guilty verdicts rarely resulted in jail time.

Kristin's law at least allowed the permissiveness to be documented. The *Globe* looked at a database of 92,183 restraining orders issued in the state since September 1992 and a companion listing of 783,354 criminal charges against those named in the orders. The conclusion: "Despite Massachusetts' reputation on paper as a state with tough laws to protect victims of domestic violence, in practice the enforcement of those laws is faltering badly in many communities."[8]

The least responsive courts, concentrated in Suffolk (Dorchester, Roxbury, and Boston) and Plymouth (Brockton) counties, dismissed 60 to 75 percent of the reported violations.[9] Other jurisdictions, including courts in Norfolk (Quincy and Brookline), Hampden (Springfield) and Middlesex (Cambridge) counties took their orders more seriously, dismissing only 10 to 20 percent of alleged violations, ordering more batterers into treatment and sometimes to jail. In Ware District Court, more than one of every three violators wound up in jail despite a policy of giving defendants a break and sending them to treatment programs the first time round. But even when batterers get jail time, they almost never get the two and a half years' maximum that district courts could hand out. Usually, the sentence, if there is a sentence, is three months or less.[10]

"Even if it gets through to the end, it's a slap on the wrist," Mel Barkley, a legal advocate for battered women in Brockton, told the *Globe*. "It's a very frustrating process for most of the women I deal with. The woman has to ask herself, 'Do I do the right thing and put myself, my kids, my family on the line, and incur his wrath when he gets out of jail after three months? Or do I drop the charges and pray he won't kill me?'"

Some officials unwisely blame the victims for most of the quick dismissals. Women often lodge a complaint and then refuse to testify for any number of reasons: they feel sorry for their batterer, they love him, they want to give him another chance, they have no money and nowhere else to go, they're afraid he'll kill them. They have reason to be terrified. The answer lies not in discarding their complaints, but in following up on them, in learning how to make a case without relying on the victim. Massachusetts prosecutor Sarah Buel, once a battered woman herself, frequently tells the story of the Quincy woman, a dentist, whose husband, a law student, used to beat her black and blue. He wrote down a long list of rules she had to follow if she didn't want to be beaten. Some of the rules:

- If I ask you what's wrong and your answer would break one of these rules, you smile and say, "Nothing." If I say, "Are you sure?" you say, "Yes, dear."
- Don't ever call the police.
- Don't ever go for a walk without first asking if you can. If I say no, you will not go.
- Don't ever scream or wake the neighbors.
- Answer all the questions that I ask you. Do not act as if I should know and not answer.
- Don't allow me to ask you a question the second time. If you do not answer within 30 seconds after the second time I ask you, be prepared to pay for it.
- Don't ever bite your lip.
- If I decide we will sleep together, you will humbly comply without a fight. You will not ever physically resist me.[11]

The case against the husband, Charles Gravina, highlighted on *60 Minutes*,[12] began in 1991, when he and his wife, Audrey Stack, walked into the Quincy police station on another matter. The detective they spoke to, Bob Curtis, noticed her face was bruised and asked who punched her. They were going to arrest him on the spot, but she was frightened about what he would do when he got out. The authorities in Quincy, known for their pioneering work against domestic violence, weren't deterred. They called her the next day and kept talking to her for eight months until finally she agreed to go to court.

You can't walk away from cases like that because the victim wants you to leave it alone, Detective Curtis told 60 *Minutes*. "People wind up dead if you leave it alone."

"I think that if I had not been in Quincy with the help that I had, that I might really be dead now," Stack agreed.[13]

The case sticks in my mind for a special reason. Quincy and Brookline, where Kristin sought help, are in the same county, under the same district attorney. What counts, in short, is individual leadership. Quincy had it. Brookline didn't.

The driving force behind the Quincy effort was Judge Kramer. He recognized that restraining orders were often inadequate, that criminal charges should also be pressed. In about eight out of ten cases that produced a petition for a restraining order, a crime was being alleged. But all that the batterers were being told was, "Don't do it again." The thing to do was to proceed on both fronts. As Kramer put it, "Why should the criminal justice system kick in right away when someone hurts a stranger and not with domestic violence? If an abuser commits a criminal act, you shouldn't just issue a restraining order and wait for the next crime."[14]

Even in Quincy, enforcement was far from rigorous. According to a recent study of 663 restraining orders issued by that court over a single year (1990), about half of the men abused the same woman again within a two-year period.[15] Nearly three in five (56.4 percent) were rearrested for a new crime. Of those who were arrested for violating the order or some other criminal charge such as assault, only one out of three was actually prosecuted and only 18 percent were sent to jail. Yet most of the men named in the restraining orders had criminal histories, with an average of thirteen criminal complaints on their record.

Andrew Klein, chief probation officer for Quincy District Court, who conducted the study, said the 18 percent incarceration figure was undoubtedly far higher than the statewide average at the time. "I'd be surprised if it was 2 percent statewide," he said. "What this research indicates is that men don't obey these orders, prosecutors don't prosecute violations of the orders, and if they do, judges don't sentence the violators."[16]

In fact, in 1992, the year Kristin was killed, some six thousand men were arrested in Massachusetts for allegedly violating restraining orders, Klein said. Eight hundred were put on probation, fewer than one hundred went to jail. "All the other cases 'went south'—they weren't prosecuted," Klein said.

District attorneys have immense authority to decide which laws will be strongly enforced and which will not, what charges will be prosecuted and which ones will be dropped. But judges can set the tone in a courthouse, especially when it comes to the violation of restraining orders. It is, after all, their orders that are being violated. They can and do make a difference. So do probation officers like Klein.

Family violence affects all social and income levels, as the case against the Quincy man illustrates, involving all sorts of seemingly upright citizens. But the statewide registry in Massachusetts bears out the Klein study: those brought into court for restraining orders usually turn out to have a demonstrated disregard for the law. Three out of every four men against whom restraining orders were issued during the registry's first few months had prior criminal records, and almost half of them had a history of violent crime. And almost three out of every ten (29.7 percent) allegedly violated the order or were arrested for some violent crime within six months of the order's issuance.[17]

None of this should be taken to mean all batterers have criminal records or that a man without a criminal record could not be violently abusive. But the study, conducted by Harvard's Injury Control Center and the state probation commissioner's office, contradicted the idea that restraining orders are granted too easily or that almost any man is at risk of being named a defendant. Those against whom orders are issued are not just a random sample of the generally law-abiding male population. "They are likely to have a criminal history, often reflective of violent behavior toward others."[18]

"These last months [since the registry law went into effect] have been an eye opener for me," said Massachusetts Probation Commissioner Donald Cochran. "The research in this field is terrible," based on samples that are far too small.[19] Conventional wisdom holds that battering cuts across all classes and that "anyone" can be an abuser, even in the best of neighborhoods.[20] That is no doubt true. But the batterers who are brought into court for restraining orders are generally not pillars of the community, "good guys" who lose it only when they get home at night. "It is an absolute myth," Cochran said, "to say that this is a guy who just couldn't get along with one woman."[21]

Despite all the talk about declining crime rates, Cochran is convinced that domestic violence is increasing. In 1992, in Massachusetts, he said, "we had 790 people put on [high-risk] probation for violating a restraining order. In 1993, it was almost 1,600." Ten to 12 percent of those deemed the riskiest probationers in Massachusetts, he said, are on probation for violating restraining orders. By 1996, Cochran said, "we expect that number to go to one in five." It will get still worse, he predicted, with any downturn in the economy that sets families to squabbling.

Joblessness is one of the ten "risk factors" most common among men who are severely violent toward their wives or girlfriends. Richard J. Gelles, one of the most prominent researchers in the field, drew up the profile on the basis of the last National Family Violence Survey. It is commonly believed that abusive behavior cuts a broad path, and, according to Gelles and his colleagues, there is much empirical support for this proposition. But certain social and demographic factors increase the risk of injury.[22]

As with all crimes of violence, battering is more likely to be committed by men under thirty. Unemployed men have higher rates of abuse than those with jobs, and blue-collar workers have higher rates than those in white-collar occupations. Severely abusive men are also more likely to use illicit drugs such as heroin or cocaine or engage in binge drinking, and to be violent toward children in the home. Their family income is likely to be below the poverty line, and they are more likely to be high school dropouts. The man is also more likely to be severely violent if he and his partner live together without being married, if they come from different religious backgrounds, and if he saw his father hit his mother when he was growing up.[23]

The dangers increase exponentially. Men with seven of the risk factors, Gelles says, engaged in extreme violence at seventeen times the rate of those with two of the markers.

But the biggest risk factor of all, obscuring social and demographic lines, is prior violent or abusive behavior. "In the absence of clear or convincing change, past behavior is probably the single most reliable indicator of future behavior, and battering is no exception."[24] It would be dangerous to think that only troubled dropouts like Michael Cartier can be violent toward women. The records in Massachusetts indicate that about one in four of the men named in restraining orders have no criminal records. Across the country, there are plenty of important, respectable people besides O. J. Simpson who are breaking the laws, whether they come to the attention of the authorities or not.

Those who have engaged in battering in just one county adjoining Washington, D.C., for instance, include lawyers, physicians, business executives, a sitting Cabinet member (in a past administration), and professional football, basketball, and baseball players.

"Many abusers are successful achievers," says Steven Stosny, director of the Compassion Workshop, a batterers' treatment program in Prince George's County that reports a surprisingly high rate of success. "They can present an impressive if not charming false self, though consumed by fear of abandonment on the one hand and a fear of engulfment on the other. . . . Their continual internal struggle encapsulates abusers in a narcissistic shell. . . . It deadens the abuser's sense of compassion for loved ones, even when they seem to exhibit compassion for those they don't love. Hence they can hurt or kill their children or hurt or kill their beloved spouse while their children sleep in the next room."[25]

It's often said that domestic violence is a "continuum," progressing steadily and inexorably, without outside intervention, from minor abuse to severe attacks, serious injuries, and worse. Gelles, a sociologist at the University of Rhode Island and director of its Family Violence Research Program, disagrees. "People keep saying it escalates, escalates, escalates—and then you kill," Gelles says. "That isn't so. There are killers, and there are non-killers. The vast majority of the two million serious batterers reach a threshold of abuse that is harmful, hurtful, and consequential, but not lethal. And then there are some people who are killers and who are working their way towards doing that. They're two different types of people. Counseling, men's programs, what have you, those fundamentally are not going to deter a killer."[26]

For people like Michael Cartier, the only solution, Gelles said, is to "lock 'em up. Lock 'em up as long as you can." If the crimes they commit carry shorter sentences, "then you have to give them a life sentence on the installment plan. And then you're playing with fire." There will always be dangerous intervals when the batterer is free to do what he wants.

There are many other brutal batterers who should also be confined, partly because justice demands it, partly because it gives their victims some respite and perhaps time to escape, partly in the faint hope that jail time might wake them up. "A guy who uses a weapon, who assaults with his fists or other objects, who violates a restraining order, is at very high risk to do it again," Gelles said. "You've got no business putting him back in the general population. Lock him up as often as you can. . . . This is really a very simple business, you know. You predict tomorrow based on what somebody did yesterday. If yesterday they were criminally violent, if they've assaulted with a weapon, if they've violated a restraining order, absent some extremely convincing evidence that they're going to change, they're not. And it doesn't much matter what you do. . . . When you try to rehabilitate somebody who doesn't want to change, guess what's going to happen? He's not going to change."[27]

Judges tend not to make such distinctions in cases of domestic violence, especially those involving restraining orders. Without the records from a "Kristin's law" to guide them, they have no idea how many previous orders have been issued, whether the alleged batterer has a criminal record, whether he might be violating probation or parole, or even whether he's wanted on other charges. The women's petitions, or the police reports, may set out what would strike a layman as an alarming account of criminal conduct. It doesn't matter. At most, where the law permits it,[28] the courts may order the defendant into a treatment program under a threat of incarceration if the course is not completed. The threats are hollow. Dropouts are common. At worst, the perpetrators are told to start the course again. The counseling is a crutch, a feel-good device the judges use to clear their dockets. A mantra like "probation" and "rehabilitation." Something is being done and it sounds good. The courts rarely try to find out whether the defendant is amenable to treatment, whether he wants to change. They don't even ask.

"It's like saying, 'All right, everybody, we're going to run the Stars and Stripes marathon. Everybody has to go out and run twenty-six miles,' " Gelles says. "There's no way everybody is going to run twenty-six miles. But that's the way intervention is done for abusers. The assumption is that everyone can run twenty-six miles. That's silly. They can't. They won't. It's not going to work."[29]

At restraining order hearings, which are civil proceedings, judges are commonly informed, under oath, of violent crimes of all sorts. One woman is thrown down the basement stairs and left bleeding from the forehead, another is chased with a machete, still another is whipped twenty times and then choked unconscious with an inch-thick cable. The restraining orders are issued, but usually that's it. There are no follow-up criminal investigations, no arrests, no prosecutions. Klein contends that judges in such circumstances should sign a criminal complaint at the same time they sign the restraining order.[30] At the least, they should tolerate no violations of those orders, but of course they do. And where children are involved, they routinely facilitate the violations by giving the abusers visitation rights without sufficient safeguards.[31]

"To me, violation of a restraining order is at least as serious a crime as assault and battery," Klein said. "The courts tell a woman, we're making a pact with you, we're going to protect you. And then they treat it as trivial. The man is saying, 'I defy you.' Any violation of a restraining order should mean jail time."

Most judges aren't going to do that. They're too committed to the notion that treatment works, and if it doesn't, the answer is more treatment. In some jurisdictions at least, violations of restraining orders get less attention than the restraining orders. An Urban Institute study in

Colorado showed that judges generally took the petitions seriously "and acted in a way consistent with the women's requests."[32] But the judges "generally relied on standard forms with standard conditions and did not personalize the conditions of the order. From our interviews with both the men and the women, this caused confusion about the content of the order and it left orders that spelled out few specifics."[33] Not surprisingly, many women called the police because their partners had violated the orders. But arrests, although seemingly required by law, were rarely made. The contrast was striking. Police helped the first time, but not the second. "Although the police were highly rated by the women when they responded to the initial incident that led to the temporary order, their rating plummeted when they responded to violation calls."[34]

So, too, with the courts. Rarely is anyone sent to jail for violating a restraining order.[35] Many judges and prosecutors, like others unfamiliar with the pathology of the problem, ask themselves: Why didn't she leave? In fact, she may have tried to get away. She may have left and been tracked down. But somehow it's her fault that she didn't escape altogether, that she was caught again. You can almost hear the muttering. The dumb broad! What's the matter with her? "A woman's 'failure' to permanently separate from a violent relationship is still widely held to be mysterious and in need of explanation, an indicator of her pathology rather than her batterer's."[36]

"Judges may blame female victims for instigating or causing the violence against them," according to a special Justice Department report on eleven family violence demonstration studies in courts across the country. "The failure of judges to respond appropriately in family violence cases was cited as the biggest single problem faced in the majority of the demonstration projects. In extreme cases, victims have been berated for failing to please the offender or jailed for refusing to testify. The seriousness of this problem is underscored by recent studies documenting gender bias in the courts."[37]

A savvy probation officer, Klein isn't counting on any mass conversion in the judiciary, no matter how many family violence conferences and training sessions are held. "You can train judges as much as you want," he said, arguing for jail time. "But if you don't have mandatory sentencing, forget it. Unless the defendant is a young male in tennis shoes who was picked up with crack cocaine in his pocket—unless he *looks* like a criminal—the sympathy of the court is going to go to the defendant, not to the victim."[38]

Klein pointed to the tougher approach to drunk driving to illustrate his point. Mandatory penalties have been the key, he said. "It wasn't that the judges got more sensitive, or less alcoholic, themselves."

Mandatory jail sentences for violating restraining orders would probably be short unless the offenses constituted serious crimes themselves, such as assault with a deadly weapon. But the courts should also be able to crack down with longer terms for blatant violations involving any kind of physical injury or damage. The New York legislature in 1994 enacted what could be a model, making it a felony for anyone aware of an order of protection to cause physical injury to the victim or to cause more than $250 in damages to the victim's property.[39]

At least some offenders, Klein concedes, would spend their time "stewing in their cells, plotting revenge." But to balk at sending someone to jail for fear of making him angry is saying we can't enforce the law because it will just stir up the lawbreakers and make them even worse.[40] Most batterers under court restraint, as Klein points out, "look like criminals, act like criminals, and re-abuse like criminals." Even if the sentence is only thirty days in jail, he said, "thirty days gives women a chance to get away." Beyond that, a jail term is a public statement that can influence others. "Even if you don't deter the abuser in the jail cell," Klein said, "you may deter five others who read about it from following in his footsteps."

Others, like Gelles, are dubious about "mandatory anything." But Gelles concedes that "the laws aren't working. Guys are walking away." A consultant for authorities in Connecticut, he pointed out that one study done for officials there on what sanctions to impose in domestic violence cases recommended waiting until the fourth offense before sending someone to jail.

"I said, 'Are you crazy?'" Gelles recalled. "You're playing with gasoline and matches. There is an enormous reluctance to use real sanctions and make tough calls on dangerous offenders. This is true all over [the criminal justice system], but it is worse in the family violence field because people say, 'It's an intimate relationship. It's not dangerous violence.' It's going to take a lot of work to convince the criminal justice system to use real sanctions early. . . . We are talking the talk of control, but we are not walking the walk of control."[41]

There is no reason to suppose that Massachusetts is different from any other state. Across the country, hundreds of laws to deal with domestic violence, especially violence against women, have been enacted since the late 1960s and early 1970s when the women's movement brought attention to it. As Gelles has written, "A review of the table of contents of social science journals published prior to 1970 would uncover virtually no articles on family violence."[42] Back then, and perhaps even today, we showed our sophistication by speaking derisively of olden times when, as eighteenth-century jurist William Blackstone observed, the law allowed a husband "for some misdemeanors, to beat his wife severely with scourges and cudgels . . . for others only moderate chastisement."[43] We forget that this rule of "moderation"—widely remembered as "the rule of thumb"—amounted to a liberal reform, supplanting sterner measures. Back in the Middle Ages, women were burned at the stake "for threatening their husbands, for talking back to or refusing a priest, for stealing, for prostitution, for adultery, for bearing a child out of wedlock, for permitting sodomy (even though the priest or husband who committed it was forgiven), for masturbation, for Lesbianism, for child neglect, for scolding and nagging, and for miscarrying, even though the miscarriage was caused by a kick or a blow from the husband."[44] Some of those traditions, and the hypocrisy behind them, were carried over to the New World. Under the criminal laws enacted in Connecticut in the mid-1600s, "there was hardly a sin not subject to the magistrate's censure,"[45] including relations between unmarried persons. One notable example cited by Tocqueville involved a 1643 case in which a Connecticut judge "directs that Margaret Bedford, convicted of loose conduct, be whipped and afterwards compelled to marry her accomplice, Nicholas Jennings."[46] Tocqueville's silence on what happened to Jennings suggests that he was spared the lash and saved for the wedding bed.

Burning at the stake is now remote history and so, supposedly, is the right to physically chastise an "errant wife."[47] But traditions linger. Even into the 1970s, the training manual promulgated by the International Association of Chiefs of Police counseled noninterference in such matters; some cities actually had an informal "stitch rule" that demanded a wound requiring more than a certain number of stitches to justify an arrest.[48] The American Bar Association, in its 1973 "Standards for the Urban Police Function," agreed that police should "engage in the resolution of conflict such as that which occurs between husband and wife . . . in the highly populated sections of the large city, without reliance upon criminal assault or disorderly conduct statutes."[49]

I couldn't help thinking about all that during a recent two-day conference for all state judges in Maryland on family violence. Changes in the state's domestic violence law, previously regarded as the worst in the country, in 1992, had led to an increase of more than 50 percent in the number of protective order cases.[50] The conference was held in Towson, Maryland, to discuss how to handle them. Ironically, there was a protest outside the hotel as the conference began, with pickets from the Women's Action Coalition and the National Organization for Women voicing their indignation over one of the judges in attendance.

Their anger was directed at Baltimore County Circuit Judge Robert E. Cahill, who the week before had sentenced a Parkton, Maryland, trucker to just eighteen months in jail, with work release, for killing his wife after finding her in bed with another man. The judge said he regarded the crime as an act of understandable rage, although the trucker, Kenneth Lee Peacock, thirty-six, spent several hours drinking and arguing with his wife before shooting her in the head with his deer rifle.

"I seriously wonder how many married men, married five years or four years, would have the strength to walk away . . . without inflicting some corporal punishment, whatever that punishment might be," Cahill told the defendant at his October 17, 1994, sentencing hearing. "I shudder to think what I might do. I'm not known for having the quietest disposition."[51]

Cahill's remarks quickly earned him nationwide notoriety. Unfortunately, that let prosecutors escape almost unscathed. Peacock was originally charged with first-degree murder, but prosecutors bargained that down to voluntary manslaughter, partly on the grounds that his drinking added to his rage. "This may sound cold, but it was only one shot," said Anne Brobest, chief prosecutor for the Baltimore County circuit court division, in defending the plea bargain.[52]

The killing took place around 4 A.M. Peacock had chased his wife's lover out of the house around midnight. He spent the intervening time drinking and arguing with her. No matter. "Finding one's spouse in a compromising situation is 'legally adequate provocation' and reduces a charge of murder to voluntary manslaughter," Baltimore County State's Attorney Sandra A. O'Connor asserted in a statement.[53]

Sandra Peacock would have done better with "the rule of thumb." And Kenneth Peacock may have been lucky he wasn't born in the latter part of the nineteenth century, when the rule was on the other thumb. In 1882, Maryland became the first state to enact a law making wife beating a crime, punishable by forty lashes or a year in jail.[54] Needless to say, the law had little lasting impact.

At the sentencing hearing, Judge Cahill noted that no one from the victim's family was present, "so I get the benefit of, in effect, sentencing in anonymity. I don't have Mothers Against Drunk Driving present. The chances are this case will not even be written up."[55] Within a fortnight, Cahill entered the conference center with a squad of bodyguards who kept him apart from the protesters out front and the TV crews scurrying around inside.

Judge Robert C. Murphy, chief judge of the Maryland Court of Appeals, welcomed his colleagues with brief remarks expressing the hope that the program would "go a long way to educating each of us to the depth of the problem we are now confronting." Sarah Buel gave the keynote address, emphasizing how much influence judges have in their communities and how important it is for them to exercise leadership. After any court appearance in a domestic violence case, Buel said, victims can always recite to her just what the judge had said, no matter how brief. "Your words have an enormous impact," she reminded them.

Cahill wasn't the only judge with a problem. "Look at this," Robert F. Sweeney, chief judge of Maryland's district court judges, said in a weary voice as the conference began. "It's five cameras following Judge Bollinger to the bathroom."[56]

Circuit Judge Thomas J. Bollinger had the year before stirred up a tempest in sentencing a forty-five-year-old man convicted of raping an unconscious, twenty-year-old woman who had passed out in his apartment after drinking too much. Bollinger gave the man probation, with his criminal record to be expunged afterward. Finding a woman passed out on the couch, the judge had observed at the hearing, was "the dream come true for a lot of males, quite frankly."[57]

The Maryland court system's Select Committee on Gender Equity received numerous complaints about Bollinger and prescribed sensitivity training. The judge refused to take it. The impasse was referred to the state's Judicial Disabilities Commission, which has the power to discipline judges, but which also operates in secret and dispenses most of its admonitions in private. Nothing more was heard about the matter. One colleague said Bollinger thought he had lived it down until the Cahill controversy revived it.

"It goes on and on," said Frances Everett of NOW, one of the protesters outside.[58]

One reason, plainly, is the benighted attitude of many judges, not to mention prosecutors and police. The judiciary is predominantly male and conservative and, in some quarters at least, annoyed by the increasing attention it is being asked to pay to violence against women.[59] As David Adams, head of Emerge, has said, "There's a kind of backlash. Some judges are sick and tired of hearing about battered women."[60]

The wider problems of the justice system come into play, too: unserved warrants, crowded dockets, overburdened prosecutors, frustrated judges, overloaded prisons, overworked probation and parole officers.[61] It's easy for judges, especially for those inclined to be lenient toward the usual run of criminal defendants, to be even more lenient toward violence in the home. They tend to forget that that is where it all begins. They tend to wait until it gets worse. And then it's too late.[62]

The administration of justice in Miami, Florida, for instance, deeply troubles Katherine Fernandez Rundle, who in March 1993 succeeded U.S. Attorney General Janet Reno as the state attorney of Dade County. "The people in the system say the criminals know they have all the advantages. They thumb their noses at us," she says. "That's what's wrong with the whole system: the punishment. Nothing's swift, nothing's severe. They know it. And we know it."[63]

Across the nation, the statistics on assault tell the story. The figures are not broken down by the kind of attacks, but this is where most of the domestic violence reported to police can be found. Despite all the talk about the need to stop violence, it is the least penalized of all serious crimes. The chances of being caught and convicted for it are about one in one hundred, in the attacker's favor. The chances of being imprisoned for it are even more remote.[64] Burglars are treated much more harshly.[65] Our justice system values our TV sets more than our teeth. It is more concerned about a drug buy than it is about broken bones.

According to the Bureau of Justice Statistics, there are some signs that the climate is changing and that arrests, convictions, and imprisonment for aggravated assault are beginning to go up quite markedly.[66] "A huge amount still goes unpunished," Patrick Langan says. "Compared to other crimes, there is still a low likelihood of conviction for aggravated assault, but I think the system is improving." He thinks the change may be due in part to demands that domestic violence be taken more seriously.[67]

Langan, it should be recorded, is an optimist, which is surprising to find in a senior scholar dedicated to the study of crime. He thinks the justice system can be harnessed, moved in a certain direction, and even made to turn in an impressive performance. "The drug problem is an example," he says. "The system was told to go after these guys and it did. I think it can do the same thing with domestic violence, once you get it rolling."[68]

Maybe. But all that's rolling right now is the rhetoric. The reality is far behind. But Langan is right to put his money on the justice system. The alternatives are not encouraging. In terms of recent history, other institutions may have actually abetted battering even more: from welfare agencies that work to "keep the family together," even when that prolongs the abuse,[69] to doctors and emergency room personnel who bandage their "sick" patients, perhaps label them as "alcoholic," "depressive," or "neurotic,"[70] and send them back home, no questions asked. Those habits need to be changed. But it is up to the justice system above all to deal with the violence that comes to its attention for what it is: a crime. Not just any crime, but one that is likely to be repeated and even turn women and children into criminals themselves unless it is treated as something more serious than a routine misdemeanor.

That is a heavy burden, especially when the system is so overloaded with what the criminal codes have long told it are more serious crimes, and when other establishments are pulling in the other direction. But it would be disastrous if, as some advocate, domestic violence came to be treated as a medical or "mental health problem." That would only lead to more excuses for the batterers at the expense of their victims. At a March 1994 American Medical Association Conference on family violence, there was little emphasis on enforcing the laws against it. "We recommend that the prevention of family violence be viewed in terms of social justice and affirmation of basic human rights rather than retributive criminal justice," one AMA work group said with a dismissive sniff of superiority. "We support the shift of social, economic and political resources toward strengthening communities and families in their many forms," the panel added, as though the ways to do that were well established. "Specific strategies," the supposed experts said, "include: 1. Instead of building more prisons, using the money to fund community-based, community-controlled, systematically evaluated prevention programs that build on strengths."[71] The "strengths," whatever they might be, were not spelled out.

The pronouncements were no doubt well intentioned but all the more presumptuous in coming from a profession that still fails to recognize a battered woman staggering into the emergency room as needing something more than a bandage and, perhaps, a tranquilizer. As a 1993 study of California's hospitals showed, most of that state's 397 emergency room departments had no idea how many battered women they were treating, and those that did have some numbers offered exceedingly low estimates.[72] The study also found that most California hospitals were not complying with accreditation requirements directing emergency departments to develop written policies and procedures for identifying, handling, evaluating, and referring battered adults and to draw up a plan for educating staff about domestic violence. "As few as one in five California hospitals may be in compliance," the survey found.[73] Yet here was the AMA meeting in national conference just a few months later telling one and all, forget about "retributive criminal justice," build on "strengths," be assured that "the AMA is committed to helping stem this horrible epidemic."[74]

What is at work here, I think, is what Senator Moynihan called the "opportunistic mode" of "defining deviancy down." While it reflects "a nominal intent to do good," he observed, "the true object is to do well, a long-established motivation among mortals. In this pattern, a growth in deviancy makes possible a transfer of resources, including prestige, to those who control the deviant population. This control would be jeopardized if any serious effort were made to reduce the deviancy in question. This leads to assorted strategies for redefining the behavior in question as not all that deviant, really. . . . Even so, now that the doctor has come, it is important that criminal violence not be defined down by epidemiologists."[75]

Gelles recalls that it was about thirty years ago that the medical profession discovered the problem of child abuse. Yet even now, he said, emergency room personnel report to child protective agencies only about a third of the cases they suspect. "And that's better than they do with battered women. Domestic violence just isn't in their mindset. Unless they're in continuous training to watch out for that kind of thing, they fall back into their old ways. A two- or three-hour course won't do anything but keep them alert for a short while. If you talk to them about it, they'll say, 'We're here to handle emergencies. We don't do social medicine here.' ".

If the doctors and the hospitals were serious about dealing with the problem, Gelles said, they would have a domestic violence advocate in the emergency room on a twenty-four-hour basis. But that would be a big investment. It's much cheaper for the hospitals to hire someone like Gelles to come in and hold a two- or three-hour training session—and then pat themselves on the back for being so advanced.

Evelyn Smith can remember how callously she was treated when she went to the emergency room of a Washington, D.C., area hospital after her husband beat her unconscious and, she later discovered, left her with a broken ankle. Her husband, Charles, a 6′5″ ex-Marine drill instructor and martial arts expert, went with her. The doctor came in and asked her how she was. "I thought I was dying," she recalled. The doctor asked her if she wanted her husband to stay. She said she told him no, that she tried to make clear she was afraid of him.

"The doctor understood, but he didn't talk to me anymore," she said. "He continued talking to my husband. He asked him if he was a football or a basketball player."

Evelyn Smith left the hospital with a prescription for Xanax, an untreated broken ankle, and her 270-pound husband. The medicine helped her get to sleep, but when she woke up, she said, "My husband was on top of me, beating and raping me."[76] She went to a different hospital after the next beating. They gave her Xanax and Tylenol 3.[77]

Criminal assaults are at the heart of domestic abuse and so are repeat offenders. About a third of the cases of domestic violence against women reported to the National Crime Victimization Survey would be classified by police as rape, robbery, or aggravated assaults—felonies in most states. The other two-thirds would be categorized as "simple assaults," a misdemeanor in most places. But as Justice Department experts have found, "Victim injury is at least as common among domestic crimes that would be classified as simple assault (42%) as it is among felonies that would be classified as rape, robbery and aggravated assault (36%)."[78] A black eye or a bloody face just doesn't count for much on the statute books. In jurisdictions such as Washington, D.C., as one former prosecutor has put it, "You can beat the hell out of somebody, but unless you do it with a pipe or a gun or a shod foot, it's just simple assault,"[79] punishable by six months in jail at most. The presence or absence of injury isn't critical to deciding whether to classify an offense as a felony or misdemeanor. What's critical is the presence or the absence of a weapon and the extent of injury. The traditional ways of sorting out felonies from misdemeanors "may have the unintended effect of masking the seriousness of domestic violence."[80]

Women, to be sure, also hit men, but how often is a matter of considerable dispute. National Crime Victimization Survey data showed that 95 percent of all assaults on spouses and ex-spouses during 1973–77 were committed by men.[81] A more recent Justice Department study of violence between intimates showed a 92 percent ratio: women are being murdered, raped, robbed, and assaulted by male partners about twelve times more often than men are treated likewise by female partners.[82] However, Gelles and his colleague, Murray A. Straus of the University of New Hampshire's Family Research Laboratory, found that "in contrast to their behavior outside the family, within the family women are about as violent as men."[83] Feminist critics have assailed the finding—and its authors. Other experts, like Langan and Klein, are highly skeptical of it. The "vast majority of abuse" reported in the Straus-Gelles surveys is "of a far lesser magnitude" than the violence that comes to the courts' attention, Klein said.

What all this suggests is that there is much more domestic violence than generally estimated.[84] The National Family Violence Surveys conducted by Richard Gelles and Murray Straus deal only with couples that are still living together. Studies of women seeking court protection indicate that many of them—perhaps most—have left their partners. Like Kristin, they were being chased, they were being stalked.[85]

"The batterers we see are engaged in sustained efforts to control people's lives," Klein said. More than 40 percent of the men named in the hundreds of restraining orders he studied were already separated from their partners at the time of the alleged abuse. A more detailed study of randomly selected cases in Quincy and Dorchester, Massachusetts, two years later showed the proportion was even higher: two-thirds of the men were not living with their victims at the time the complaints were filed.

"The violence [reflected in restraining orders] is really something that's gone on after the relationship has ended," said sociologist James Ptacek of Tufts, who conducted the second study. "We need to realize how common it is that women are harassed, abused, and threatened after they leave these men."[86]

The dangers they face are indeed much greater. According to one Justice Department study, separated or divorced women are fourteen times more likely than married women to report being battered by a spouse or ex-spouse.[87] The act of separation, beginning with the threat of it, poses the biggest risks. Justice Department data over a five-year period show that attacks on separated women are 30 times as numerous as violence against married women and 3.4 times more likely than attacks on women who have already obtained a divorce.[88]

"Some of the women who are separated may be reporting beatings that took place before they left," said Langan, who did the study. "That may be the reason they left. But this still suggests that the period of separation is very volatile, very dangerous for a woman."

Perhaps a new name is needed for such attacks. Law professor Martha R. Mahoney of the University of Miami has proposed the term "separation assault" to cover the violence used to prevent women from leaving, as well as to punish them for leaving and to force them to come back. Naming the phenomenon, she suggests, could direct public attention to where it belongs: on the nature of the attacks rather than on the failure of the women to leave.[89]

"The story of the violent pursuit of the separating woman must become part of the way we understand domestic violence to help eliminate the question 'Why didn't she leave?' from our common vocabulary. . . . The woman defines successful flight from attack as a victory. The man insists this is not victory but defeat. The persistent accounts of the difficulty women encounter on separation, especially condemnation from their families and employers, suggest society's perceptions track man's interpretations. . . . [Yet] the dangers women face in the effort to separate make separation a victory. These need a name."[90]

Failure to recognize those dangers can be fatal, as it was for Kristin. According to the FBI's nationwide reports, 29 percent of all female murder victims each year are killed by husbands or boyfriends or ex-husbands and ex-boyfriends.[91] Even those stark statistics understate the problem because the police reports on which they are based are often incomplete. Almost four of ten homicides reported in 1993 were "unclassified," meaning the relationship between the victim and the offender was unknown. More than 2,000 of those "unclassified" victims were female.[92]

The files of state prosecutors across the country sampled in a new Justice Department spouse-murder study reflect the hazards of breaking up:

In Oklahoma City a husband has threatened his wife in the past and she has left him because of those threats. One day she returns to his apartment with her mother to pick up clothing and food. He stabs both of them to death.[93]

In Seattle a husband is jailed for attacking his wife. She and the children move out of the house. Two weeks later, the children are being watched by a baby-sitter when the wife returns to her new lodgings. The husband appears out of hiding and tells his wife to watch while he kills the baby-sitter, whom he begins to stab in the back. The baby-sitter manages to get away, and the husband turns on the wife, stabbing her to death.[94]

Men can be on the receiving end, too, but such fatalities have been dropping. Women used to kill their husbands and boyfriends and exes about as often as the men killed them. But no longer. By 1992, the year Kristin was killed, females were the victims in so-called intimate murders 70 percent of the time.[95] Women may be resorting less to killing their partners because they increasingly have other alternatives, such as battered-women's shelters.[96]

The surveys conducted by Gelles and Straus indicate that a little more than 2 million husbands are subjected to "severe violence" each year, but Gelles himself protests that the numbers are too often rattled off in simplistic fashion. "Kicking a man in the shins, for instance, is not the same as kicking a man in the groin, and both of these instances are distinct from kicking a pregnant woman in the abdomen."[97] Men are less likely than women to own up to their violence.[98] In addition, Gelles says, "most [women] use violence as a defensive reaction to violence. Some women initiate violence because they know, or believe they are about to be attacked."[99] Women do sometimes throw things and occasionally lash out with a slap, a punch, a kick or worse, often in self-defense, but not always. I'm sure Kristin would have agreed that women aren't perfect. But men are bigger and more aggressive. They hit harder and they do more damage. Women beaten by their male partners are seven times more likely to need medical attention.[100] They spend twice as long in bed as other sick women, have twice as many headaches, four times as much depression, and try to kill themselves five and a half times more often.[101]

What's clear, too, is that the beatings go on and on. Often there's a cycle to them. Like Michael Cartier, batterers are frequently contrite, affectionate, and full of undying promises—until they do it again. About one in five women victimized by a spouse or ex-spouse told the National Crime Victimization Survey that "they had been a victim of a series of 3 or more assaults in the last 6 months that were so similar that they could not distinguish one from another."[102] And only a small fraction of assaults by intimates is reflected in the NCVS. The last National Family Violence Survey conducted by Gelles and Straus found that almost two million women suffered severe violence four to six times a year.[103] The real extent of the violence is probably twice that, involving as many as four million women who were badly and repeatedly beaten. The estimate would be higher still if dating, divorced, and separated couples were surveyed.

"The sad part is that numbers just don't speak for themselves," Gelles says. "It stands to reason," Gelles says, "that if a woman will admit over the phone that she's been threatened with a knife, there is another who will admit that in a face-to-face interview and others who have had the same experience but wouldn't admit it under any circumstance. If I go into a home and really bear down, I get a much higher rate [of violence] than a professional over the phone who is working for $6.50 or $8.50 an hour. And even on the phone, you'll find a guy who says, yes, he pulled a gun on his wife. If one guy says that, you've got to think there are a lot more out there who wouldn't admit it."[104]

What are we to do then with people like Michael Cartier? And

O. J. Simpson? And Charles Gravina? The first thing is not to blame their victims. The second thing is to ask not why the victims tolerated what they did—and Kristin, I think, tolerated very little—but why society and, more particularly, our justice system tolerate it. And by tolerating it, sanction it, foster it, encourage it. Batterers are even less susceptible to rehabilitation than garden-variety criminals who pick on strangers. Lawbreakers of any stripe can be helped, if they're willing to be helped, if they're "amenable" to change. But those who beat up women may be the least amenable of all, especially under a system that sets them loose to do it again and again. There are plenty of louts out there to cheer them on. Just listen to talk radio for a sampling, such as this O. J. Simpson defender, a chap named Daryl, in a testy exchange with feminist attorney Gloria Allred, described by Howard Kurtz in the *Washington Post:*

> "O.J. was in a state of shock," Daryl says, arguing that Simpson should be released on bail.
>
> Allred cuts him off, her voice rising. "Wait a minute, when he was accused of beating his wife [in 1989] . . . was he also in a state of shock then?"
>
> "We are not talking about 1989. Every man in this country has whooped his woman's butt before. . . . There's nothing wrong with spanking your woman."
>
> "*Ex-cuse me*," Allred snaps.
>
> After a brief exchange of epithets with another caller, Daryl retreats to his last line of defense.
>
> "He owns that woman. That's his woman! . . . O.J. was in a state of shock," he says.[105]

Batterers enrolled in treatment programs, especially when forced to enroll by court order, don't need to listen to talk radio to find support for what they've done. They can just sit in the back of the room and swap stories with their classmates.[106] A study by the Urban Institute showed how much of a sham some of these sessions are, no matter how well intentioned. The judges who ordered the counseling had no idea whether treatment was effective or not. Training typically did not begin until about two months after it was ordered. One in four failed to complete the programs, but no penalties were imposed, not even on those whose prosecution was suspended on condition they undergo the training. And after three months of counseling, offenders who underwent the treatment were "no more likely to abstain from severe violence or threats of violence" than a comparison group of offenders not ordered into treatment at all.[107] Whether a defendant was ordered into counseling or not depended mainly on the assigning judge's preference, or distaste, for treatment rather than on an assessment of the batterer's treatability. The biggest difference in the two groups of offenders was that those ordered to treatment were more often married. "This may reflect a tendency of judges to view the treatment as a form of marriage therapy appropriate for couples who intend to remain together," the study said.

Whatever the reason, the result may simply have been to lull the battered woman into sticking around a bit longer, thinking that her partner was learning to mend his ways. Unfortunately, the Urban Institute's most appalling finding indicated that those required to undergo treatment had learned nothing at all. Indeed, they scored worse on two critical questions on a "wife-beating index" than those who had no counseling. Significantly more of those who underwent treatment assented when asked if they thought "occasional violence can help a marriage," and more of them said yes, again, when asked whether "most wives secretly desire to be beaten."

So much for your standard batterer's treatment program. Michael Cartier's lasted only half as long as those in the Urban Institute study, but Kristin thought it would do him some good. She took his phone calls, and even his roses, so long as he went. The flowers were still in her flat the day he killed her.

On average, Gelles estimates, treatment programs for abusive men "have a 25 to 30 percent effectiveness"—which means they fail the overwhelming majority of the time. According to Adele Harrell, who conducted the Urban Institute study, "There's been no reversal of my findings," although a promising new approach is under way in

Maryland.[108] Instant experts are reportedly moving in, too, looking for work now that the drunk-driving market is starting to dry up. "These same experts who have done a lousy job on drunk drivers are all now applying to suddenly become spousal experts," Klein said. "Everyone wants to get into the act because that's where the money is now."[109] The National Council of Juvenile and Family Court Judges has put the matter more delicately, noting that several jurisdictions "have experienced the hasty development of services by providers who have little or no experience in the area of battering."[110] There is even a correspondence course, advertised to judges for $225 a head, that is "meant to be enjoyable"—for the batterers. It includes pamphlets, an Ann Landers column on "12 rules for a happy marriage," and a mail-in quiz with the answers in the back.[111]

Cartier was beyond rehabilitation. He was what Massachusetts Governor Weld and others have called "a walking time bomb," a so-called borderline personality, someone who can appear to be among the nicest of human beings until they encounter stress and then blow up. Some who dealt with him have suggested he was too clever and manipulative for them to have seen the dangers, that he knew too well how to bow and scrape and give all the right answers. At times perhaps. But he also sent out warning signals that cried out for attention. He spoke of killing himself and others. He told officials at Deer Island, "If he doesn't get the help he needs, he will mess up."[112] Yet when he was released, amid reports that he was harassing Rose Ryan, probation officials didn't even assign him to the maximum supervision or "risk/needs" category that the top probation official in the state says is supposed to be "automatic" for anyone convicted of a crime of violence. Little things. They ought to have added up, but they didn't. The justice system is so hungry for signs of compliance, so grateful for at least an outward show of respect, that it tends to accept them without question. "If you can figure out what is expected of you, you've slipped through," says William Hudgins, the psychologist who interviewed Cartier shortly before the murder. "You can call your own tune."[113]

Just be 'umble, as Uriah Heep might say. Heep would do very well in an American courtroom or in a police encounter. Criminologist

Lawrence Sherman offers a classic account of a conversation with Minneapolis police officers about their reactions to domestic violence calls in the early 1980s.

"What kind of people do you arrest now?" Sherman asked them.

"Assholes," they replied. "People who commit aggravated POPO."

"What is aggravated POPO?"

"Pissing off a police officer," they answered. "Contempt of cop. But we also arrest people who look like they're going to be violent, or who have caused more serious injuries."

Sherman asked them what kind of people they didn't arrest in misdemeanor domestic assault cases.

"People who act calm and polite, who lost their temper but managed to get control of themselves," they told him.[114]

Most violence in the home or in dating relationships is never reported to the police or brought to the attention of the courts. Even the victims may fail to see what happened as a crime. Or they may fear reprisals. "He didn't beat me. He just grabbed me, turned me upside down and banged my head on the floor," one woman said in explaining why she didn't call authorities.[115] And just as there are petty thieves and shoplifters who would never dare rob a bank, there are petty bullies who keep getting away with the physical harm they inflict because it isn't that severe. Gelles likens the situation abused women face to the damage that falls below the deductible on an insurance policy; the dents are frustrating, even maddening, but there's no point in calling your agent. He isn't going to do anything about it.

That makes it all the more important for authorities to pay attention when the calls are made. They are likely to be signs of serious trouble. The damage has gone far past the deductible. Even then, most victims say nothing. Only about one in every ten women who are severely beaten by their partners reports the attacks to police.[116] And according to the 1985 National Family Violence Survey, only one in one hundred assaults on wives resulted in an arrest.[117] Since those sorry numbers were compiled, laws making arrests mandatory in domestic violence cases, particularly for violations of restraining orders, have gone into effect in more than half of the states and the District of Columbia, and pro-arrest policies have been adopted in many other jurisdictions.[118] Before a mandatory arrest law was enacted in Washington, D.C., police usually failed to arrest the apparent abuser even in cases where the woman was found bleeding. The officers in the nation's capital made arrests twice as often in incidents involving damaged cars.[119]

Yet arrests alone won't work if prosecutors don't follow them up. And there's the rub. Prosecutors traditionally dismiss most family violence cases brought to their attention, if attention is what it can be called. It doesn't matter whether the complaints are directed to them by the police or by the victims themselves.[120] They have virtually untrammeled "prosecutorial discretion." They dispose of more than nine out of every ten criminal cases of any kind that come before them, with dismissals or pleas. They say they're constantly overloaded, and they are. They say they don't have enough time to learn about the heartbreak and the brutality tucked into the folders they lug into court every day. On some Monday mornings, a single prosecutor has to be ready to go to trial on any one of one hundred pending criminal cases. At that point, as one of them told the *Miami Herald,* "It's sweetheart deal time."[121]

The big $30.2 billion crime bill Congress passed in 1994 will probably add to those pressures. It has more money for police, which is to say more for arrests. It has more money for prisons at the other end of the line. But very little money for the logjams at the courthouse, where it counts. The new Republican majority in Congress is pushing to substitute last year's prescription with block grants for state and local governments, but there is little reason to think that the GOP strategy will bring much relief either. Prosecutors, judges, and probation officers can't do their job if they're too busy, if they give short shrift to most of their work because it's "routine." Heavy caseloads promote permissive attitudes, and vice versa. Ask Billy Dwyer, the Boston detective who investigated Kristin's murder.

"We don't need more cops," he said.[122] "A very small amount of people commit most of the crimes. The criminal element has already been identified. The courts let them go. The message we send them is, 'Listen, you can live a life of crime.' . . . I could take you down to Boston police headquarters right now, and in thirty minutes, I could come up with files on one hundred people with in excess of twenty-five arrests . . ."

"They get suspended sentences on top of suspended sentences," said Detective Mark Molloy, Dwyer's partner. "And then they get put 'on file.' Because the judges know they can't suspend the sentences any more. 'On file' basically means they don't exist."[123]

Every jurisdiction has euphemisms for it. "Probation Before Judgment." "Filed Without Finding." "Diversion." All are devices for looking the other way, for forgetting about what happened. Conditions are set, warnings are issued, all are widely ignored. Defendants often do deserve a second chance, but not a third and fourth and fifth. In cases of violence against women, what is especially frustrating is the habit of judges in restraining order cases—even in Massachusetts, where the criminal records are readily available—to look on the facts of the complaint as an isolated incident.

"We put everybody in some rinky-dink treatment program because it's his first offense," says Klein. "It isn't going to work. Most of these guys have been through the system already. They have an average of thirteen prior complaints against them on all sorts of charges. The judges should see them as fourteen-time losers instead of first offenders."

The controversial new omnibus crime law still has much to recommend it, particularly in some of its provisions concerning violence against women, and these will remain intact. It makes restraining orders in one state enforceable in any other and makes it a federal felony for batterers to cross state lines to continue their abuse.[124] It will also take years to implement and even longer to change official attitudes. Meanwhile, the population, which is growing older, will paradoxically be getting younger, too. There will be two million more teenagers aged fifteen to nineteen at the turn of the century than there are right now. Half of them will be male.[125] "Six percent of them will become high-rate, repeat offenders"—60,000 more strong-arm robbers, killers and thieves than we have now.[126] Prosecutors trying to juggle all sorts of crimes will be looking even more anxiously for their "sweetheart deals" because they will have more cases stacked up on their desks. More judges will be ready for deals because their dockets will be even more crowded. Except for high-profile cases, the defendants and their attorneys will have the upper hand.

So what happens when some battered young or not-so-young woman intrudes on a busy day and asks for justice? She may get a more sympathetic ear than she would have ten or twenty years ago. She certainly will have more laws to invoke. But justice? That is still the last thing she is going to get.

Kristin didn't demand justice. Like so many other women who have been beaten or stalked, she just wanted to be left alone. She expected her stalker to be arrested. She was given a piece of paper that said he had to stay away from her and told herself that would be good enough. In a way she told me, too. I can still remember how confident she was in the lighthearted laughter of our last conversation, the day before she was killed. We were talking about boyfriends and I asked her if there were any hanging about. She sounded as happy as she had ever been. "Not now," she said.

ACKNOWLEDGMENTS

Unfortunately, I cannot thank everyone who in one way or another helped me with this book. My gratitude goes far beyond those I mention here. I could not have written it without the generosity and support of *Washington Post* publisher Donald E. Graham and *Post* executive editor Leonard Downie Jr., who gave me an extended sabbatical to do the work. The Pope Foundation of New York provided an investigative journalism award that enabled me to complete the project.

I am especially indebted to a friend and colleague at the *Post*, Jeffrey Frank, who edited my original article about Kristin for the *Post*'s Outlook section and who continued to provide his insights and encouragement as I kept going. Other friends I relied on for their advice and good judgment were Morton and Anita Mintz, George Wilson, and Dan Morgan.

In Massachusetts, Brookline Police Lieutenant George Finnegan gave me immense help, both in getting started and in finding answers to a constant list of questions. I am thankful in many ways as well to Rose Ryan and her sister, Tina Ryan Tucker; probation officers Tom Casey in Brighton and Andrew Klein in Quincy; state Probation Commissioner Donald Cochran and retired District Court Judge Albert Kramer of Quincy; Charles McDonald of the Massachusetts Executive Office of Public Safety and Joseph Landolfi of the state's Executive Office of Health and Human Services; Peter F. Caulfield of the Massachusetts Society for the Prevention of Cruelty to Animals; Suffolk County Sheriff Robert Rufo; Boston police detectives William C. Dwyer and Mark Molloy; attorney Jeffrey Newman; Shelagh Lafferty of the Massachusetts Office for Victim Assistance; David Adams, cofounder and president of Emerge; Ross Ellenhorn; David Lowy, formerly a legal advisor to Governor William F. Weld and now a federal prosecutor; John Connors of the District Court Department in Salem; Octavia Ossola, Ferd "Chip" Wilder, and Thomas Walsh, formerly of the New England Home; Kristin's friends and roommates; and the teachers and staff of the Museum School. I also owe special thanks to my longtime friend and college roommate, Peter Mitchell, now president of the Massachusetts Maritime Academy, and his wife, Lou, who frequently took me into their home on my trips to Boston and who were especially kind to Kristin while she was a student there.

For education in the everyday workings of the criminal justice system, I owe special thanks to the Bureau of Justice Statistics, an underfunded arm of the Justice Department that manages to do outstanding work despite a tiny budget. The entire staff was helpful in countless ways, but none more than BJS senior statistician Patrick A. Langan, who was unfailingly generous with his time and insights, no matter what the question, from probation and parole to big-city crime to violence against women.

One of the leading scholars in the country on the subject of family violence is Richard J. Gelles, director of the Family Violence Research Program at the University of Rhode Island. I have benefited greatly from the work that he and his colleague, Murray A. Straus of the University of New Hampshire, did in their unprecedented national surveys of American families, best presented in their book *Physical Violence in American Families.* Gelles graciously spent hours with me, both in person and on the telephone, patiently explaining the findings of the surveys and much more. I am also indebted to him and Langan for their comments on various portions of the manuscript. They are in no way responsible for any errors of fact or judgment in these pages, nor is anyone else I mention here, but I could not have completed this book without the benefit of their knowledge.

To others cited in the book and many more who are not, I am also indebted in many ways. Among them are Leslye E. Orloff, founder of a domestic violence program at Ayuda Inc. in Washington, D.C., for immigrant and refugee women, and Catherine E. Klein, director of Catholic University's clinical domestic violence program since 1981. Others are Adele Harrell of the Urban Institute; Charles A. Lauer, retired special assistant to the assistant attorney general in the Justice Department's Office of Special Programs; James Q. Wilson, professor of management and public policy at UCLA; economist Mark Cohen of Vanderbilt University; Meredith Hofford of the National Council of Juvenile and Family Court Judges; Lisa Doyle Moran of the National Criminal Justice Association; Donna Hunzeker of the National Conference of State Legislators; Alan Najarian and Gay Sheldon of Gay's Flowers and Gifts; Sgt. Mark Wynn of the Nashville, Tenn., police department; U.S. District Court Judge Gladys Kessler; Maryland Circuit Judge Dennis Sweeney; Maryland District Court Judge Martha F. Rasin; Commonwealth's Attorney Robert Horan of Fairfax County, Va.; Gerald McKelvey of the Manhattan (N.Y.) District Attorney's office; Barbara Hart of the Pennsylvania Coalition Against Domestic Violence; James Ptacek of Tufts University; Angela Browne, author of *When Battered Women Kill;* Sarah Koch, formerly of the *Boston Herald,* now with ABC News; Esta Soler, executive director of the Family Violence Prevention Fund; Robert James Bidinotto of *Reader's Digest;* Kathie Neff of the *Lawrence* (Mass.) *Eagle-Tribune;* John J. DiIluio Jr. of the Brookings Institution and Princeton University; Mark Lipsey of Vanderbilt University; Kevin Ohlson of the U.S. Attorney's Office in Washington, D.C.; D.C. Assistant Corporation Counsel John McCabe; S. Molly Chaudhuri of the Norfolk County (Mass.) District Attorney's office; Officer John F. Sapienza of the Lawrence Police Department; Detective Donald H. Pattullo of the Andover (Mass.) Police Department; John Firman of the International Association of Chiefs of Police; Ann Grant of the Fund for Investigative Journalism; and Catherine E. Pope of the Pope Foundation.

At Atlantic Monthly Press, my editor, Anton Mueller, was patient, understanding, and always helpful. Best of all, he made whatever

I turned in better, and he did it with a wise and easy hand. My copy editor, Jill Mason, made a great contribution by applying her painstaking precision when and where it was needed. At the *Post,* John Cotter graciously reviewed the manuscript on short notice. I cannot express enough thanks to all the members of the *Post* research staff for their invaluable help, always cheerfully given, and especially to Pam Smith, who managed to find one arcane book and journal after another with great dispatch. I am grateful, too, to my agent, Tim Seldes, who was always available when I needed his advice.

I owe thanks to my daughter Helen for her invaluable suggestions and editing; to my son Richard for his help in reporting, especially at times when there seemed to be just too much to do; and to my sons Charles and Edmund for their thoughts and recollections. Lastly I want to thank my wife, Rosemary, for being so patient.

NOTES

CHAPTER 2

1. Dan Greenfield, "Slain Brookline Woman Recalled As 'Great Sport,'" *Brookline Citizen,* June 5, 1992, p. 1. The rest of Hyde's remarks come from conversations with the author.

2. Mary Ann Hinkle, assistant district attorney for Norfolk County, speaking at the 1994 Massachusetts Victim's Rights Week Conference at the State House in Boston, Tuesday, April 26, 1994. Hinkle is head of the sexual assault unit for the Norfolk County DA's office.

3. Author interview with Donna Hunzeker, National Conference of State Legislatures, May 19, 1994.
   Arizona and Maine remain the only states without stalking laws. Arizona uses its harassment statute and Maine uses its terrorizing statute to deal with stalking behavior. Maine added provisions related to stalking cases to its protective order statute in 1993. See "Project to Develop a Model Anti-Stalking Code for States," Research Report, National Institute of Justice (Washington, D.C.: U.S. Department of Justice, October 1993), p. 13.

4. Thomas B. Edsall, "Failure to Punish Misdemeanors Fuels Violence, St. Louis Officials Say," *Washington Post,* April 10, 1994.

5. Especially in jurisdictions like the District of Columbia, which until 1994 had no aggravated assault law. The District has long had a law making assault with a dangerous weapon a felony, but its meticulous jurists have sliced that

so fine as to exclude stationary bathroom fixtures such as tubs and toilet bowls from the definition of a "dangerous weapon." The case involved a man who permanently disfigured his wife, a model, by slamming her into the fixtures. His conviction, on a charge of assault with a dangerous weapon, was overturned. Loud words can bring much more judicial wrath. In D.C., for instance, threatening to kill someone can get you twenty years in prison, even if you don't lift a finger (D. C. Code 22-2307). But beating someone senseless will get you no more than six months, as long as you keep your mouth shut while you're doing it.

6. Massachusetts does not expunge its juvenile records, according to state Probation Commissioner Donald Cochran.

7. Interview with author, June 26, 1992.

8. Lawrence A. Greenfeld, *Prisons and Prisoners in the United States* (Washington, D.C.: Bureau of Justice Statistics, April 1992), NCJ-137002, p. 16. According to the study, "An estimated 93% of State prison inmates in 1991 were serving a sentence for a violent crime, had a history of violence, or were recidivists." The report was based on interviews in the summer of 1991 with a national representative sample of 14,000 inmates in state prison facilities.

9. Tracy L. Snell, *Correctional Populations in the United States, 1992* (Washington, D.C.: Bureau of Justice Statistics, January 1995), NCJ-146413, table 1.1, p. 5. Although the prison and jail populations keep going up, so do the numbers on probation and parole.

10. John J. DiIulio Jr., "Political Booknotes," *The Washington Monthly*, April 1995, p. 56.

11. Author interview with Rose Ryan, June 25, 1992. Also see Ryan remarks in Victoria Benning and Colleen Brush, "Legal Procedures Examined after Slaying in Allston, Critics Say Grounds for Arrest Existed," *Boston Globe*, June 1, 1992, p. 1.

12. Benning and Brush, "Legal Procedures Examined."

CHAPTER 3

1. Recent studies confirm that girls who keep their adolescent confusion and anger to themselves are more susceptible to depression, exploitation, substance abuse, eating disorders, and suicide attempts. According to a nation-

wide poll of nine- to fifteen-year-olds, commissioned by the American Association of University Women in 1990, 60 percent of the girls said they were "happy the way I am" when they were in elementary school, but only 29 percent agreed with that statement once they were in high school. Boys remained relatively more pleased with themselves, 67 percent in grade school and 46 percent in high school.

"Girls aged 8 and 9 are confident, assertive, and feel authoritative about themselves," the AAUW study said. "They emerge from adolescence with a poor self-image, constrained views of their future and their place in society, and much less confidence about themselves and their abilities."

Women's groups told the *Washington Post* that they think the reason for the decline in self-esteem is that girls realize the world is not listening to them or valuing them. "They start noticing how the world devalues their mothers, how the world devalues them," said Marie C. Wilson, president of the Ms. Foundation. Quoted in Sandra Evans, "Adolescent Girls and the Self-Esteem Gap," *Washington Post,* Health section, May 3, 1994.

2. The friendships lasted well after high school was over. Jennifer used to date Mark Arden, now an army helicopter pilot. They were married last spring (1994) at the Fort Myer, Virginia, post chapel; Kevin VanFlandern, who dated Eleanor the longest but at one point Jennifer and very briefly Kristin, was one of the groomsmen.

3. Almost 54 percent of high school seniors in the class of 1988, the year Kristin graduated, had tried some illicit drug, primarily marijuana or hashish (47.2 percent), according to the University of Michigan's Monitoring the Future Study, 1975–92. Ninety-two percent had taken alcohol. Ecstasy (MDMA) was not measured among high school students "because of concern that its alluring name might have the effect of stimulating interest." Lloyd D. Johnston, Patrick M. O'Malley, and Jerald G. Bachman, *National Survey Results on Drug Use from the Monitoring the Future Study, 1975–1992,* vol. 11, p. 40, University of Michigan Institute for Social Research (National Institute on Drug Abuse, NIH Publication no. 93–3598).

CHAPTER 4

1. Philip Bennett and Doris Sue Wong, "Judge Regrets He Didn't See Cartier's Record," *Boston Globe,* June 2, 1992, p. 1.

2. Ibid.

3. Remarks during Senate debate on omnibus crime bill, *Congressional Record,* Nov. 3, 1993, p. S-14905.

4. That is a widespread but erroneous impression, as an unprecedented study of more than 18,000 male defendants in restraining order cases in Massachusetts subsequently showed. "The high frequency with which ROs [restraining orders] are issued might lead some skeptics to assume that these orders are granted too easily for minor offenses and almost any man is at risk of being a defendant. The data available from the new RO database reflect otherwise," the study said. See Nancy E. Isaac, Donald Cochran, Marjorie E. Brown, and Sandra L. Adams, "Men Who Batter," *Archives of Family Medicine,* January 1994, vol. 3, pp. 50–54.

5. L. Kim Tan and Sarah Koch, "Hub Killer Dodged Jail for Therapy," *Boston Herald,* June 2, 1992, p. 6.

6. Yves Simon, *Nature and Functions of Authority* (Milwaukee: Marquette University Press, 1948), pp. 24–25.

7. There is no definitive count of battered women. Advocacy groups sometimes exaggerate the numbers, but the media don't make it any easier to understand them. In a July 25, 1984, article titled "The Numbers Game," for instance, *Newsweek* purported to explain how it could report that the number of women beaten by their "husbands, ex-husbands and boyfriends" was two million a year when *Time* said four million a year were attacked by a "domestic partner." *Newsweek* said its data came from a 1985 survey by an acknowledged authority in the field, Richard J. Gelles. *Time*'s report, *Newsweek* said, was based on a 1992 article in the *Journal of the American Medical Association,* which cited a "landmark" study in 1975.

In fact, that 1975 landmark study was also done by Gelles and his co-author, Murray Straus of the University of New Hampshire. Their 1975 and 1985 surveys, described widely as the only representative studies of family violence in America, showed that 1.8 million women living in households were severely assaulted by their husbands and mates each year and said that the actual number was probably twice that. Neither study dealt with "ex-husbands," as *Newsweek* claimed.

Gelles and Straus also found that over the course of a marriage, 28 percent of those surveyed in 1975 and 30 percent of those interviewed in 1985 had experienced one or more incidents of physical violence at the hands of their partners. "Moreover," they said, "there are several reasons to think that the true rates may be twice as high. If so, the majority of American couples have experienced at least one violent incident."

Newsweek was not the only publication to cite Gelles as an authority while rejecting or even deriding his findings, evidently under the impression that they came from someone or somewhere else. The *Washington Post* ("Battered-Truth Syndrome," July 3, 1994) and the *Nation* ("Truth Abuse," Aug. 1, 1994) also did so. "It's incredibly ironic," Gelles told me. "I feel there must be two of me." He said he suspected the reporters had been reading not his work, but secondhand descriptions and misrepresentations of it.

CHAPTER 5

1. L. Kim Tan and Sarah Koch, "Court Officials: We Didn't Know of Killer's Psych Woes," *Boston Herald,* June 3, 1992, pp. 1ff.

2. James Q. Wilson, *The Moral Sense* (New York: The Free Press 1993), pp. 133ff. "Difficult" infants may develop more behavioral problems than babies who are "easy" to handle, but it's hard to know what to make of that in terms of moral development. As Wilson points out, "An easy child can become a spoiled monster and a difficult one a moral visionary; people can have behavioral problems and still understand and act in a considerate and fair-minded fashion" (p. 138).

3. "Children acquire aggressive habits through interaction with their environment. Although biological factors (temperament, hormones, physique) also contribute to the learning of aggression, the dominant influences are environmental. . . . According to one theory, developed by Gerald Patterson of the Oregon Learning Center, children often resort to aggression because they find that aggression is the only way to stop the flow of noxious stimuli emanating from other people—it is used to demand attention, to stop the teasing, to stop being frustrated, or, in some cases, to interrupt the boredom" (David G. Perry, "How Is Aggression Learned?" *School Safety,* Fall 1987). Perry, a psychologist, said his own research showed that aggressive children expect more payoffs for behaving aggressively and are relatively unconcerned by the prospect of injuring another person in the process. For them, aggression works. It gets them what they want.

4. A twenty-two-year study of third-grade children in a semirural New York county found that aggressive behavior was remarkably consistent and stable. Children at age eight who fought over nothing, who pushed and shoved other children, who took other things without asking, who were rude to the teacher or said mean things to other children—behaviors that are often dismissed as normal, as "boys being boys"—were at age nineteen more likely to be cited in

juvenile court records and to have performed poorly in school. Compared to their less aggressive classmates, they were, by age thirty, "much more likely to have been convicted of crimes, to have been convicted of more serious crimes, to have more moving traffic violations, to have more convictions for drunken driving, to be more abusive to their spouses, to have more aggressive children, and to have not achieved as well educationally, professionally and socially. These results were independent of intelligence and social class as measured at age 8." ("Leonard D. Eron, "Aggression Through the Ages," *School Safety,* Fall 1987.) Eron found that some of the most powerful predictors of aggression at age eight were rejection by one or both parents, extensive use of physical punishment, lack of nurturance, and parental disharmony. Punishment for aggression served as a deterrent only for boys who were close to their fathers. For boys who were poorly or only minimally identified with their fathers, punishment led to increased aggression.

5. Emily Brontë, *Wuthering Heights* (London: Penguin Books, 1985), "Editor's Preface to the New [1850] Edition."

6. Doris Sue Wong, "Weld Signs Bill Establishing Computerized Warrant System," *Boston Globe,* Dec. 29, 1994.

7. The new law probably puts Massachusetts on the "cutting edge" of advanced-warrant systems, according to David Lowy, Governor Weld's deputy legal counsel. Unserved warrants are a mini-scandal across the country. Millions of them are stacked up on any given day in police stations from coast to coast. In San Diego alone, the county marshal's office recently counted 662,-000 unserved misdemeanor warrants for a host of minor crimes, including battery, petty thefts, and drunken driving, sometimes involving multiple charges against the same individual. "We just don't have a place to book these people," Lt. Paula Robinson of the San Diego County Marshal's office told the *Washington Post.* See Edsall, "Failure to Punish Misdemeanors," p. A-8.

8. Frank Phillips, "Weld Says Quick Move on Crime Bill Could Have Prevented Death," *Boston Globe,* June 2, 1992, p. 7.

9. Philip Bennett and Doris Sue Wong, "Judge Regrets He Didn't See Cartier's Record," *Boston Globe,* June 2, 1992, pp. 1 and 6.

10. Patricia Nealon and Sean P. Murphy, "Thwarting the Killers Is Complex, Elusive Goal," *Boston Globe,* June 2, 1992, p. 1.

11. Gerard F. Russell, "Bar Chief Calls Effort to List Batterers Ineffective," *Boston Globe,* June 6, 1992, p. 22.

12. Eric Fehrnstrom, "Weld: Death Could Have Been Stopped If Bail Reforms Adopted," *Boston Herald,* June 2, 1992, p. 6.

13. Author interview with Weld, June 26, 1992.

14. Doris Sue Wong, "Judges Get More Leeway on Bail—State Law to Allow Look at Dangerousness of Defendants," *Boston Globe,* July 15, 1994.

15. Author interview with Sapienza, Jan. 6, 1995.

16. Kathie Neff, "Skinhead Crew: We Are a Family, Not Racist Bunch," *Lawrence Eagle-Tribune,* June 16, 1989.

17. Ibid.

18. Kathie Neff, "When Will the Killing Finally End?" *Lawrence Eagle-Tribune,* June 7, 1992, p. A-1.

19. Ibid.

CHAPTER 6

1. Author interview with Rose Ryan, June 25, 1992.

2. The list goes on. Kristin and Rose were not the only women with brown hair and brown eyes, of similar height and weight, who fascinated Cartier. At the New England Home, according to Tom Walsh, he was infatuated with a teacher named Sherri. According to Sean Coleman, a young man from South Boston, Cartier was stalking a woman acquaintance of Coleman's, Elissa, in 1990 before he met Rose Ryan. Like Kristin and Rose and Penny Cartier, Elissa and Sherri had brown hair, brown eyes, stood about 5′5″ and weighed between 110 and 120. Cartier wanted a girl who looked like his mother to love him, or else.

3. "Courts and Communities: Confronting Violence in the Family," conference sponsored by the National Council of Juvenile and Family Court Judges, State Justice Institute, Family Violence Prevention Fund, and Urban Institute, San Francisco, March 25–28, 1993.

4. David Adams, "Treatment Models of Men Who Batter, A Profeminist Analysis," in *Feminist Perspectives on Wife Abuse,* K. Yllo and M. Bograd, eds. (Beverly Hills: Sage, 1988).

5. Ibid.

6. Tovia Smith, "Get Out of My Face or I'll Kill You," *Boston Globe* magazine, Jan. 2, 1994.

7. Ibid.

8. See James Ptacek, "Wifebeaters' Accounts of Their Violence: Loss of Control As an Excuse and As Subjective Experience," unpublished thesis, University of Wisconsin, 1985, p. 87 and passim.

9. "Courts and Communities," *Conference Highlights,* p. 10.

10. Author interviews with James Q. Wilson, Oct. 17, 1994, and William Hudgins, Oct. 4, 1994. Hudgins, a psychologist who interviewed Cartier shortly before he killed Kristin, said he regarded deliberate mistreatment of an animal as "a sure sign you are dealing with a very, very disturbed person." He was not aware of Cartier's record. Also see Randall Lockwood and Guy R. Hodge, "The Tangled Web of Animal Abuse," *Humane Society News,* Summer 1986, and Stephen R. Kellert and Alan R. Felthous, "Childhood Cruelty toward Animals among Criminals and Noncriminals," *Human Relations,* vol. 38, no. 12 (1985), pp. 1113–1125. According to Lockwood and Hodge, "There is compelling evidence linking both serial and mass murderers to acts of animal abuse prior to age 25." Examples include Albert DiSalvo, the "Boston Strangler," who killed thirteen women in 1962–63 and in his youth trapped dogs and cats in orange crates and shot them with arrows; David Berkowitz, the "Son of Sam" gunman, who shot a neighbor's Labrador retriever, claiming that it compelled him to kill; and Carroll E. Cole, who was executed in 1985 for five of thirty-five murders of which he was accused and said his first act of violence as a child was to strangle a puppy. A more recent case involves Richard A. Davis, who killed twelve-year-old Polly Klaas in California in 1993; his history of violence began in adolescence, when "he would set cats on fire for fun" (*Washington Monthly,* Sept. 1994, p. 25).

11. Cited in Lockwood and Hodge, "The Tangled Web," p. 6.

12. Author interviews with Caulfield, July 13 and Aug. 3, 1994.

13. Cartier's parents contend that it was a bad rap, that he claimed to have done it himself to protect a friend who would otherwise have gone to jail. "It was a practical joke," Gene Cartier said. "His friend was on probation, so Michael took the rap for it. He didn't think it was such a big deal." Cartier, however, had as much to worry about. He was on probation, too, with a six-month suspended sentence waiting for him. Pattullo said, "There's no doubt

that Michael was the guy who was doing the blood. He admitted to it. He was described as being the guy that did it. When we talked to the kid with the needles, the kid immediately—because he knew he was in trouble for giving Cartier the needle, he could have been charged also—the kid immediately told us who it was." The diabetic youth, Pattullo added, "had a clean record."

14. The CORI law still has extensive restrictions on public access to criminal records although Gov. Weld has proposed a bill to eliminate most of them. Records of arraignments in open court, for instance, are not available unless they result in convictions.

15. On a total of six counts. In addition to the grocery store burglary (which involved three felony counts), illegal contamination of food, and the apartment bashing, Cartier had also been convicted on a felony charge of malicious destruction for busting the front glass door of a Lawrence store on September 23, 1988. He was put on six months' probation for that incident.

16. Lockwood and Hodge, "The Tangled Web," p. 2.

17. "The system in Massachusetts isn't much different from when the pilgrims got off the boat," said Edward Dolan of the Massachusetts Parole Board. "It's a nightmare. Take manslaughter. What is it? There are guys who get sixty days for it. There are guys who do life."

For suspects who deserve stiffer sentences, plea bargaining usually offers a way out. The courts are clogged everywhere. Except for high-profile cases, prosecutors are almost always ready to deal. "The system settles to the path of least resistance," said one Massachusetts correction official. "It says, in effect, let's see what this guy will settle for with the least fight." That isn't justice, not if you think the punishment should fit the crime. But it preserves the pretense of it. It holds up the house of cards.

18. "Antistalking Proposals," *Hearing Before the Committee on the Judiciary of the United States Senate on Combating Stalking and Family Violence* (Washington, D.C.: Government Printing Office), March 17, 1993, p. 62.

CHAPTER 7

1. It was covered with wall board during renovations on my last visit in 1994.

2. At an April 13, 1994, hearing before the District of Columbia Council on a bill to extend coverage of the domestic violence law to dating relationships,

the sponsor, council member James E. Nathanson, said he had been able to find only eight states, including Massachusetts, that provided such protection. One of the witnesses, Catherine Klein of the Families and Law Clinic at Catholic University, said there were sixteen states that afforded extended protection to individuals in a nonmarital, dating, or engagement relationship. States with laws to that effect were Alaska, California, Colorado, Illinois, Indiana, Massachusetts, Montana, New Hampshire, New Mexico, North Dakota, Washington, and West Virginia. In addition, courts in New Jersey, Oklahoma, Pennsylvania, and Wisconsin have supported this approach and issued civil protection orders based on dating relationships. Cf. Klein testimony, pp. 17–18.

3. Case of Harvey v. Randall, IF-2690-92, D.C. Superior Court hearing, Jan. 26, 1993. Several advocates for battered women contend that the judge erred in posing the question and that relationships can be intimate under relevant law without necessarily being sexual. The woman in the case did not have an attorney; her former boyfriend, whom she accused of threatening her with a machete, did.

4. Catherine Klein testimony, D.C. Council hearing, April 13, 1994, p. 7.

5. Massachusetts Bay Transit Authority police did not get around to filing their paperwork and obtaining a warrant against Cartier for the Government Center attack until April 19, 1991, five days after the felonious assault.

6. Keith A. Harriston and Saundra Torry, "D.C. Called Lax on Escapees, City Failing to Seek Warrants, Memo Says," *Washington Post,* Oct. 8, 1993, p. A-1.

7. Author interview with Firman, July 18, 1994, and letter from Firman on informal survey results, Aug. 31, 1994.

8. Ibid.

9. Ibid.

10. In conversations October 3 and October 5, 1994, Annunziata refused to talk about any of his discussions with or impressions of Cartier, citing doctor-patient privilege. But he insisted that he interviewed Cartier in an office at the courthouse rather than in the cage. He may have been remembering an interview the previous fall when Cartier was at Brighton District Court for trashing the apartment. Probation officer Casey said he distinctly remembered the April 29, 1991, interview taking place in the big cell built into the courtroom. Rose Ryan said a male psychologist or psychiatrist—she can't re-

member his name—talked to Cartier at the Brighton courthouse in the fall of 1990 and again in the spring of 1991. She said she saw the same man when she went to the courthouse in May and as she recalled it, "he said joking, 'You guys back together? I thought you were going to keep him out of trouble.' "

11. The law was finally repealed, effective January 1994. Called the "de novo" law, it dated back to the days when defendants unhappy with a justice of the peace's ruling wanted another chance. "Abolishing de novo was a terrific accomplishment," Governor Weld's deputy legal counsel, David Lowy, told me in an interview. "It had no relevance to the 1990s. It wasn't even relevant to the 1890s."

12. This artificial insulation can work to the detriment of the defendant as well as the victim. See William Finnegan, "Doubt," *The New Yorker,* Jan. 31, 1994, pp. 48–67. Finnegan, who sat on a jury that convicted a New York man of assault and robbery, checked up on the case after the trial and to his dismay discovered evidence that the man may not have been guilty beyond a reasonable doubt, evidence that was kept from the jurors under the guise of giving the man a fair trial.

13. Tape of proceeding, Case nos. 9101-CR3503A and CR3503B, Boston Municipal Court, June 20, 1991.

14. Author interview with Wayne Murphy, April 29, 1994.

15. According to official records, Deer Island in 1992 was 53 percent black, 31 percent white, and 14 percent Hispanic.

16. Massachusetts since 1984 has had a victim rights law entitling victims to be notified "upon request" when the defendant is released from custody, but the rules and regulations implementing the law require the request to be made in writing. Neither this law nor a stronger version enacted in May 1995 contains any penalties for officials who fail to follow its requirements. The 1984 law did not even say that notification must be made "in advance" of release from custody. The new law added those two little words, but without saying how far "in advance."

17. For inmates in the state prison system, release notifications are the responsibility of the Massachusetts Department of Corrections.

18. Background conversation, April 11, 1994. The officer asked not to be identified.

19. Case of Richard V. Wasilewski, Fairfax County, Virginia, General District Court, Docket no. 93-15724, tried Dec. 16, 1993.

20. Linda Pride, "A Worst Case Scenario—Stalked from Jail," as told to Bill Holton, *Women First* magazine, vol. 6, no. 13, March 28, 1994, pp. 36–38.

21. Ibid.

22. According to a nationwide survey in 1994 by the National Council on Crime and Delinquency, only Pennsylvania, Utah, and Hawaii provide no "good time" credits. BJS statistician Lawrence Greenfeld said in an interview that good-time calculations vary widely from state to state and can be incredibly complicated. Alabama's rulebook, for instance, runs about two hundred pages. Many jurisdictions have different earnings rates for different types of offenders, such as maximum and minimum security. Some have special awards. Massachusetts used to give a special deduction for blood donors; California, for fighting fires. "Basically," Greenfeld said, "it's an administrative fudge factor to keep the population from being overcrowded. With the demise of parole [under truth-in-sentencing laws] 'good time' is actually becoming more and more prevalent. One thing you could say about parole is that it is a matter of record, considered by people appointed by the governor, people with some sense of what would outrage the public. 'Good time' is immune from public scrutiny."

23. Robert James Bidinotto, "Revolving-Door Justice: Plague on America," *Reader's Digest*, February 1994, pp. 33–39.

24. Ibid.

25. Author interview with Suffolk County Sheriff Robert Rufo, Oct. 6, 1994. Deer Island was run by a city penal commission, now defunct. Sheriff Rufo, who runs the new facility, inherited the records.

26. As part of a new "truth in sentencing" law, Massachusetts repealed its statutory "good time" law, effective July 1, 1994, and now gives credits only for earned good time, such as participation in programs related to education, substance abuse, and the like. But despite talk across the country about ending or restricting "good time," James Austin, Washington director of the National Council on Crime and Delinquency, predicts most states will keep their current form of good-time credits. He said the Council recently conducted a survey of "good time" credits in all the states.

CHAPTER 8

1. It was started in 1977 at the request of some women who were working in battered-women shelters in the Boston area. A group of eleven men started it with the help of the Boston Men's Center. It was incorporated in April 1978 as a nonprofit organization.

2. Author's conversation with John Tobin, chief probation officer, Boston Municipal Court, Sept. 16, 1992.

3. In an October 14, 1994, interview with Tobin and Chief Justice William J. Tierney of Boston Municipal Court, Tobin said that in 1991, assignments of probation officers were routinely made "after release" in cases involving a split sentence. He said a probation officer is now assigned at the time of disposition, when the sentence is meted out. The new policy was adopted at the end of 1992, apparently after the article I wrote about Kristin was reprinted in the *Boston Globe* and cited extensively in the *Boston Herald*.

4. "Administrative Probation Report" on Michael Cartier, Boston Municipal Court, opened Dec. 5, 1991, File no. 816357.

5. Author interview with Cochran, Nov. 22, 1994.

6. Asked in a March 28, 1995, interview about the costs of maximum risk supervision, Cochran said "we haven't done a study in years," but he estimated them to be "a couple of thousand dollars" a probationer. He said minimum risk supervision costs "a couple of hundred dollars" while administrative probation "is basically intended to make sure they pay their fines, make restitution." Rose Ryan, it should be pointed out, never got a penny from Cartier for her dental bills.

7. Author interview with Tobin, March 31, 1995.

8. The proportion of public funds allocated to probation and parole across the country has been dropping steadily as the populations supposedly being supervised have been rising. In 1977, 17.6 percent of all state and local tax dollars allocated to corrections went to probation and parole, while 74.4 percent went to correctional institutions. In 1990, probation and parole got only 11 percent. On a federal level, the proportion allocated for probation, parole, and pardon operations went from 21.1 percent in 1979 to 13.9 percent in 1990. See Sue A. Lindgren, "Justice Expenditure and Employment, 1990,"

Bureau of Justice Statistics Bulletin (Washington, D.C.: U.S. Department of Justice, September 1992). See also Marc Perrusquia, "More Cases, Low Morale Sap Watch on Parolees, Audit Shows Some Officers Ignored Convicts for 4 Years," *Memphis Commercial-Appeal,* March 8, 1993, p. A-1; and Howard Goodman, "A Crushing Load for Corrections Officers, Cases Are Doubling, Sometimes Tripling," *Philadelphia Inquirer,* April 20, 1992, p. A-1.

9. BMC Probation Chief Tobin identified the handwriting on the first page of the file as that of Regan, who has since retired.

10. "Administrative Probation Report," File no. 816357.

11. Ibid. Evidently the calls were made by Regan before the case was turned over to Diane Barrett-Moeller, who also spells her first name "Dyann."

12. Rose Ryan is skeptical. She said, "I don't remember Mike ever beating up any male [I was acquainted with]."

13. Author interview with Judge Tierney, Oct. 14, 1994.

14. Author interview with Judge Donovan, April 21, 1995.

15. Author interview with Tobin, June 24, 1992.

16. It was eliminated in July 1993, about a year after Kristin's murder.

17. Robert Martinson, "What Works?—Questions and Answers About Prison Reform," *The Public Interest,* Spring 1974, no. 35, pp. 22–54. State officials in New York, for whom the study was done, suppressed the findings for a time. Martinson and his colleagues did the study for a state planning agency working under a mandate from the New York State Governor's Special Committee on Criminal Offenders. But its conclusions were "viewed as a serious threat to the programs which, in the meantime, [state officials] had determined to carry forward." By the spring of 1972, a full year after it had been re-edited for final publication, Martinson wrote, "The state had not only failed to publish it but had also refused to give me permission to publish it on my own." It became public only after a lawyer subpoenaed it from the state as evidence in a Bronx court case.

The failures reflected in the study were staggering. James Q. Wilson, then of Harvard, now of UCLA, summed up the results in his book *Thinking About Crime:* "It did not seem to matter what form of treatment was attempted—whether vocational training or academic education, whether counseling inmates individually, in groups, or not at all; whether therapy was administered by social workers or psychiatrists; whether the institutional context of the treatment was custodial or benign; whether the sentences were short or long; whether the person was placed on probation or released on parole; or whether the treatment took place in the community or in institutions. Indeed, some forms of treatment (notably a few experiments with psychotherapy) actually produced an *increase* in the rate of recidivism."

18. Author interview with David Adams, Jan. 15, 1995.

19. Massachusetts Guidelines and Standards for the Certification of Batterers' Treatment Programs, effective July 1991, p. 12.

20. "Treatment Standards for Abuser Programs," *Violence Update,* vol. 5, no. 1, Sept. 1994, p. 5.

21. Donovan interview, April 21, 1995.

22. "Probation officer Barrett-Moeller excluded me from any involvement in both the development and operation of the program," Assistant Chief Probation Officer Ann L. Fuller said in a July 14, 1993, letter to Chief Justice Tierney. Fuller said she asked "at least three or four times to observe a session in progress, but was denied access on the grounds that my presence would be disruptive and interfere with the group's dynamics." Fuller said she expressed her concerns in a December 1992 conversation with Barrett-Moeller and emphasized to Barrett-Moeller "the importance of keeping statistics . . . for her own protection (and my own) should a tragedy similar to the Michael Cartier case recur." In a March 28, 1995, interview, Tobin distanced himself from the program, saying "it was an idea she [Barrett-Moeller] developed on her own and received authorization for from the chief justice."

23. Memo of July 6, 1993, from Tobin to Diane M. Barrett-Moeller and letter of July 15, 1993 from Tobin to Diane Barrett-Moeller. The correspondence was provided to the author by Chief Justice Tierney. In a memo of July 9, 1993, Barrett-Moeller reportedly expressed her "shock" and "dismay" that the program had been terminated and suggested that the entire probation department be terminated because of recidivism.

24. Tobin to Barrett-Moeller, July 15, 1993.

25. Donovan interview, April 21, 1995.

CHAPTER 9

1. Tobin expressed chagrin in March 31 and April 20, 1995, interviews about Cartier's having been allowed back into the program after being expelled from it and said he did not know about this when he first spoke with me in late June 1992. He said it was his understanding then that Barrett-Moeller simply told the judge, Linda Giles, that Cartier "had not had an opportunity to complete the program" and that Barrett-Moeller "asked for an extension" so that he could start over.

Tobin, however, acknowledged that he had reviewed Cartier's administrative probation file when he first talked to me. It states plainly, on the second page, that Cartier "never appeared" for his second AVG class and was expelled or "terminated" from the program, only to be given another chance by Judge Giles two days later. I asked Tobin how he squared that entry with his saying he didn't know about it. "It doesn't square," he said. Was the page held out of the file that had been made available to him then? Tobin said he couldn't bring himself to say that. "I can only say what I said before," he replied. He said the information about Cartier's expulsion from the program "was not available to me at the time. I did not have it in my possession and it was not given to me orally either."

In any case, Tobin said Cartier should never have been allowed back into the program and in fact should not have been enrolled in it in the first place. "It was not designed for people who abuse spouses and girlfriends," he said. "It was designed for people who tend to become violent under stress and smash windows, kick at cars. It was not for people who are into control, power, and dominance." Tobin said that enrolling Cartier in Barrett-Moeller's program and then letting him repeat it "was a violation of her own rules and the program's rules."

2. Author interview with Judge Donovan, April 21, 1995.

3. In a letter dated Aug. 10, 1994, Judge Tierney said he had no objection to my speaking with Barrett-Moeller, but she has not responded to my renewed request for an interview.

4. Phone conversation with Barrett-Moeller, June 23, 1992.

5. L. Kim Tan and Sarah Koch, "Hub Killer Dodged Jail for Therapy," *Boston Herald,* June 2, 1992, p. 1ff.

6. Alexis de Tocqueville, *Democracy in America,* ed. J. P. Mayer, tr. George Lawrence (New York: Harper Perennial, 1988), p. 590.

7. A study of wife beating in 36 states showed that such violence is most common in states where the economic, educational, political, and legal status of women is lowest, but the rate of violence is almost as high in the top fifth of states where women have achieved the greatest equality, in terms of equal-pay laws, unrestricted property rights, representation in Congress, median income, and the like. This appears to be true "because of the conflicts inherent in the *inconsistency* between the relatively equal structural status of women and the attempt to maintain a traditional patriarchal power structure within the family." See Kersti A. Yllo and Murray A. Straus, "Patriarchy and Violence Against Wives: The Impact of Structural and Normative Factors," in *Physical Violence in American Families* (New Brunswick, N.J., 1992), pp. 394–398.

8. David Adams, "Identifying the Assaultive Husband in Court: You Be the Judge," *Boston Bar Journal,* July-August 1989, p. 24.

9. Author interview with Brian Fazekas, Jan. 29, 1995.

10. "Some perpetrators will batter only in particular ways, e.g., hit certain parts of the body, but not others; only use violence towards the victim even though they may be angry at others (their bosses, other family members, etc.); break only the abused party's possessions, not their own. They are making choices even when they are supposedly 'out of control.' Such decision-making indicates they are actually in control of their behavior." See Anne L. Ganley, "Domestic Violence: The What, Why and Who, as Relevant to Civil Court Cases," in *Domestic Violence in Civil Court Cases: A National Model for Judicial Education,* The Family Violence Prevention Fund (San Francisco, 1992), p. 35.

11. Gene Cartier denied doing this.

CHAPTER 10

1. "Administration Probation Report," File no. 816357. I did not obtain a copy until August 1994, when Chief Justice William J. Tierney of Boston Municipal Court provided it in response to an inquiry I sent to him.

2. Hudgins is a psychologist, not a psychiatrist.

3. Peter Finn and Sarah Colson, *Civil Protection Orders: Legislation, Current Court Practice and Enforcement* (Washington, D.C.: National Institute of Justice, U.S. Department of Justice, March 1990), pp. 2–3.

4. Ibid.

5. This is the way Lauren remembered the conversation. I'm not sure how Kristin knew at that point that Cartier had killed any cats unless Sgt. Simmons managed to get details beyond those contained in the summary history. The offense listed there said only "cruelty to animals."

6. "A Judge of Character," *Boston Globe*, Nov. 23, 1992, p. 10.

7. "For Judge, Retirement Not the End," *Boston Globe*, City Weekly / Brookline edition, Nov. 15, 1992, p. 1.

8. Andreae Downs, "Abusers Slip through Local Court," *Brookline Citizen*, June 5, 1992.

9. Andreae Downs, "Repeat Offender Gets 3 Years Jail," *Brookline Citizen*, June 12, 1992.

10. Author interview with Judge Kramer, Nov. 10, 1992.

11. Andreae Downs, "Abusers Slip through Local Court," *Brookline Citizen*, June 5, 1992.

12. The Quincy program was one of twenty across the nation cited by the National Council of Juvenile and Family Court Judges in 1992 as the best in the country in dealing with family violence. It was hailed for combining innovative policies and approaches "that not only provide maximum protection, but also empower victims of domestic violence." Its sentencing practices include intensive supervision; mandatory, long-term batterers' group treatment; alcohol and drug abstinence monitored through random urine and hair tests; and contact with the victim to ensure that the defendant is obeying court orders to refrain from contact and abuse. See *Family Violence—State-of-the-Art Court Programs* (Reno, Nev.: National Council of Juvenile and Family Court Judges, 1992), pp. 76–77. Yet even in Quincy, repeat offenders rarely got jail time.

13. "Judge Regrets He Didn't See Cartier's Record," *Boston Globe*, June 2, 1992, p. 1. Also see "Hub Killer Dodged Jail for Therapy," *Boston Herald*, June 2, 1992, p. 1.

14. Andreae Downs, "Court Vows Vigilance," *Brookline Citizen*, June 19, 1992.

CHAPTER 11

1. Author interview with Rose Ryan, Oct. 4, 1994. She said she discovered this from Cartier's friends after he killed himself. "The time I was going out with him I didn't know he was doing drugs," she said. "I just thought he drank a lot."

2. "Suffolk County House of Correction Intake Summary for Michael Cartier," May 13, 1991, p. 7. Cartier listed "mesc" as one of the drugs he was taking, but according to Drug Enforcement Administration spokesman James McGivney, it was most likely PCP. "Real mescaline is harder to come by and can be unpleasant to take," McGivney said. He said that Cartier would appear to have been "past casual" as a drug user, but "not a junkie yet"— unless he was taking the heroin daily rather than on weekends.

3. Interestingly, the abuse prevention law gives the courts authority to order a violator to undergo treatment, in addition to any other penalty, but only in cases "where the defendant has no record of any crime of violence." The law also states, "If a defendant ordered to undergo treatment has received a suspended sentence, the original sentence shall be reimposed if the defendant fails to participate in said program as required by the terms of his probation."

Cartier, of course, had been convicted of the crimes of assault with a dangerous weapon and assault and battery for his attack on Rose Ryan, and not of the crime of violating a restraining order, but the intent seems clear. His continued harassment of Rose was a violation of the restraining order she had gotten, as well as a violation of his probation, and should have been sufficient to send him straight back to jail.

4. Author interview with Judge McGill, June 24, 1992.

5. *Family Violence: Improving Court Practice, Recommendations from the National Council of Juvenile and Family Court Judges* (Reno, Nev.: National Council of Juvenile and Family Court Judges, 1990), adopted July 12, 1990, p. 25.

CHAPTER 12

1. "Killer Preyed on Women," *Lawrence Eagle-Tribune*, June 2, 1992, p. 1.

2. "Legal Procedures Examined after Slaying in Allston," *Boston Globe*, June 1, 1992, p. 1.

3. "Court Officials: We Didn't Know of Killer's Psych Woes," *Boston Herald,* June 3, 1992, p. 1ff.

4. Author interview with J. D. Crump, manager of Bunratty's, June 23, 1992.

5. "Probation Referral for Evaluation," report of W. Hudgins regarding Michael Cartier, Department of Mental Health Court Clinic at Government Center, May 27, 1992. The interview was conducted May 21, 1992.

6. Author interview with Hudgins, Oct. 4, 1994.

7. Martinson, "What Works." Some rehabilitation efforts, Martinson found, can even make things worse. One he cited involved individual psychotherapy on young incarcerated female offenders. A study of that program found that if the individual therapy was administered by a psychiatrist or a psychologist, subsequent parole violations were almost two and a half times higher than they were when the therapy was administered by a social worker without specialized training. Another study in 1964 involving "self-government" group psychotherapy on young males designated as psychopaths found that "group therapy" boys went on to commit twice as many offenses as those given "authoritarian" individual counseling.

8. Illustrative of this mindset is an editorial from the newsletter of the Association of State Correctional Administrators entitled "It's the Inmates, Stupid," October 1993 (vol. 9, no. 8). "In our business," it said, "the customer is not the public, not the legislature or other elected officials, not our staff, and not the victims in the community. Our customers are our inmates, probationers, and parolees."

9. That tattoo was a castle. "I didn't get a close look," Hudgins later explained.

10. Author interview with Hudgins, Oct. 4, 1992.

11. Ibid.

12. Author interview with Adams, Jan. 18, 1995.

13. Tovia Smith, "Get Out of My Face or I'll Kill You."

14. Author interview with David Bowden, June 22, 1992.

15. Cartier admitted putting his blood in the bottle both to Detective Pattullo of the Andover Police Department and later to Dr. Zeizel at Deer Island.

Cartier volunteered the information to Zeizel when he asked Cartier why he was going to be sent back to Lawrence following his release from Deer Island. "He told me he did it," Zeizel recalled. "There was no reason for him to lie to me."

16. Author interview with Dan Graham, Oct. 6, 1994.

17. Author interview with Scott Morales, June 23, 1992.

18. Boston Police Homicide unit investigative report, "Interview of Paul Pitts," May 30, 1992.

19. Author interview with Chris Toher, June 23, 1992.

20. One of the investigating officers told me that no drug or alcohol tests were conducted as part of the autopsy.

21. During 1985–91, arrest rates for murder and non-negligent manslaughter increased 127 percent for males aged fifteen to nineteen and 43 percent for males aged twenty to twenty-four. The rates went down 1 and 13 percent for men aged twenty-five to twenty-nine and thirty to thirty-four, respectively. In 1991, fifteen- to nineteen-year-old males were more likely to be arrested for murder than men of any other age group. See *Morbidity and Mortality Weekly Report,* U.S. Public Health Service, vol. 43, no. 40, Oct. 14, 1994.

CHAPTER 13

1. The Clothesline Project is a visual display that was started in Hyannis, Massachusetts, in the fall of 1990.

2. I gave only a short summary. What follows is an elaboration.

3. Sydney Hanlon, "Saving Battered Women," *Boston Globe,* Dec. 30, 1992. Hanlon is a judge in Dorchester District Court.

4. Lindgren, "Justice Expenditure and Employment."

5. James P. Lynch, Steven K. Smith, Helen A. Graziadei, and Tanutda Pittayathikhun, *Profile of Inmates in the United States and in England and Wales, 1991* (Washington, D.C.: Bureau of Justice Statistics, October 1994), NCJ-145863, p. 2. The cost of the justice system per resident in 1991 was $299 in the United States and $310 in England and Wales.

6. *Criminal Justice in Crisis* (Washington, D.C.: American Bar Association, Criminal Justice Section, November 1988), p. 5.

7. Some of the money will go to other agencies, such as the Department of Health and Human Services, rather than to the justice system. The new Republican-controlled Congress is trying to change the law to give much of the money in block grants to the states and eliminate the federally prescribed crime prevention programs in the 1994 law, but that proposal has shortcomings of its own. For instance, more attention needs to be paid to the structural defects in the administration of justice.

8. James Q. Wilson, *Thinking About Crime* (New York: Vintage Books, 1985), p. 260.

9. Lindgren, "Justice Expenditure and Employment."

10. Remarks of Senator Bob Dole (R., Kan.), *Congressional Record,* Feb. 8, 1994, p. S-1102.

11. *Survey of State Prison Inmates, 1991* (Washington, D.C.: Bureau of Justice Statistics, March 1993), p. 11.

12. The estimate was derived from nationwide compilations by the *Corrections Compendium,* a monthly magazine, of the state and federal corrections budgets for fiscal 1993, totaling $21.9 billion, and of the state and federal prison populations, totaling 888,861 prisoners (excluding New Mexico and Puerto Rico, which did not respond to the survey). Eleven percent, or $2.4 billion, was subtracted from the budget total to allow for the most recently calculated level of spending on probation and parole. Those figures suggest an average cost of $21,900 per prisoner. This is significantly higher than the last official estimates of the Justice Department for fiscal 1990, when total state and federal spending on prisons was about $11.5 billion. The average annual cost per prisoner then was $15,603. See Lindgren, "Justice Expenditure and Employment," p. 5, and Greenfeld, *Prisons and Prisoners in the United States,* p. 12.

13. Jeffrey A. Roth, *Understanding and Preventing Violence,* a research brief summarizing the findings of the National Academy of Sciences Panel on the Understanding and Control of Violent Behavior, published by the National Institute of Justice, February 1994, p. 5. The actual number of serious violent crimes remained about the same in 1989 as in 1975—2.9 million—because of other factors, the panel said. But it would have been much larger without the increased imposition of prison sentences.

14. "Crime Solution—Lock 'Em Up," *Wall Street Journal,* Dec. 17, 1993. Wattenberg is a senior fellow at the American Enterprise Institute.

15. Patrick A. Langan, "Between Prison and Probation: Intermediate Sanctions," *Science,* vol. 264, May 6, 1994, pp. 791–793.

16. Author interview with Langan, Nov. 9, 1994. There would have been 65,000 more rapes, 160,000 more robberies, 240,000 more aggravated assaults, and 4,000,000 more burglaries.

17. Interview with Langan, Oct. 25, 1994. Also see Jeff Leen and Don Van Natta, Jr., "Dade Justice Puts Felons on the Street," *Miami Herald,* Aug. 28, 1994, p. 22A.

18. Mark A. Cohen, "Early Prison Release, Consider Cost of Pain, Fear," *Houston Chronicle,* April 27, 1992, p. 11A.

19. Patsy A. Klaus, *The Costs of Crime to Victims,* Crime Data Brief (Washington, D.C.: Bureau of Justice Statistics, February 1994), NCJ-145865.

20. Jeff Leen and Don Van Natta, Jr., "Plea Bargain Leaves Victim Angry, Afraid," *Miami Herald,* Aug. 28, 1994, p. 22A.

21. Ibid. Also see Don Van Natta, Jr., and Jeff Leen, "Dade Courts, An Expressway to Freedom," *Miami Herald,* Aug. 28, 1994, p. 24A.

22. Klaus, *The Costs of Crime to Victims.* The survey does not count insurance payments, medical costs after six months, psychological counseling, moving expenses, decreased productivity at work, or other items. Nor does it ask about mental health costs, which other studies show dwarf medical costs.

23. Ted R. Miller, Mark A. Cohen, and Shelli B. Rossman, "Victim Costs of Violent Crime and Resulting Injuries," *Health Affairs,* Winter 1993, pp. 187–197. The study did not count much larger and more controversial punitive damage awards, "since they are not meant to compensate victims for pain and suffering." Of the total lifetime costs of $208 billion, aggravated assaults constitute the biggest chunk, $112.8 billion, because there are so many of them. There is nothing written in stone about these or other cost-of-crime estimates. Mark Cohen, the Vanderbilt University economist who pioneered the studies reported in *Health Affairs,* is constantly refining his methodology, but the refinements are resulting in higher, not lower, estimates. The National Academy of Sciences' expert panel endorsed the approach in its 1993 report "Understanding and Preventing Violence," putting the average cost at $54,000 for rape, $19,200 for robbery, and $16,000 for assault. About 15 percent of the costs are financial, the panel said, and 85 percent reflect values imputed for pain, suffering, risk of death, pshychological damage, and reduced quality of life.

24. Lindgren, "Justice Expenditure and Employment," table 2. Total justice spending in fiscal 1990 was $74.25 billion. The *Health Affairs* study, stated in 1989 dollars, put the total lifetime costs at $177 billion.

25. John J. DiIulio Jr., "Crime and Punishment in Wisconsin," *Wisconsin Policy Research Institute Report,* vol. 3, no. 7, December 1990, and *Final Report of the New Jersey Sentencing Policy Commission,* January 1994. The New Jersey study was done by DiIulio and Anne Morrison Piehl, formerly at Princeton, now at Harvard University. Also see DiIulio and Piehl, "Does Prison Pay?" *Brookings Review,* Fall 1991, and "Does Prison Pay? Revisited," *Brookings Review,* Winter 1995.

26. *Report of New Jersey Sentencing Policy Commission,* op. cit., pp. 19–20.

27. DiIulio and Piehl, "Does Prison Pay? Revisited." They say, "The best estimate of the incapacitation effect (number of drug sales prevented by incarcerating a drug dealer) is zero," because there is usually someone ready and willing to take the place of the imprisoned dealer. Drug offenders, however, do commit other crimes, including murder, rape, and robbery. According to the Bureau of Justice Statistics, *Prisoners 1993,* 30.5 percent of the new inmates sent to state prison in 1992 were committed for drug offenses; in 1980, only 6.8 percent were committed for drug offenses. Those imprisoned for violent crime, meanwhile, dropped from 48.2 percent of new state prison commitments in 1980 to 28.5 percent in 1992.

28. James Q. Wilson, "What to Do About Crime," *Commentary,* Sept. 1994, pp. 27–28. The figures on peak age for criminals and average age for prison inmates also come from Wilson.

29. Wicker, "The Punitive Society," *New York Times,* Jan. 12, 1991, p. 25. This myth, which Wicker reiterated, had been given currency by the National Council on Crime and Delinquency in a misleading 1990 report asserting that the "vast majority" of those "now" being sent to prison were "petty" offenders who were not dangerous and should not be sent to prison. The report was based on interviews with just 154 incoming prisoners in three states. Criminologist Charles H. Logan said a close look at the data showed that the NCCD's "vast majority" was actually 52.6 percent, and almost half of that "majority" (25.4 percent) whose crimes were dismissed as "petty" told the interviewers they were high-rate offenders who were committed to a criminal lifestyle. In an article for the *Federal Bureau of Prisons Journal* (Summer 1991), Logan, a professor of sociology at the University of Connecticut, pointed out

that if the 25.4 percent were added to the 47.4 percent whose crimes were concededly not petty, then the NCCD study would show that nearly three-quarters of the new admissions were either serious or high-rate offenders. Even that number, Logan said, would not account for the 21 percent "who, while not identified as high-rate offenders, are described [in the NCCD study] as having been on a 'crime spree' at the time of their commitment offense."

30. John J. DiIulio, Jr., *Governing Prisons, A Comparative Study of Correctional Management* (New York: Free Press, 1987), pp. 206–207.

31. Public attitude about prisons has changed over the past twenty years, reflecting a growing belief that their main job is to punish, not rehabilitate. In 1971, 15 percent said the primary purpose of prisons was to punish, while 76 percent said it was to rehabilitate; in 1980, the split was 32 percent for punishment, 53 percent for rehabilitation; and in 1994, 49 percent supported punishment as the primary function and 49 percent rehabilitation. According to a report in the *Washington Post* ("Do Crime, Do Time," Dec. 4, 1994, p. C-5), whites supported punishment as primary by 53 percent to 46 percent; blacks supported rehabilitation 65 percent to 29 percent. The question was: Which one of the statements comes closest to expressing your point of view on prisons: a) the main role of prisons is to punish criminals and keep them apart from the rest of society, or b) the main purpose of prisons is to keep criminals separate from the rest of society until they can be rehabilitated and returned to society.

32. Charles H. Logan and Gerald G. Gaes, "Meta-Analysis and the Rehabilitation of Punishment," *Justice Quarterly,* vol. 10, no. 2, June 1993, pp. 245–263.

33. Author interview with Octavia Ossola, Jan. 24, 1995.

34. Author interview with Wilson, Oct. 17, 1994.

35. See Logan and Gaes, "Meta-Analysis." In practice, they say, its claim that rehabilitation works, in the sense of being significantly and reliably effective, is "seriously flawed, unsubstantiated and largely circular."

36. Wilson, "What to Do About Crime," pp. 25–54.

37. Mark Lipsey of Vanderbilt University, who conducted the mega-evaluation Wilson mentioned, said in a March 23, 1995, interview that the best of the programs in his review of nearly 500 studies show a reduction in recidi-

vism on the order of 25 to 30 percent, but he declined to identify any of those individual programs because it would "put too much emphasis on the particulars of a program model." He said he was working on a profile that might point the way to development of successful programs, based on the characteristics of the ones he found that worked, but he also agreed that successful programs are sometimes difficult to replicate and that it would be best in any case to concentrate on children at an earlier age. "If we're serious about this," he said, "the best thing to do is get in there earlier. The problem kids have when they mature is learned behavior. Some do have wiring problems when they're born, but the bulk of what we're talking about is learned behavior."

38. Crime trends are best reflected by the the Justice Department's National Crime Victimization Survey, which is based on interviews each six months with about 100,000 individuals living in randomly selected households. In contrast to the trends reflected in the survey, the FBI's annual Uniform Crime Reports show a huge increase over recent decades, indicating, for instance, that overall crime rates have tripled since 1960 and that violent crime rates have nearly quadrupled. But the UCR measures only those crimes reported to and recorded by police, and a major reason for the increases in the FBI's numbers, perhaps the biggest reason, is better police recording practices. For example, in 1973, the nation's crime victims said they reported 1.5 million violent crimes (rapes, noncommercial robberies, and aggravated assaults) to police, but the police (and therefore the FBI) recorded only 750,000. The disparity gradually grew smaller and by now has virtually disappeared, according to data compiled by Patrick A. Langan of the Bureau of Justice Statistics. In 1992, the nation's crime victims said they reported 1.8 million of those same kinds of violent crimes to police, and police recorded more than 1.76 million.

39. *Criminal Victimization in the United States* (Washington, D.C.: Bureau of Justice Statistics, March 1994), p. 6, table 4. The latest National Crime Victimization Survey, covering 1993 and released in May 1995, employed a new methodology designed to elicit more complete responses, especially about domestic violence. It shows a total of 10.9 million violent crimes in 1993. The 1992 total of violent crimes, adjusted for the new method, was 10.3 million, rather than the 6.6 million computed under the old method. However, comparisons with earlier years are not yet available.

40. *Crime in the United States, 1992* (Washington, D.C.: Federal Bureau of Investigation, October 1993), p. 58.

41. Wilson, "What to Do About Crime," p. 26.

42. Gallup polls in recent years show that the criminal justice system ranks lowest when Americans are asked how much confidence they have in various institutions. Even Congress fares better. The 1994 poll showed that only 15 percent had a great deal of confidence in the justice system, compared to 18 percent for Congress, the next lowest on the list, and 64 percent for the military, which did the best. Unlike the justice system in general, police are highly regarded. Fifty-four percent said they had a great deal of confidence in the police, tying them for second place with organized religion. Most blacks, however, have "not very much" (52 percent) or no confidence at all (11 percent) in the ability of the police to protect them from violent crime. Only 34 percent of the black population has a great deal of confidence in the police as an institution, but blacks have even less faith in the criminal justice system. Only 26 percent of black Americans have a great deal of confidence in the system, while 50 percent have "very little or none." See *Sourcebook of Criminal Justice Statistics 1993* (Washington, D.C.: Bureau of Justice Statistics), NCJ-148211, table 2.6, p. 157; tables 2.8 and 2.9, p. 159; and table 2.17, p. 165.

43. Less than 40 percent of all serious offenses and less than 50 percent of all crimes of violence are reported to police (*Sourcebook of Criminal Justice Statistics 1993*, Bureau of Justice Statistics, NCJ-148211, table 3.6, p. 252). Of the offenses that are reported, only about one in five result in an arrest (table 4.23, p. 450). That works out to one arrest for every 12.5 crimes. For arrest and adjudication outcomes, see table 5.73, p. 546; Jacob Perez, *Tracking Offenders, 1990* (Washington, D.C.: Bureau of Justice Statistics, June 1994), NCJ-1148200, p. 1; and Patrick A. Langan and John M. Dawson, *Felony Sentences in State Courts, 1992* (Washington, D.C.: Bureau of Justice Statistics, December 1994), NCJ-151167, p. 5.

44. Langan and Dawson, *Felony Sentences in State Courts, 1992*, p. 2, table 2, and Craig Perkins, *National Corrections Reporting Program, 1992* (Washington, D.C.: Bureau of Justice Statistics, October 1994), NCJ-145862, table 2–12, p. 46.

45. Author interview with Langan of Bureau of Justice Statistics, Feb. 27, 1995.

46. An estimated 62.5 percent of those released from prison are rearrested for a felony or serious misdemeanor, while 62 percent of the probationers are either arrested for a new felony or charged at a hearing with violating a condi-

tion of their probation. The released prisoners accumulate an average of 4.8 charges each. Greenfeld, *Prisons and Prisoners in the United States,* p. xvi. Also see Allen J. Beck and Bernard F. Shipley, *Recidivism of Prisoners Released in 1983* (Washington, D.C.: Bureau of Justice Statistics, April 1989), NCJ-116261, p. 1, and Patrick Langan and Mark Cunniff, *Recidivism of Felons on Probation, 1986–1989* (Washington, D.C.: Bureau of Justice Statistics, February 1992), NCJ-134177, pp. 1 and 5.

47. Wilson, "What to Do About Crime," p. 26.

48. President Clinton last year, acting in conjunction with a new federal law, ordered a cutoff in federal education funds to any state that fails to adopt a "near-blanket" policy of expelling for at least one year anyone who brings a gun to school. See Pierre Thomas, "U.S. Acts to Curb Youth Handgun Use," *Washington Post,* Nov. 18, 1994, p. A-4. Also see text of Clinton memo for the Secretary of Education regarding implementation of the Gun-Free Safe Schools Act of 1994 and the Safe and Drug-Free Schools and Communities Act, Oct. 22, 1994.

49. Retha Hill, "Boy, 5, Takes Loaded Gun to P. G. School," *Washington Post,* Feb. 4, 1995, p. A-1.

50. Joseph F. Sheley and James D. Wright, "Gun Acquisition and Possession in Selected Juvenile Samples," *Research in Brief* (Washington, D.C.: National Institute of Justice, Office of Justice Programs, December 1993), NCJ-145326.

51. Bill McAllister, "Handgun Crime Up Sharply," *Washington Post,* May 16, 1994, p. A-1. Also see James Q. Wilson, "Just Take Away Their Guns," *New York Times* magazine, March 20, 1994, p. 47.

52. Wilson, "Just Take Away Their Guns," p. 47. Tests in Kansas City, Missouri, and Indianapolis, Indiana, developed by criminologist Lawrence A. Sherman have shown that vigorous enforcement can work, just as it has with drunk drivers. Gun seizures, by specially assigned teams of police officers, increased 65 percent and gun-related crimes went down 50 percent in the Kansas City neighborhoods chosen for the experiment. Although other factors may have been involved in the drop, Sherman thinks the decrease in violent crime was largely due to the gun seizures. See Fox Butterfield, "Cities Finding a New Policy Limits Guns," *New York Times,* Nov. 20, 1994, p. 22, and Ruben Castaneda, "One City's Attack on Handguns," *Washington Post,* Jan. 30, 1995, p. B-1.

53. Elijah Anderson, "The Code of the Streets," *Atlantic Monthly,* May 1994, pp. 80–94. Anderson was writing about inner-city black neighborhoods where there is "a profound lack of faith in the police and the judicial system." I would submit that "the code" he talks about has in some respects infected troubled white teenagers and neighborhoods as well. Women are not the primary casualties of such violence, but they are inevitable ones. Young men ready to attack at the slightest sign of being "dissed" are not going to take any arguments from some "bitch" who happens to be a girlfriend. In black communities, unfortunately, the women probably have the same distrust of police as the men and so may be reluctant to see the men arrested, even for beating them. They're used to "the code." Indeed, as mothers, many of them probably promote it, especially in one-parent homes where the women administer the discipline. As Anderson says, "Many mothers in the community subscribe to the notion that there is a 'devil in that boy' that must be beaten out of him or that socially 'fast girls need to be whupped.' "

54. Rorie Sherman, "Juvenile Court Judges Say: Time to Get Tough," *National Law Journal,* vol. 16, no. 49, Aug. 8, 1994. Sixty-eight percent of the judges said they believe today's youths are increasingly depraved. Only 17 percent said they were "no different," and 5 percent said they were "less" depraved. The remaining 10 percent said "don't know."

55. Gary Taylor and Rorie Sherman, "Judges Oppose Adult Court for Kids," *National Law Journal,* Aug. 8, 1994, p. A24. The expert cited was Malcolm W. Klein, director of the Social Sciences Research Institute at the University of Southern California.

56. Author interview with Hunter Hurst, Nov. 8, 1994.

57. Peter W. Greenwood and Susan Turner, "Evaluation of the Paint Creek Youth Center, A Residential Program for Serious Delinquents," Rand Corp., 1993, reprinted from *Criminology,* vol. 31, no. 2, May 1993, pp. 263–279. The program drew on a combination of treatment philosophies, including "positive peer culture," "reality therapy," and "criminal thinking errors." Upon release from the center, three out of four of the Paint Creek graduates saw their "aftercare workers" at least twice a week, and 52 percent saw them more than six times a week.

58. Ibid.

59. Wilson, *The Moral Sense* (New York: The Free Press, 1993), pp. 130 and 141.

60. Ibid., pp. 143–144.

61. Ibid., p. 145.

62. Susan Chira, "Study Confirms Worst Fears on U.S. Children," *New York Times,* April 12, 1994, p. 1.

63. Ibid.

64. Toni Locy, "D.C. Social Services Face Court Takeover," *Washington Post,* Feb. 4, 1995, p. A-10. "The bureaucracy seems to be more worried about bureaucratic posturing than . . . the care of the children," a federal judge said of the troubled D.C. child welfare system. He seized control of it on May 22, 1995.

65. Richard Perez-Pena, "Report Finds the Limbo of Child Care Is Growing Longer," *New York Times,* Dec. 22, 1994, p. B-1.

66. Cathy Spatz Widom, *The Cycle of Violence,* research brief published by the National Institute of Justice, U.S. Justice Department, October 1992.

67. Ibid., p. 5.

68. American humorist Finley Peter Dunne's character, Mr. Dooley, made the remark in 1901: "No matter whether th' Constitution follows the flag or not, th' Supreme Court follows th' illiction returns." The observation was prompted by the Republican party's slogan following the conquest of the Philippines: "The Constitution follows the flag."

69. One of my colleagues at the *Post,* columnist Richard Cohen, for instance, wrote an election-day column denouncing the fact that crime had become an issue as an "election-year obscenity." He noted that crime rates had been declining, but it did not seem to occur to him that the increasing number of prison sentences and the protective measures prompted by the fear of crime might have had something to do with it. Cohen contended that the public belief that crime is worsening was based on television's crass attempts to nudge up ratings by serving up a "nightly diet of crime and mayhem" on the evening news. The same complaint could have been made about all the attention paid to the war in Vietnam. I doubt that Cohen has ever excoriated the networks for trying to "nudge up ratings" with their nightly reports on Vietnam. The war was real, and so is the crime problem. See Cohen, "The Great Tantrum of '94," *Washington Post,* Nov. 8, 1994, p. A-17.

70. Remarks of Mario Cuomo, from "In Their Own Words," *New York Times,* Metro section, Oct. 13, 1994.

71. Miedzian, *Boys Will Be Boys* (New York: Anchor Books, 1991), p. 288. She points out that a review of eighty popular comic book series by the National Coalition on Television Violence, reported in NCTV's June–July 1988 newsletter, found that violent themes including cannibalism, satanism, and rape were becoming increasingly common.

72. The preceding were quoted in Miedzian, *Boys Will Be Boys,* p. 255.

73. Cited in Nathan McCall, "My Rap Against Rap," *Washington Post,* Outlook section, Nov. 14, 1993.

74. James Q. Wilson and Richard J. Herrnstein, *Crime and Human Nature* (New York: Simon & Schuster, 1985), chapter 13.

75. Wilson, "What to Do About Crime," p. 27.

76. The pioneering study, conducted by Marvin Wolfgang, involved 10,000 boys born in 1945 who grew up in Philadelphia. Six percent of them accounted for 53 percent of all the arrests of that 10,000-member group. That same small fraction committed 71 percent of all the homicides, 70 percent of the robberies, 73 percent of the rapes, and 69 percent of the aggravated assaults attributable to the group. Wolfgang did another study of a group born in 1958 and found the same pattern: 7.5 percent were responsible for 61 percent of all arrests and 71 percent of all murders, rapes, robberies, and aggravated assaults attributable to the birth cohort. See, for example, "Delinquency in Two Birth Cohorts," *American Behavioral Scientist,* 1983, vol. 27, no. 1, pp. 75–86. Studies conducted in such diverse places as London, Copenhagen, and Orange County, California, produced roughly the same result, according to Wilson.

77. Ibid.

78. The bill was not signed into law until May 16, 1995, more than a year later.

79. Bob Hohler, "State Found Shy on Aid to Victims of Home Violence," *Boston Globe,* May 26, 1993.

CHAPTER 14

1. Title IV, Subtitle F, Sections 40601–40611, Violent Crime and Law Enforcement Control Act of 1994.

2. Author interview with Horan, Feb. 16, 1994.

3. Author interview with Lisa Doyle Moran, assistant director for legal affairs at the National Criminal Justice Association and member of the task force staff, Feb. 7, 1995. At the time of the task force study, only eight states allowed stalking to be treated as a felony, punishable by more than a year in prison, for the first offense.

4. Kennedy had the backing of House Judiciary Committee chairman Jack Brooks (D-Tex.); Charles E. Schumer (D-N.Y.), chairman of the Judiciary Subcommittee on Crime; Rep. Patricia Schroeder (D-Colo.), co-chair of the Congressional Caucus on Women's Issues; and Rep. Jim Ramstad (R-Minn.). House Rules Committee chairman Joseph Moakley (D-Mass.) was also "very supportive," Kennedy said. Suzanne Hoeg lived in Moakley's district.

5. *Congressional Record,* April 20, 1994, p. H2525.

6. Toni Locy, "Weld Signs Bill Creating Registry of Batterers," *Boston Globe,* Sept. 23, 1992.

7. Allison Bass, Patricia Nealon, and David Armstrong, "The War on Domestic Abuse—State Records Reveal Discrepancies in Enforcing Restraining Orders," *Boston Globe,* Sept. 25, 1994.

8. Ibid.

9. Ibid. Among big urban counties, Suffolk also has the worst adjudication record in the country for felony cases. In 1990, only 32 percent of its felony cases resulted in convictions of any kind, while 58 percent resulted in dismissals or acquittals. Another 11 percent resulted in "deferred adjudication" or "diversions." Suffolk also has the highest proportion of felony defendants charged with violent crimes (44 percent). See Pheny Z. Smith, *Felony Defendants in Large Urban Counties, 1990* (Washington, D.C.: Bureau of Justice Statistics, May 1993), NCJ-141872, pp. 24 and 27.

10. Ibid.

11. "The Dynamics of Family Violence," a speech by Sarah Buel delivered to "Courts and Communities: Confronting Violence in the Family" conference sponsored by the National Council of Juvenile and Family Court Judges, State Justice Institute, Urban Institute, and Family Violence Prevention Fund, March 25–28, 1993.

12. "Alive and Well in Quincy," 60 *Minutes,* CBS Inc., Feb. 7, 1993.

13. Ibid.

14. Author interview with Judge Kramer, Nov. 10, 1992.

15. There were fewer than a dozen cases in which the defendant was a female and the petitioner a male, and slightly over one hundred in which the defendant was the adult child of the petitioner. Those cases were not included in the study. It found official records indicating about half of the abusers (48.8 percent) reabused their victims within two years and noted that the findings were conservative because only records were examined; the victims were not interviewed. Prior research has shown that arrest records represent only a small percentage of actual abuse cases.

16. Author interview with Klein, Sept. 3, 1993.

17. Isaac, Cochran, Brown, and Adams, "Men Who Batter." In an analysis of 18,369 male defendants against whom restraining orders were issued in the state from September 8, 1992, to March 9, 1993, the study found 74.8 percent had prior criminal records and 48.1 percent had histories of violent crime. The criminal records were probably understated since they did not contain any information on offenses outside Massachusetts.

18. Ibid., p. 53.

19. Author interview with Cochran, April 25, 1994. "The image of the 'batterer as everyone' is typically based on clinical samples and the reports of victims. Since comparison groups of nonviolent men are not used, there is no way to calculate the risk-to-violence of any social or demographic variable," Straus and Gelles, *Physical Violence in American Families* (New Brunswick, N.J.: Transaction Publishers, 1992), p. 437.

20. Interview with Gelles, Sept. 21, 1994. Also see "Men Who Batter—The Risk Markers" by Richard J. Gelles, Regina Lackner, and Glenn D. Wolfner of the University of Rhode Island's Family Violence Research Program, published in *Violence Update*, vol. 4, no. 12, August 1994.

21. Author interview with Cochran, April 25, 1994.

22. Gelles interview, Sept. 21, 1994, and Gelles, Lackner, and Wolfner, "Men Who Batter—The Risk Markers."

23. Ibid.

24. Ibid.

25. "Compassion Training for Domestic Violence," program outline, undated, by Steven Stosny, director, Silver Spring, Maryland.

26. Author interview with Gelles, Sept. 21, 1994.

27. Ibid.

28. Twenty-nine states allow a judge to order treatment and supervision as part of a restraining order, according to Klein. Massachusetts does not.

29. Gelles interview, Sept. 21, 1994.

30. According to the National Council of Juvenile and Family Court Judges, "Prosecutors should initiate, manage and pursue prosecution in all family violence cases where a criminal case can be proved, including proceeding without the active involvement of the victim, if necessary. . . . [I]t is the responsibility of the state to move the case forward. Victims must not be placed in the position of initiating and managing their own cases. . . . A relatively high percentage of them will request that their cases be dismissed. However, a number of jurisdictions have discovered the withdrawal rate is significantly lower when victims are relieved of the burden of the decision to prosecute. . . . In fact, a number of courts have discovered that victims are more willing and able to testify when they receive emotional support and advocacy from victim assistance personnel. . . . By controlling the criminal process, the prosecutor provides a powerful message that the offender or other family members may not avoid criminal sanctions through their control over the victim or refusal to cooperate." From "Family Violence: Improving Court Practice, Recommendations from the National Council of Juvenile and Family Court Judges," adopted by the council July 12, 1990.

31. "Judges and victims alike agree that nowhere is the potential for renewed violence greater than during visitation." Finn and Colson, *Civil Protection Orders,* p. 43.

32. Adele Harrell, Barbara Smith, and Lisa Newmark, *Court Processing and the Effects of Restraining Orders for Domestic Violence Victims* (Washington, D.C.: Urban Institute, May 1993), p. 78.

33. Ibid. For instance, many women said the order did not set out the specific conditions they needed, especially concerning child care and visitation. Others wanted more explicit conditions about the distance their partner was to keep from them. Many of the men seemed to think that contacting their partners or ex-partners to "work things out" did not violate the court orders.

34. Ibid., p. 79. Of the 290 incidents reported to the police within a year after the orders were issued, only 59 arrests were made in Denver and Boulder (20 percent). "According to the women, the police called to the scene during the first three months after the order asked her to leave the scene almost as often as they arrested the man. Not surprisingly, ratings of police helpfulness at violations were dramatically lower than ratings of police helpfulness at the response to the initial incident" (p. 74).

35. As the *Boston Globe* series and Klein's studies show.

36. Martha R. Mahoney, "Legal Images of Battered Women: Redefining the Issue of Separation," *Michigan Law Review,* October 1991. According to Maryland District Judge Martha Rasin, co-chairman of a 1994 conference of Maryland judges on family violence, many judges described how the sessions taught them above all never again to ask, Why didn't she leave? Obviously, they had been accustomed to asking themselves just that question when confronted with the problem.

37. Meredith Hofford and Adele V. Harrell, "Family Violence: Interventions for the Justice System," program brief for the Bureau of Justice Assistance, U.S. Justice Department, October 1993, pp. 19–20.

38. Author interview with Klein, Dec. 9, 1994.

39. New York Penal Law 215.51; Chapter 222. The law went into effect Jan. 1, 1995, along with other provisions dealing with domestic violence, including creation of a computerized registry of all orders of protection issued by family courts in the state. See "Gould's Criminal Law & Procedure Reporter," vol. 6, no. 1, Fall 1994.

40. The same self-defeating objections have been raised to arresting violent partners and taking out restraining orders. Restraining orders may fail to deter some, perhaps many, abusers, but they also serve as a notice to police and promote a higher arrest rate. In Massachusetts, for instance, Klein reports, there is a slightly greater arrest rate for men with restraining orders against them compared to men whose orders have lapsed. "Without ROs [restraining orders]," he said, "it is often left to the women to bring their abusers back to court for another RO petition or criminal complaint."

41. Author interview with Gelles, Sept. 21, 1994.

42. Straus and Gelles, *Physical Violence in American Families,* p. 17.

43. Cited in Angela Browne, *When Battered Women Kill* (New York: Free Press, 1987), p. 165.

44. Straus and Gelles, pp. 113–114, citing Elizabeth Gould Davis, *The First Sex* (New York: Putnam, 1971).

45. Tocqueville, *Democracy in America,* p. 42.

46. Ibid.

47. It was not until 1871 that a U.S. court revoked a man's legal authority to beat his wife. An Alabama court led the way, holding that "the privilege, ancient though it be, to beat [one's wife] with a stick, to pull her hair, choke her, spit in her face or kick her about the floor, or to inflict upon her like indignities, is not now acknowledged by our law. . . . In person, the wife is entitled to the same protection of the law that the husband can invoke for himself." Cited in Barbara J. Hart, "State Codes on Domestic Violence, Analysis, Commentary and Recommendations," *Juvenile and Family Court Journal,* 1992, vol. 43, no. 4, p. 22.

48. Straus and Gelles, *Physical Violence in American Families,* p. 433.

49. Cited in Lawrence W. Sherman, "Policing Domestic Violence" (New York: The Free Press, 1992), p. 26.

50. Until 1992, Maryland law provided less relief than almost any state in the country, limiting protective orders to thirty days and allowing them only for current spouses living with the alleged abuser; a new statute that went into effect in October 1992 greatly expanded eligibility, the forms of relief, and the duration of the orders. The changes produced a 66 percent increase in the orders granted during the last three months of 1992, compared to the final quarter of 1991.

51. "Transcript of Remarks Made During Sentencing of Man Who Killed His Wife," *Baltimore Sun,* Oct. 21, 1994, p. 3B.

52. Megan Rosenfeld, "Mercy for a Cuckolded Killer," *Washington Post,* Oct. 19, 1994.

53. Karl Vick, "Md. Judge Taking Heat in Cuckolded Killer Case," *Washington Post,* Oct. 30, 1994.

54. Hart, "State Codes," p. 22.

55. "Transcript of Remarks Made."

56. Vick, "Md. Judge."

57. Ibid. Also see Rosenfeld, "Mercy."

58. Sheridan Lyons, "Judges Attend Conference on Domestic Violence," *Baltimore Sun,* Oct. 28, 1994.

59. Many judges simply bristle when the problem is cast in terms of violence against women, according to a judge at a planning session for the Maryland conference. An official from Baltimore's House of Ruth had opened the preparatory meeting with a documentary film depicting a brutal beating and a mass of statistics about the extent of violence women suffer at the hands of their partners. One of the planners, Circuit Judge Dana Levitz, frowned on the presentation. This was supposed to be a conference on "family violence," he cautioned. He said he knew very well, as did everyone else in the room, that it is almost always women who seek protective orders. But if the theme of the conference were to be violence against women, he warned, "You'll lose a third of the judges right at the beginning." Elaborating later, he said he was afraid many of his colleagues would tend to see the issue not in terms of violence, which is the way they should see it, but in terms of "the feminist agenda, which is quite frankly a difficult agenda for many conservative men to accept."

60. Bass, Nealon, and Armstrong, "War on Domestic Abuse."

61. The *Miami Herald*'s series "Crime and Punishment," Aug. 28–Sept. 5, 1994, offered a stunning look at the shortcomings there.

62. As one of the organizers of the Maryland conference, Circuit Judge Dennis Sweeney, said at a previous meeting, "Go to the pre-sentence investigations of all the people on death row. I'll bet you'll find [domestic] abuse."

63. Leen and Van Natta, "Dade Justice Puts Felons on the Street."

64. Paul H. Robinson, "A Failure of Moral Conviction?" *The Public Interest,* Fall 1994, no. 117, p. 42.

65. *Drug and Crime Facts, 1993* (Washington, D.C.: Bureau of Justice Statistics), p. 15. For every 100 felony arrests for assault by state and local authorities, only 13 are convicted and only 6 are sent to prison. For every 100 burglary arrests, 38 are convicted and 20 are sent to prison. Yet the lifetime costs of assaults committed each year, including attempted murders and those that resulted in murder, stood at more than $96 billion a year in 1989. Since

then, according to the National Crime Victimization Survey for 1992, the aggravated assault rate has increased 8.3 percent and the simple assault rate has gone up 12 percent.

66. Conviction rates for aggravated assault rose 57 percent between 1988 and 1992, the biggest factor in an overall 34 percent increase in felony convictions in state courts during that period. Forty-four percent of the felons convicted for aggravated assault were sent to prison and 28 percent to jail. See Patrick A. Langan and Helen A. Graziadei, "Felony Sentences in State Courts, 1992," *Bureau of Justice Statistics Bulletin* (Washington, D.C.: U.S. Justice Department, January 1995), NCJ-151167.

67. Interview with Langan, Dec. 1, 1994.

68. Ibid.

69. Richard Perez-Pena, "Report Finds the Limbo of Child Care Is Growing," *New York Times,* Dec. 22, 1994.

70. "One nonbattered woman in 50 leaves [the hospital] with these [and similar] labels, 1 battered woman in 4 does." Cf. Evan Stark, Anne Flitcraft, and William Frazier, "Medicine and Patriarchal Violence: The Social Construction of a 'Private' Event," *International Journal of Health Services,* vol. 9, no. 3, 1979.

71. Prevention Work Group 1, "Work Group Recommendations," National Conference on Family Violence, American Medical Association (Washington, D.C., March 11–13, 1994), pp. 12–13.

72. "California Hospital Emergency Departments Response to Domestic Violence—Survey Report," published by the Family Violence Prevention fund, San Francisco, August 1993. Several studies have indicated that one-fifth to one-third of the patients who enter hospital emergency rooms are victims of domestic violence. Interestingly, one of these frequently cited studies said it found no "statistically significant difference between the number of male and female domestic violence victims, although a greater proportion of the victims were female (62 percent)." The women tended to be more alarmed about their predicaments, worried about children who had also been hurt, and more desirous of counseling than the men. In any case, "only 5% of the domestic violence victims were identified as such on the ED [Emergency Department] record." Cf., Wendy G. Goldberg and Michael C. Tomlanovich, "Domestic Violence Victims in the Emergency Department, New Findings," *Journal of*

the American Medical Association, vol. 251, no. 24, June 22–29, 1984, pp. 3259–3264.

73. "California Hospitals Fail to Train Most Emergency Room Staff to Diagnose & Aid Battered Women, New Survey Finds," news release, Family Violence Prevention Fund, San Francisco, Aug. 17, 1993.

74. Statement of Dr. Robert E. McAfee, president-elect, American Medical Association, March 13, 1994.

75. Daniel Patrick Moynihan, "Defining Deviancy Down," *American Educator,* Winter 1993–1994, pp. 10–18. Moynihan's last sentence was a reference to the June 10, 1992, issue of the *Journal of the American Medical Association,* which was devoted entirely to the subject of violence, mainly gun-related violence, and which said in an editorial: "Regarding violence in our society as purely a sociological matter, or one of law enforcement, has led to unmitigated failure. It is time to test further whether violence can be amenable to medical/public health interventions." *JAMA*'s next issue, June 17, 1992, was devoted to domestic violence against women.

76. Press conference at the U.S. Capitol on a proposed bill to require medical and health professional schools to include training on domestic violence in their curriculums, Sept. 30, 1993. Evelyn Smith killed her husband the night of Nov. 12, 1991, when he came home "saying this was the night I was to die," choked her with a phone cord, and punched her bloody. She said he was charging at her when she fired once with a .38-caliber revolver. She was later tried for first-degree murder and acquitted. Her jurors decided she had acted in self-defense after three years of beatings and emotional abuse. It was the first trial in Prince George's County, Maryland, under the state's new "battered spouse syndrome law," permitting her lawyer to offer evidence of past abuse and its psychological effect on her. Several jurors said they might have voted to acquit her anyway on the basis of what happened that night. See Paul Duggan, "Jury Finds Wife Killed in Self-Defense," *Washington Post,* June 19, 1992, p. D-1, and "Survivor Speakout," an account by Evelyn Smith, distributed at press conference.

77. Xanax is a strong sleeping pill and tranquilizer; Tylenol 3 is a painkiller containing codeine.

78. Patrick A. Langan and Christopher A. Innes, *Preventing Domestic Violence Against Women,* Special Report (Washington, D.C.: Bureau of Justice Statistics, August 1986), p. 3. In terms of actual bodily injury, as many as half of all

incidents of domestic violence that police would classify as misdemeanors are as serious or more serious than 90 percent of all the violent crimes—rapes, robberies, and aggravated assaults—that police would classify as felonies.

79. Author interview with then U.S. Attorney Jay Stephens of the District of Columbia, Dec. 1, 1992.

80. Langan and Innes, p. 3.

81. Gail A. Goolkasian, *Confronting Domestic Violence: The Role of Criminal Court Judges,* National Institute of Justice, U.S. Department of Justice, November 1986, p. 7, note 1.

82. *Violence between Intimates,* Bureau of Justice Statistics, November 1994, NCJ-149259, p. 2. The study covered the years 1987–1991.

83. Straus and Gelles, *Physical Violence in American Families,* p. 11.

84. Straus and Gelles say their surveys showed 3.4 million intact households where the husband or the wife has been severely beaten (for instance, kicked, choked, or punched) in the past year. No comparable total has been compiled for cases that come up in court, but Probation Commissioner Cochran points out that in 1994, almost 47,000 restraining orders were issued against 40,000 individuals in Massachusetts alone, a state with a population of about 6 million. The proportion is probably lower nationwide because many states do not allow issuance of restraining orders in circumstances such as Kristin's, involving a former boyfriend. But if the proportion were applicable to the U.S. population of 255 million, that would suggest as many as 1.7 million restraining orders a year, most of them obtained by women and many, probably most, by women who have already left their batterers.

85. I use the word here not with reference to any particular legal definition, but in the broader sense of conduct that puts a reasonable person in fear of bodily injury or death of oneself or of a member of one's immediate family. That, of course, would include a physical attack as well as furtive approaches and intimidating messages.

86. Author interview with Ptacek, Dec. 20, 1994.

87. Carolyn Wolf Harlow, "Female Victims of Violent Crime" (Washington, D.C.: Bureau of Justice Statistics, January 1991), NCJ-126826, p. 5. The strikingly high proportion may be due in part to the greater willingness of women who have left their batterers to talk about the beatings. In any case,

the report noted: "Although separated or divorced women comprised 10 percent of all women, they reported 75 percent of the spousal violence."

88. Interview with Patrick Langan, Bureau of Justice Statistics, Feb. 14, 1995. He reviewed National Crime Survey data from 1987 through 1992 for crimes of violence by intimate males against females. They showed a rate of 48 crimes per 1,000 for separated women; 14 per 1,000 for divorced women; and 1.6 per 1,000 for married women. For those in dating and common-law relationships or formerly in such relationships, the rate was 6.9 per 1,000.

89. Martha R. Mahoney, "Legal Images of Battered Women: Redefining the Issue of Separation," *Michigan Law Review,* vol. 90, no. 1, October 1991.

90. Mahoney, "Legal Images," p. 63.

91. "Crime in the United States 1992," Uniform Crime Reports, FBI, p. 17, and "Crime in the United States 1993," p. 17. The reports also show that 3 to 4 percent of all male murder victims are killed by wives or girlfriends and ex-wives or ex-girlfriends.

92. The Center for the Prevention and Understanding of Violence at the University of Colorado estimates that the actual number of women killed by their husbands and boyfriends or former husbands and boyfriends is close to 42 percent of all female homicide victims. In a study commissioned by the Family Violence Prevention Fund of San Francisco, the center applied the proportion of known husband-boyfriend killings to the "unclassified" female homicide victims from 1987 to 1991. Other experts, such as Langan and James Q. Wilson of UCLA, say they do not think such an approach is justified, but agree that the proportion is higher than 29 percent.

93. Patrick A. Langan and John M. Dawson, "Spouse Murder" (Washington, D.C.: Bureau of Justice Statistics, in progress, 1995). The report is based on a sampling of spouse-murder cases disposed of in 1988 in the nation's most populous counties.

94. Ibid.

95. *Violence Between Intimates* (Washington, D.C.: Bureau of Justice Statistics, November 1994), NCJ-149259, p. 3. "In 1977, 54 percent of the murder victims who were killed by intimates were male. . . . In other words, the number of male victims fell from 1,185 in 1977 to 657 in 1992 and the number of female victims increased from 1,396 to 1,510 during the same period."

96. The new spouse-murder study supported that impression when it found that evidence of provocation was "far more often present when wives killed husbands than when husbands killed wives." The report said more wives (44 percent) than husbands (10 percent) were assaulted at or around the time of the murder, more wives (21 percent) than husbands (10 percent) killed an armed spouse, and fewer wives (8 percent) than husbands (34 percent) had a prior arrest for a violent crime. The study said such circumstances appeared to be a key factor behind the less severe treatment the wives received from the justice system. Judges and juries acquitted them more often than husbands. Of those convicted, fewer wives than husbands received prison sentences, while wives who were sent to prison received shorter terms (an average of 9½ years) than husbands (an average of 21 years).

97. Straus and Gelles, *Physical Violence in American Families,* p. 53.

98. Ibid., p. 239.

99. Richard J. Gelles, "In Domestic Abuse, Men Do by Far the Heaviest Damage," *Providence Journal,* Aug. 20, 1994.

100. Straus and Gelles, *Physical Violence in American Families,* p. 157.

101. Ibid., p. 510.

102. Op. cit., *Violence between Intimates,* p. 2.

103. Author interview with Gelles, Nov. 29, 1994. According to *Physical Violence in American Families* (p. 89), six million women a year are attacked an average of six times a year. The more severe attacks, such as kicking, biting, punching, or choking, were inflicted on about two million women, according to the percentages in the 1985 survey.

104. Author interviews with Gelles on Sept. 21 and Oct. 14, 1994.

105. "Radio Daze, A Day with the Country's Masters of Gab: Is America Talking Itself Silly?" Howard Kurtz, *Washington Post,* Oct. 24, 1994, pp. B-1 and B-7.

106. Smith, "Get Out of My Face."

107. Adele Harrell, *Evaluation of Court-Ordered Treatment for Domestic Violence Offenders, Final Report,* Urban Institute, October 1991. The study focused on three treatment programs in Baltimore County, Maryland, coincidentally the home base of Judges Cahill and Bollinger.

108. It is called the Compassion Workshop, conducted by Stephen Stosny. He teaches his charges to feel compassion for their partners rather than to be angry at them, and he says he has achieved a violence-free rate one year after treatment of more than 80 percent. "We define violence as any unwanted touching," he says. Of his approach, he says, "The brain cannot experience anger and compassion at the same time." I hope he succeeds. But I also know that model programs are rarely replicated and usually deteriorate in the hands of others.

109. Smith, "Get Out of My Face."

110. "Family Violence: Improving Court Practice," p. 50.

111. Brian Ross, "Soft on Domestic Violence," *Day One,* ABC News, Feb. 2, 1995.

112. Caseworker's report, Cartier file, Deer Island, Sept. 9, 1991.

113. Author interview with Hudgins, Oct. 4, 1994.

114. Lawrence W. Sherman, with Jannell D. Schmidt and Dennis P. Rogan, *Policing Domestic Violence* (New York: Free Press, 1992), p. 67.

115. Cited in Straus and Gelles, *Physical Violence in American Families,* p. 485, from a 1983 study by D. Reed et al., entitled "All They Can Do . . . Police Response to Battered Women's Complaints."

116. Straus and Gelles, *Physical Violence in American Families,* p. 486. "Only 6.7 percent of all husband-to-wife assaults are reported to police. When severity of violence is considered, 3.2 percent of minor violence and 14.4 percent of severe violence is reported." By contrast, the Justice Department's National Crime Victimization Survey says that 52 percent of domestic violence victims reported crimes to the police, but the most likely reason for this high proportion is that most assaults by husbands are not even mentioned to NCVS interviewers.

117. Ibid., p. 4. Girlfriends were not included in this calculation.

118. Testimony of Joan Zorza, senior attorney, National Battered Women's Law Project of the National Center on Women and Family Law, House Judiciary Subcommittee on Crime and Criminal Justice, June 30, 1994. The 1994 federal crime law provides federal funds for state and local governments to implement mandatory arrest and pro-arrest policies in domestic violence cases. Controversy still exists over the wisdom of mandatory arrest, with crit-

ics such as criminologist Lawrence Sherman arguing that while it deters employed suspects, it can increase repeat violence among unemployed batterers who seem to have nothing to lose. Zorza contends that the jobless abusers in the studies Sherman cites almost always had prior arrest histories and so were less likely to be deterred in any event. She says that arrests of black and white suspects are virtually proportionate only when a mandatory arrest policy is in place and that in jurisdictions where police still have discretion, they use it "not to arrest white and/or privileged abusers, as probably happened many times when they responded to domestic violence calls regarding O. J. Simpson."

119. Study conducted by the D.C. Coalition Against Domestic Violence in 1987–88, cited in Catherine Klein, "Domestic Violence, D.C.'s New Mandatory Arrest Law," *Washington Lawyer,* November–December 1991, pp. 24–29. The arrest rate for incidents involving damage to a car was 28.6 percent. The arrest rate in incidents involving a bleeding victim was 13.7 percent. The study involved extensive interviews of 274 victims of domestic abuse in the District who sought help *after* the Metropolitan Police Department adopted a "pro-arrest" domestic violence policy.

120. Delbert S. Elliott, "Criminal Justice Procedures in Family Violence Crimes," in *Crime and Justice, A Review of Research,* Lloyd Ohlin and Michael Tonry, eds., vol. 11 (Chicago: University of Chicago Press, 1989), p. 459.

121. Leen and Van Natta, "Dade Justice Puts Felons on Street," p. 22A.

122. Author interview with Detective Dwyer, Oct. 3, 1994.

123. Author interview with Detective Mark Molloy, Oct. 3, 1994.

124. The law includes more money for battered women's shelters and some grants-in-aid for the hiring of more prosecutors, but ignores the needs of beleaguered probation officers, who will still be expected to mind the biggest part of the store. The statute also permits victims of gender-based felonies to sue their attackers for compensatory and punitive damages without waiting for criminal prosecution. The principal sponsor of the $1.6 billion measure, and of the civil rights remedy, Senator Biden, argues that women should not be left "at the sufferance of the state to determine whether something will be done to their abusers." But it could also give prosecutors an excuse not to pursue criminal action. Critics contend that "the big winners" in this kind of civil litigation will be lawyers and therapists.

125. Author interview with Martin O'Connell, chief of the U.S. Census Bureau's fertility statistics branch, Dec. 29, 1994. The Census Bureau estimates the population of fifteen- to nineteen-year-olds will be 17.8 million in 1995 and will increase to 19.8 million in 2000. It will keep going up until it reaches a peak of 22.4 million in 2010.

126. Wilson, "What to Do About Crime," p. 34.

INDEX

Index

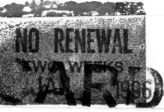